ENHEDUANA

ENHEDUANA

THE COMPLETE POEMS OF THE WORLD'S FIRST AUTHOR

SOPHUS HELLE

Yale
UNIVERSITY PRESS
NEW HAVEN & LONDON

Frontispiece: A manuscript of Enheduana's *Exaltation to Inana.* Courtesy of the Penn Museum, image no. 296656 and object no. B7847.

Published with assistance from the Mary Cady Tew Memorial Fund.

Yale University Press books may be purchased in quantity for educational, business, or promotional use. For information, please e-mail sales.press@yale.edu (U.S. office) or sales@yaleup.co.uk (U.K. office).

Designed by Dustin Kilgore.
Set in Spectral type by Newgen North America.
Printed in the United States of America.

Library of Congress Control Number: 2022937721
ISBN 978-0-300-26417-3 (hardcover : alk. paper)
ISBN 978-0-300-27676-3 (paperback)

A catalogue record for this book is available from the British Library.

10 9 8 7 6 5 4 3 2

CONTENTS

INTRODUCTION

ENHEDUANA IS THE FIRST POET WHOSE NAME WE know. There are stories and poems far older than hers—as much as five hundred years older—but they are all anonymous. In the annals of world literature, Enheduana marks the earliest known appearance of authorship: the idea that there is a person behind the text, speaking to us across time. And yet, despite her pride of place in history and despite the exceptional beauty of her hymns, the world has forgotten about Enheduana. Western literary history instead begins with Homer, a man who sang his songs some fifteen hundred years after her death. Today, Enheduana is known only by a small circle of academics and enthusiasts, but she deserves better.

Enheduana lived around 2300 BCE, and it can be hard to grasp the gap in time that lies between us and her: Julius Caesar lived closer in time to *us* than to Enheduana. It is nothing short of miraculous that this ancient woman's voice has survived the passing of centuries, if only as an echo etched into clay, revised and rewritten over many generations. Enheduana served as high priestess in Ur, a city nestled in the southernmost corner of the country we now call Iraq. She was the daughter of Sargon of Akkad, an emperor who would be remembered for millennia as the paragon of kingship. She lived through a period of profound transformation; the world she was born into was not the same as the one she left behind. Sargon founded the first empire that history had ever seen, and he and his successors worked hard to reshape the cities they had conquered. Enheduana's installment as high priestess in Ur, one of the largest cities in the empire, was probably part of this political overhaul. But the new empire was also highly unpopular among the old Sumerian nobles, and Enheduana's life would have been beset by constant revolts. The story of one of those revolts is told in her best-known poem, *The Exaltation of Inana.*

All the poems attributed to Enheduana are hymns. They were not meant to be bedside reading; they do not seek to enlighten or entertain. Hymns are a strange sort of poetry, full of power and persuasion. Their goal is not to describe the world but to change it by invoking the gods and enlisting their help. To properly praise the gods, the writer of hymns must bring out their terrifying strength, so to read Enheduana's poems is to enter a world ruled by the violent whims of reckless gods. The hymns that we now label literature were in fact a way for ancient people to defend themselves from the mood swings of the gods: their lavish praise might soothe the heart of an angry deity and so keep its wrath at bay, at least for a time. Enheduana was a master of this genre until she lost her gift: The *Exaltation* tells us that she was ousted from her temple when a usurper named Lugal-Ane seized power in Ur. The text summons a world riven by rebellion, in which Enheduana struggles to regain her place of power. She prays for help to Nanna, the moon god, whom she had served as high priestess, but to no avail. Nanna ignores her petition, and it seems that Enheduana has lost command of her famous eloquence. "My honey-mouth is full of froth," she writes; "my soothing words are turned to dust" (ll. 72–73). Without those soothing words, she cannot rally the gods to her side, and this leaves her powerless in the face of the revolt. In despair, Enheduana turns instead to Nanna's daughter Inana, begging her to intervene in the Moon God's stead.

Inana is the single most complex and compelling goddess of the ancient world.[1] Also known as Ishtar, she was the patron deity of war, sex, change, and destruction. She was said to break every rule and flout every norm. Two of Enheduana's poems, the *Exaltation* and *The Hymn to Inana*, sing the praises of this awe-inspiring figure. That is no easy task, for as Enheduana herself says to Inana in the *Exaltation*, "It is daunting to sing of your might" (l. 64). Inana is too puzzling and capricious to be captured in words: in one text, she is a love-struck girl pining for the young shepherd Dumuzi, in another, she is a ruthless warrior grinding skulls to dust and feasting on the corpses of her enemies.[2] But in the *Hymn*, Enheduana finds a way to bring out the central character of the goddess— paradox itself. Through a long litany of contradictions, Enheduana conveys the terrifying and unpredictable power of Inana:

To destroy and
to create, to plant
and to pluck out
are yours, Inana.
To turn men into
women, to turn
women into men
are yours, Inana.
[. . . . .]
To step, to stride,
to strive, to arrive
are yours, Inana.
To turn brutes
into weaklings
and to make the
powerful puny
are yours, Inana.
To reverse peaks
and plains, to raise
up and to reduce
are yours, Inana.
To assign and allot

the crown, throne,
and staff of kings
are yours, Inana.

                              (ll. 119–21, 139–42)

In both the *Hymn* and the *Exaltation,* Enheduana makes clear that
Inana is not a deity like any other but the ruler of the universe. By
designating Inana as the queen of the gods, Enheduana makes a
statement not just about religion but about reality more broadly:
since the gods controlled the cosmos, their position in the pan-
theon reflected how the universe was organized. In elevating
Inana, Enheduana shows that the world is ruled not by a pre-
dictable and everlasting order but by change, conflict, chaos, and
contradiction—and not least by a stubborn and defiant female
force, to whom even the greatest gods must bow.

That is the goddess to whom Enheduana turns for help in the
Exaltation, asking her to intervene against Lugal-Ane. Enheduana's
hymn grows increasingly desperate, since her survival depends on
Inana's grace, something the goddess rarely grants. Enheduana
wanders through the thorns of foreign lands and bemoans her fate
before describing how her despair led her to compose a song to
Inana—that is, the very poem we are reading. Enheduana depicts
herself meeting Inana at the dead of night and metaphorically
giving birth to the text. In this climactic scene, the poem essen-
tially turns back on itself: in the narrative equivalent of a snake
biting its own tail, the text ends by showing us how it came into
being. In the epilogue that follows, we are told that the hymn
succeeded in exalting and appeasing Inana: the goddess heard
Enheduana's prayer and restored her as high priestess. Through
this act of self-reference, the poet thus shows us what hymns
can achieve when they are sung with eloquence and force. The
Exaltation is a poem about poetry, about what beautiful words

can do and what it means to write them. Not only is Enheduana the world's first known author, her poems also include a complex and self-reflective account of authorship, as she depicts herself stepping into literary history.

That history has since come to be dominated by white men, so the fact that the first known author was a "woman of color"—to use a deliberately anachronistic phrase—comes as an empowering revelation to many modern readers.[3] Even today, female authors continue to be labeled "women writers," as if they were anomalies in an inherently male profession. But Enheduana's authorship overturns that assumption: the concept of authorship began with a woman. Her hymns are a rare flash of female voice in the ancient world, and they treat themes that are as relevant today as they were four thousand years ago: exile, social disruption, the power of storytelling, gender roles, the devastation of war, and the terrifying forces of nature. In this book, the first to include a complete translation of Enheduana's poems from the original Sumerian, I seek to do justice to this overlooked figure.

The *Exaltation* and the *Hymn* are both addressed to Inana, and they combine a celebration of the goddess with an account of Enheduana's own troubled life, though in the *Hymn*, the "autobiographical" section has unfortunately been lost. A third text attributed to Enheduana is a collection of poems known as *The Temple Hymns*: forty-two short odes to the temples, cities, and gods of ancient Sumer, all described in a rich and intensely metaphorical language. By guiding the reader through the sights of ancient Iraq, the collection offers a whistle-stop tour of the long-lost world in which Enheduana lived. There are two more texts, both short and fragmentary, that mention Enheduana: both are hymns to the Moon God, though at least one of them seems not to be told in Enheduana's own voice, instead addressing her as a character in the text.[4] Some modern scholars have also assigned a sixth poem to Enheduana, *Inana and Ebih*, the story of Inana's raid on a mountain that failed to honor her. While *Inana and Ebih* is a fascinating poem in all sorts of ways, the grounds for attributing it to Enheduana are extremely slim, so I have not included it.[5] That being said, allusions to Inana's battle against Ebih are scattered throughout the *Hymn* and the *Exaltation*.

Besides these five poems, we have several other traces of Enheduana's life, most notably a limestone disk inscribed with her name that shows her presiding over a ritual sacrifice to Inana. The inscription on the back of the disk identifies Enheduana as the daughter of Sargon and the high priestess of Nanna, proving beyond doubt that she was a real historical figure. But what the disk cannot tell us is whether she composed the hymns that were attributed to her by the ancient Babylonian scribes, and philologists have long grappled with the possibility that the hymns may have been written after her death.[6] In "Enheduana's World," below, I return to this argument and lay out the evidence for and against it. The poems may indeed have been written much later, perhaps as a way for Babylonian poets to celebrate what was to them a famous figure. According to this view, the *Exaltation* and the *Hymn* are to be read not as autobiographical accounts but as a kind of ancient historical fiction, dramatizing the life and poetic struggles of Enheduana. If they were later compositions, the poems may have built on a real memory of Enheduana as a gifted orator devoted to Inana, embellishing that memory into a fictional tale. For now, we cannot tell one way or the other.

Regardless, the fact that the ancient scribes saw Enheduana as the author of these poems is significant: in this case it really is the thought that counts. The *idea* of authorship, the notion that a poetic text could be traced back to a named and identifiable individual rather than to a collective and anonymous tradition was born when these hymns were ascribed to Enheduana, and that is true regardless of whether the attribution was correct. It is in Enheduana's poems, and especially the *Exaltation*, that authorship was born. Today we take the importance of authors for granted, as we sort books by the names on their covers, bestow prizes on poets, and interview novelists about their intentions. But a historical view that stretches back to and beyond Enheduana reveals that the literary world can be—and once was—organized differently. I like to think that history can make the present strange. A knowledge of the past overturns the conventions we usually take for granted, be they gender roles, national borders, or the ordering of literature, by showing that conventions like these are neither natural nor necessary but instead are accidental and liable to change. Authorship is not a fixed feature of tales and texts, but a practice that arose at a specific moment in time. Enheduana's poems were a key part of that process, so if we want to understand the history of authorship, we must begin with her.[7]

But precisely because we live in the modern world, where authorship has become such an established fact of life, we feel an urge to know for sure: Was she or was she not the author of these texts? What in these poems is real and what is fiction? Where do we draw the line between not man and myth but woman and wonder? The debate about the truth of Enheduana's authorship has gone back and forth over the past forty years, and it has yet to come to any meaningful conclusion. Not only has the debate failed to produce agreement, it has also caused collateral damage. Because philologists have spent so long arguing about the dating of the hymns, they have paid little attention to their poetic power or popular appeal.[8] This is one reason why Enheduana's hymns are not better known. Philologists in general have been reluctant to proselytize her poems because they are dogged by the suspicion that they may not really be *her* poems. This must stop. The hymns are a stunning poetic achievement, and regardless of whether they are by or only about Enheduana, they are enough to make her a fascinating figure, one who deserves much greater fame than she currently enjoys. True, we cannot always separate life from legend when it comes to Enheduana: she did, after all, live more than four millennia ago. But the texts that circle around her paint a compelling portrait, and rather than trying to decide whether she is the author or "merely" the main character of the poems, we should be tracing her transformation over time—from real priestess to remembered poet.

The philologist Gina Konstantopoulos has laid out a useful framework that sidesteps the question of Enheduana's authorship and so gives us a much better starting point for studying her life, legend, and literary heritage. As Konstantopoulos puts it, drawing on a phrase coined by the historian Eleanor Robson, Enheduana has led three lives.[9] In the first life, she was a powerful priestess in Sargon's empire. In the second, she was a literary star in the Babylonian schools. The third life is the one she leads now: that of an ancient poet in the modern world. We can follow Enheduana's transformation from one life to the next without faulting her for the changes she underwent. The Babylonian students of the eighteenth century BCE, for example, prized her poems for the insights they yielded into a dead language: Sumerian, in which the hymns are written, had died out in the intervening centuries. The Babylonian students grew up speaking the Akkadian language, so for them, studying Sumerian would have been like our studying Latin today, and Enheduana was a prime example of eloquent Sumerian. Meanwhile, some modern readers see in Enheduana's celebration of Inana something like a proto-feminist statement: an unstoppable goddess who defies all norms and forces the older gods into submission is a compellingly inspirational figure in the fight against patriarchy. Neither approach would have made sense in Enheduana's own lifetime, when the Sumerian language was still alive and feminism had not yet been born. But that is the way of all literature. Texts are transformed by those who read them. Enheduana's status as an exemplar of Sumerian and female empowerment was grafted on to her retroactively, long after her lifetime, but it cannot be rooted out now. These readings have become an integral part of her long history, growing around her memory like rings on a literary tree.

Enheduana's twenty-first-century revival has a distinct political edge, as she illuminates by sheer contrast the dearth of female and nonwhite voices in what currently passes for literary history. But as some aspects of Enheduana's story are brought into the limelight, others are overlooked. When we celebrate the subversive force of her poetry, we tend to ignore her historical role as an apologist for empire and her poetry's frankly disturbing glee at the crushing of revolts. To modern feminists, Enheduana can seem like a "wish-fulfillment figure," in Robson's words, but for that same reason her less savory qualities are often pushed to the side, downplaying the complexity of her history.[10] One way to approach that complexity is to note that in each of her three lives, Enheduana has stood at the heart of a community that reshaped her in its image. As high priestess, she was the center of the religious and political community in Ur, including the empire founded by her father and the networks of the temple. In her second life, Enheduana became obligatory reading for would-be scribes: the *Exaltation* was a central part of the school curriculum that future priests and civil servants were made to learn. The elite leaders of ancient states and temples would have been able to swap references to Enheduana's poetry, and their shared learning bound them together in a cultural clique.[11] And today, in her third life, Enheduana is being rediscovered by communities of readers all over the world. So to understand Enheduana's poems, we must understand the wider social world in which they were, and continue to be, embedded and read. Since we know so little about her, Enheduana's story must also be the story of the people who have sought to make sense of her legacy.

Each in its own way, these communities have used Enheduana to define themselves.[12] In return, they have sustained her memory and ensured her continued relevance. The poets whose works last longest are often those who can tap into several communities, so that their words continue to circulate even after a particular community has faded away—as the community of Babylonian scholars faded away. In Enheduana's case, it is particularly noteworthy that she can continue to reach and touch her readers four thousand years after her death. Following the philologist Sheldon Pollock, I would argue that the best understanding of Enheduana is achieved when we keep these three perspectives in mind at the same time: one rooted in her historical life, one in the ancient reception of her work, one in the modern world.[13] But as a result of this threefold understanding, the meaning of the name "Enheduana" will often shift and grow. According to context, I find myself using it to refer to the historical priestess, the cultural memory she left behind, the character and narrator of the poems, and the author who wrote them. Only sometimes do I explicitly distinguish between these various meanings of "Enheduana." This practice may be confusing to the reader, but, as I argue below, it is a confusion that the poems themselves generate and play with.[14]

What the poems attributed to Enheduana have in common is that they overwhelm the reader with a torrent of images. There is an intensity to her work, a condensed fervor which even today feels like an explosion, and which I have done my best to convey in translation. Line after line, the reader is bombarded with metaphors and similes, often focused on reversals and the destructive forces of war and nature. The link between one image and the next is often unclear. In one line, Inana is compared to a giant chain that holds the gods in place, in the next, the awe-inspiring splendor that surrounds Inana's body is said to cover the mountains like a shroud and still the noise of busy streets (*Hymn*, ll. 9–10). The jump from one image to the next, from chain to splendor, comes without warning, and the reader is kept sprinting to catch up while the text just as quickly moves on. Any sense of narrative progression in the poems must be reconstructed from hints that are strewn throughout the text. What the hymns give us, at least at first glance, is not a carefully constructed argument but a blizzard of disturbing scenes.

This strategy is partly a reflection of the confounding nature of Inana herself. When reading about ancient gods and goddesses, we find it easy to pigeonhole them in our minds, reducing them to a handful of episodes in the mythological tradition and a list of their main functions—"the god of justice," "the goddess of fertility," "the patron of merchants," and so on. The deities of the ancient world can seem to be quaint characters, each equipped with a convenient set of symbols and stories. But the ancient gods were complex, colossal, fathomless figures, difficult to grasp and still more difficult to soothe. The power of the gods was everywhere, and even a far-famed priestess like Enheduana could not be sure of commanding their attention. No one exemplifies their fickle and violent nature better than Inana, as shown by the *Hymn*'s list of contradictory qualities.

What makes a text like the *Hymn* even more confusing is that it has not reached us intact. Enheduana's poems are written in a script called cuneiform, which was most often incised on tablets made of clay. As I discuss in "Enheduana's World," below, the poems survived because they were copied out by ancient students learning the Sumerian language, providing us with plentiful but also fragmentary manuscripts, since dried clay is prone to breaking. So not only was the *Hymn* written long ago in a now-dead language, and not only does it allude to myths the ancient scribes knew well but which are obscure to modern readers, the text also comes to us in an incomplete state, with large breaks that interrupt the already puzzling flow of the poem. This is a common conundrum facing readers of literature from the ancient Near East. The *Exaltation* is an exception to the rule that Sumerian and Babylonian poems are always full of holes. Those holes can be frustrating, but they can also be beautiful, for they infuse the text with a sense of mystery, forcing modern readers to guess at what missing lines might once have held. Further, new manuscripts of Sumerian poetry are constantly being discovered, filling these holes one by one. But as our knowledge of Sumerian language and literature grows, our understanding of the poems changes too. The field of Sumerology is still young and unsettled: fierce debates about key aspects of Sumerian grammar continue to rage. The translations given in this book are necessarily temporary. Within the next decade, the philological interpretation of Enheduana's poetry will probably change, because it is always changing, and updated translations will have to be produced. This is an exciting prospect. In her third life, Enheduana is still in the process of being born.

One example of a Sumerian word that is central to Enheduana's poems but is still poorly understood is **me**, traditionally pronounced with a long, open vowel, so as to rhyme with Spanish *que*.[15] (Note that Sumerian words are conventionally given in bold, while Akkadian words are given in italics.) It is a crucial component of the Sumerian worldview, but its exact meaning remains a source of doubt.[16] Since the instances of **me** (which is both singular and plural) often denote the influence of a god over the human world, I have consistently translated it as "power," allowing readers to track its repetition and varied use across the poems. I discuss the word at greater length in "The Honeyed Mouth," below, but a simplified way of explaining the **me** is that if a god was a god *of* something, that something was a **me**. Justice was a **me**, kingship was a **me**, war was a **me**, and so were the various professions practiced by the Sumerians—farming, carpentry, metalworking, and so on. But the **me** also included victory and defeat, honesty and deception, comfort and strife, sex and labor, fire and its extinction. The **me** were the building blocks of civilization in both its positive and its negative aspects, and those blocks were controlled by the gods. In many texts, including the *Exaltation*, the **me** are depicted as physical objects that the gods could hold in their hands.[17]

The importance of the **me** to Enheduana's poetry is shown by the fact that the word appears in the first line of the *Exaltation*. The line also serves as its Sumerian title: this was standard practice in cuneiform cultures. Like an auto-named Word file today, compositions were known by their opening words, which are called the *incipit* of the text. *The Exaltation of Inana* and *The Hymn to Inana* are both modern names. In the ancient world, the *Hymn* was known as **innin ša gura**, "Queen of vast heart"; and the *Exaltation* as **nin me šara**, "Queen of all the me."[18] More often than not, the opening words of a cuneiform poem also give us a hint for how to read the text that follows, and the *Exaltation* is no exception. The phrase **nin me šara** spells out the gist of Enheduana's message. Inana is depicted not as one goddess among many but as the ruler of all the world's fundamental elements. To be the "Queen of all the **me**" was to hold the cosmos in one's palm. Crucially, this was not a universally accepted view of Inana.[19] Though she was of course a celebrated goddess in Sumerian culture, she was generally considered inferior to the main male deities of the pantheon: Enlil, An, and Ea. The *Exaltation* sets out to change this by making Inana supreme among gods, and this aim is emphatically announced in the first three words of the text.

The case of the **me** shows just how difficult it can be to translate even a single Sumerian word, let alone the fast-paced and fragmentary drift of the text as a whole. In my translation, I have taken a number of liberties to render the Sumerian diction in a way that makes the poems compelling to modern ears. That does not mean that I want the poems to fit neatly into modern expectations—that would kill their strangeness and poetic force. I have done my best not to tame the text, but neither did I want to produce an exact word-for-word translation that might convey the sense of the lines but none of their magic. I wanted to do justice to the myriad verbal games that are found in the Sumerian originals, which teem with puns, wordplay, and double meanings. To take just one example, in the *Exaltation* we find a couplet that in a phonemic transcription and a literal translation would read:[20]

biluda galgala niĝzu aba munzu
kur gulgul ude a baešum

Who can understand the great rites that are your possession?
Destroyer of the enemy land, you give force to the storm.

(ll. 16–17)

This literal translation gives no hint of the elegant construction of the original. The word **galgala**, "great," in the first line is echoed by **gulgul**, "destroyer," in the second, just as the word **aba**, "who," is echoed by the phrase **a baešum**, "you give force." The first line repeats the syllable **zu** in two different meanings, "your" (in **niĝzu**, "your possession") and "understand" (in **munzu**). Meanwhile, the second line contains an allusion to the myth of Inana's destruction of Mount Ebih, since the word **kur**, "enemy," can also mean "mountain." Finally, the lines display a delicate patterning of vowels, which becomes particularly clear if they are split into half-verses. The sequence runs as follows: i-u-a-a-a-a / i-u-a-a-u-u // u-u-u / u-e-a-a-e-u, revealing both symmetries (i-u-a-a) and contrasts (u-e-a | a-e-u). In my translation, I have tried to re-create these sound games through alliteration: "Who can fathom the great duties that befall you? It is you who strike down the enemy, you who give the storm its strength."

A major challenge of translating Sumerian poetry is the compactness of the lines. Consider again this couplet: it consists of ten words in Sumerian, but more than twice as many in both the literal and the free English translation. Lines that are short and succinct in Sumerian often become bulky in English, simply because the translator must unfurl at length what is rolled up in a few Sumerian syllables. I wanted to replicate this feeling of close-packed intensity, so I decided to deviate from the line breaks of the original, splitting the text into much shorter verses. At first I was afraid that these short lines would interrupt the flow of the text, but I found that they actually helped me read the hymn as a steady stream of words and images, which is how I experience it in Sumerian. However, when I turned to the *Temple Hymns,* I opted for a different strategy. There I wanted to make each hymn stand as a separate building, not a stream of words but a series of houses. For this text, it seemed more fitting to keep the line breaks where the ancient scribes had put them. For those who want to go beyond these translations and explore Enheduana's world and poems in more depth, a number of excellent online tools are available.[21]

Special characters are used to represent Sumerian and Akkadian words. The letter š is pronounced like *sh* in *ship,* the letter ĝ like *ng* in *song,* though in Sumerian it can also stand at the beginning of a word, as in **ĝipar** (the home of the high priestesses). When transliterating cuneiform signs (as opposed to transcribing how those signs may have been pronounced, which is what I do above), subscript numbers are used to distinguish signs that have the same meaning: the sign **kur,** for example, means "mountain," while **kur**$_2$ would mean "different." The pronunciation of Sumerian is difficult to reconstruct, but some evidence indicates that stress was placed on the final syllable of a word: ĝi-PAR, Enhedua-NA.[22] Because cuneiform can be transcribed into Latin letters using different conventions, the name Enheduana is sometimes rendered Enheduanna, but the former is now more common. Likewise, Inana can also be spelled Inanna, and some scholars have recently argued that it should be spelled Innana.[23] These variations rest only on the technicalities of transcription; they do not indicate different figures.

It is my hope that by making Enheduana's poems available in English and by unpacking her history in the essays that follow the translations, I can help recall this fascinating figure to new life. Restoring Enheduana to her place at the beginning of literary history is important not least because of the light she would shed on later poetry. What would the history of Western literature look like if it began not with Homer and his war-hungry heroes but with a woman from ancient Iraq, who sang her hymns to the goddess of chaos and change?

POEMS

THE EXALTATION
OF INANA

THE *EXALTATION* IS THE MOST CELEBRATED OF ENHE-
duana's poems, and the most complex.[1] Its Sumerian title is **nin
me šara**, literally "Queen of all the **me**"; it is also known as *Inana B*.
The poem begins with a hymnic invocation of Inana, dwelling on
her powers of destruction and the cruelty with which she crushes
all who oppose her, including a mountain she invades and a city
that rebels against her rule. About halfway through the hymn,
the narrator reveals her own identity and explains her reason for
invoking Inana. Enheduana says that she has served faithfully as
high priestess to Nanna, the moon god, but now a rebel leader
named Lugal-Ane has seized power, ousting Enheduana from
the city and defiling the temple that Inana shares with An, lord
of the heavens. The conflict between Enheduana and Lugal-Ane
is depicted as a court case, with the gods as judges and the two
humans as opposing claimants.[2] Enheduana interprets her own
ambiguous situation—exiled but still alive—as proof that the case
has not been resolved. "Still my case stays open," she says. "An evil
verdict coils around me—is it mine?" (l. 117). It becomes clear that
Enheduana has already tried praying to Nanna, but to no avail,
and that this is why she now turns to Inana.

As I understand the story—and scholars disagree on how to
interpret it—Enheduana confronts a triple challenge as she in-
vokes Inana.[3] First she must convince Inana to rule in her favor,
which is difficult enough in itself: the goddess's wrath is impla-
cable. Enheduana fears that Inana has become angry with her,
and prays desperately for the goddess to let go of her fury: "Will

your heart not have mercy on me?" (l. 138). Second, Enheduana must convince Inana to rule at all. As noted in the Introduction, the supreme status that Inana is given in these hymns was not a matter of course in the Sumerian world; as Enheduana herself says to Inana, "You were born to be a second-rate ruler" (l. 114). But once more, Enheduana engages in some clever interpretation. She claims that because Nanna has not resolved her ambiguous situation one way or the other, he has effectively passed the matter on to Inana, who can now step into her father's role as ruler among gods: "Nanna said nothing, so he has left it up to you. My queen! This has made you even greater, this has made you the greatest" (ll. 133–34). In other words, Nanna's silence leaves a vacuum of power for Inana to fill, and Enheduana urges the goddess to seize her chance.

Enheduana's third challenge is to make the other gods and the human population recognize Inana's might. Without that recognition, her verdict will be meaningless. Inana's power must be widely accepted for her words to carry weight.[4] This is why the poem combines an autobiographical section detailing Enheduana's plight with a hymnic section extolling Inana's might. The fate of the two women is wound together. Only if Inana's rulership is widely recognized will the goddess be able to judge Enheduana's case and restore her as high priestess. That is, the hymn must convince the audience of Inana's awe-inspiring power if Enheduana is to extricate herself from exile.

As Enheduana faces these challenges—swaying Inana's heart, convincing her to take Nanna's place, and elevating her in the eyes of the audience—words fail her: "My honey-mouth is full of froth, my soothing words are turned to dust" (ll. 72–73). Her eloquence disappears at the moment she needs it most. If Enheduana is to save herself, she needs to regain her command of language. In a sense, the *Exaltation* is a poem about itself, about whether Enheduana will succeed in elevating Inana, overcoming her loss of eloquence, and so saving her own life. As noted by the philologist Louise Pryke, the first known story of a writer is also the first known story of a writer's block.[5]

The poem culminates with Enheduana inviting Inana to join her in a nighttime ritual, in which she composes a song to the goddess—that is, the text we have been reading. Having been at a literal loss for words, Enheduana at last succeeds in recapturing her poetic gift, as shown by the beauty of the poem itself. In a short epilogue, we are told that the hymn had the intended effect. Inana accepted Enheduana's prayer, she was exalted among the gods, and Nanna approved of her new powers. Tellingly, the final epilogue is told in the third person. It is as if Enheduana, who narrated the preceding events in her own voice, steps out of the text and hands it over to others. When she says that the poem was sung on the next day by a ritual lamenter, she is transformed from "I" to "her," from character to composer.

I.

Queen of all powers,
downpour of daylight!
Good woman wrapped
in frightful light, loved
by heaven and earth,
holy woman of An.
You hold the great
gems, you love the
good crown, to rule
is your right:[6] you
have seized the seven 5
powers of the gods.[7]

II.

My queen, you are
the guardian of the
gods' great powers:
you lift them up and
grasp them in your
hand, you take them
in and clasp them
to your breast. As if
you were a basilisk,[8]
you pour poison
upon the enemy,
as if you were the 10
Storm God, grain
bends before your
roar. You are like
a flash flood that
gushes down the
mountains, you

are supreme in
heaven and earth:
You are Inana.[9]

Raging rainfall of
fire! It was An who
gave you power. You
are a queen astride
a lion, you give orders   15
by the holy order of
An. Who can fathom
the great duties that
befall you? It is you
who strike down
the enemy, you who
give the storm its
strength. Enlil loves
you for teaching the
land how to fear, An
has ordered you to
stand by for battle.

My queen, hearing   20
your battle cry the
enemy bows down.
Fleeing sandstorms,
terror, and splendor,
humanity assembled
to stand before you
in silence, and of all
the gods' powers, you
took the most terrible.
Because of you, the

people must march
past the threshold
of tears. Because of   25
you, they go to the
great house of grief.
Because of you, they
yield all they own
without a fight.

My queen, your
strength can make
teeth crush stone.[10]
You strike like the
strike of a storm.
You roar like the
roar of a storm.
Your howl is like   30
the Storm God's
howl. You wear
yourself out with
wind after wind,
but your feet stay
strong. With the
harps of the temple,
they strike the beat
of a sorrowful song.[11]

My queen, even the
Anuna flee from you
like bats fluttering   35
through ruins: they
could not withstand
your terrifying gaze,

no one can stand
firm before your
staring eyes. Who
can calm the rage
in your heart? To
soothe your wrath
is a daunting task.
Queen, who can   40
ease your mind?
Queen, who can
please your heart?

III.
Your rage cannot
be cooled, O great
daughter of Nanna!
Queen, outstanding
on earth, who can
rob you of your rule?

The mountain fell
under your rule. Its
harvest has failed,
its city gates burn,
its rivers run with   45
blood—the thirsty
must drink it. All
its armies march
before you, all its
troops disband
before you, all
its soldiers stand
before you. While   50

the wind fills the
squares where they
danced, their best
men are led before
you in chains.[12]

The city that did not
say, "This country
is yours!" that did
not say, "It belongs
to your father!"—
the holy order has
been given: it is
back beneath your
feet. But something
is wrong with the
wombs of the city.[13]
The woman there   55
no longer speaks
beautiful words to
her spouse—in the
dead of night, she
will not converse
with him. She does
not show him what
shines inside her.

You charge like an
aurochs,[14] O great
daughter of Nanna!
Queen, outstanding
in heaven, who can
rob you of your rule?

IV.
Queen of queens,   60
born from a holy
womb to wield
great power, you
now surpass even
your own mother.
Wise and clever
queen of all lands,
of living beings and
the innumerable
people: I will sing
you a sacred song.
Good goddess who
is fated for power,
it is daunting to sing
of your might. Good   65
woman, inscrutable
and radiant, I will
sing of your power.
For you, I stepped
into my holy home.[15]

I am Enheduana, I
am the high priestess.
I carried the basket
of offerings, I sang
the hymns of joy.
Now they bring me
funeral gifts—am I
no longer living?[16]
I went to the light,   70
but the light burned

me; I went to the
shadow, but it was
shrouded in storms.
My honey-mouth
is full of froth, my
soothing words are
turned to dust.

This fate of mine,
Nanna, this man
Lugal-Ane: tell An   75
about it, and let An
resolve the matter![17]
Tell An now, and he
will resolve it right
away. He will let the
woman wrench off
this fate, Lugal-Ane.
She is mighty, floods
and mountains lie at
her feet, cities shake
before her. Stand by   80
me, Nanna! May she
have mercy on me.

I am Enheduana. I
will pray to you, holy
Inana: I will let my
tears stream free to
soften your heart, as
if they were beer. I
will say to you, "The
decision is yours." I

cannot make Nanna
care for my case. But   85
Lugal-Ane has defiled
the holy rites of An,
wrenching the Temple
of Heaven from the
God of Heaven.[18] Even
the greatest god he
does not fear. He has
turned the temple
of infinite joy and
endless delight into
a home of evil. He   90
has made himself
my equal, but envy
hounds him.[19] O,
my righteous aurochs,
chase him, chain him!

In the land of life, what
am I? May An abandon
this rebel land, loathed
by Nanna. This city: let
An crush it. This city: 95
let Enlil curse it. Let its
mothers not comfort
their crying children.
But when they sing
their lamentations,
my queen, then sail
your boat of sorrow
to another shore.

Am I to die because   100
of my holy song? Me!
My Nanna does not
care for me, and so
I waste away in this
land of lies. Nanna
is silent in my case,
and what do I care
if he speaks or not?
Lugal-Ane stood in
triumph, he stepped
out from the temple.
I fled like a swallow   105
swooping through a
window—my life is
all spent. The thorns
of foreign lands—is
that what you have
decreed for me? He
took the crown of
the high priestess
from me, giving me
a knife and dagger
instead: "These suit
you better," he said.[20]

    V.
Queen, beloved of
heaven! Your holy   110
heart is great: may
it come back to me!
Darling lover of the

dead Dumuzi,[21] your
rule extends from
zenith to horizon.
Even the Anuna bow
before you: you were
born to be a second-
rate ruler, but now!
How far you surpass
all the greatest gods;
they press their lips
to the dust beneath
you. But still my case
stays open, and an evil
verdict coils around
me—is it mine? I have
not defiled the shining
bed, I have not divulged
the words of Ningal.[22]
I am still the splendid
high priestess of Nanna!

Queen, beloved of
heaven! May your
heart have mercy on
me. Nanna has said
nothing, so he has
said, "It is up to you!"
Let it be known! Let
them know that you
are as mighty as the
skies. Let them know
that you are as great
as the earth. Let them

115

120

125

know that you crush
every rebel. Let them
know that you deafen
the enemy. Let them
know that you grind
skulls to dust. Let
them know that you
eat corpses like a lion.
Let them know that
your gaze is terrifying,
and that you lift your
terrifying gaze. Let   130
them know that your
eyes flash and flicker.
Let them know that
you are headstrong
and defiant. Let them
know that you always
stand triumphant.
Nanna said nothing,
so he has left it up to
you. My queen! This
has made you even
greater, this has made
you the greatest.

Queen, beloved of   135
heaven! I will sing
of your fury. I have
piled up the coals, I
have purified myself.
The Holy Inn awaits
you.[23] Will your heart

not have mercy on
me? The pain filled
me, overwhelmed me.
Queen, lady! For you,
I have given birth to
it: what I sang to you
at dead of night, let   140
a lamenter repeat at
midday. For your
captive spouse and
your captive child,
your fury grows ever
greater, your heart
can find no rest.[24]

VI.
The mighty woman,
the greatest in the
gathering of gods,
has heard her plea.
Inana's holy heart   145
came back to her.

The light pleased
her. She spread joy
and beamed with a
passionate delight,
like a downpour of
moonlight, wrapped
in charm.[25] Nanna
extolled her, Ningal
blessed her, and the
temple's thresholds   150

welcomed her home.
What she said to her
holy woman was
magnificent.[26]

You who crush the
mountains, you who
were given powers
by An. My queen   153
cloaked in charm:
All praise Inana!

THE HYMN TO INANA

MORE STRONGLY THAN ANY OTHER POEM FROM
the ancient Near East, the *Hymn* brings out the power and para-
doxical nature of Inana.[1] In Sumerian its title is **innin ša gura**,
"Queen of vast heart"; philologists also refer to it as *Inana C*. To-
day, the text is less widely read than the *Exaltation*, largely because
it is less fully preserved. But the *Hymn* is in many ways a wilder
poem than the *Exaltation*, especially in its praise of Inana. It was
customary for ancient hymnists to boost the status of the deity
they addressed, but in the *Hymn* we see an uncompromising eleva-
tion of Inana over and above any other god. If we were to read the
Hymn and no other work of Sumerian literature, we would think
that Inana was the head of the pantheon. This is not usually the
way she is presented. In most Sumerian texts, the king of the gods
is Enlil, and the moral authority among them is An. Even in the
Exaltation, Inana's power is qualified: she is said to rule with per-
mission from An and Enlil. No such caveat is found in the *Hymn*,
which bluntly asserts that even these august deities must submit
to Inana: "Without Inana, An can reach no decisions, Enlil can
fix no fates" (l. 14).[2]

After the initial hymn, the text moves on to recount in minia-
ture format several myths associated with Inana (ll. 73–115). These
include the story of how Inana came to share a temple with An,
how she created a group of ritual performers who disrupted
conventional gender roles, and how she destroyed Mount Ebih.
What these stories reveal is Inana's ability to transform everything
and anything: the humans are changed from men to women and

POEMS

vice versa, the other gods are bullied until they give her what she wants, and even the landscape is transmuted by her might. The central theme of the *Hymn* is Inana's ability to upend all rules and conventions: humans, gods, and mountains are all subject to her unpredictable powers of transformation.

Then follows the set piece of the poem: the long list of Inana's attributes, including all sorts of irreconcilable aspects. At first each line of the list ends with the words "is yours, Inana," playing off opposite terms and binding them together through wordplay and assonance. But eventually the text disintegrates into smaller and smaller units, until it is simply a long stream of words. The effect can be compared to what the author Umberto Eco has dubbed "the vertigo of lists," the dizzying sense that a list can go on forever, moving from entry to entry through associations that are far from clear.[3] Though this list does eventually stop, it gives the reader an immediate sense of Inana's ineffability: the length, self-contradictions, and chaotic structure of the list show us that Inana defies all attempts at description.

After this powerful central section comes another hymnic passage, again focusing on Inana's supremacy among the gods (ll. 174–218). The beginning of this section is marked by a strong parallelism in the Sumerian sentence structure, which cannot be fully re-created in translation.[4] Enheduana then introduces herself, with the same assertive words that we find in the *Exaltation:* "I am Enheduana" (l. 219). But the autobiographical section that presumably followed is missing, with some twenty-two lines lost altogether. The concluding passage (ll. 254–74) turns once more to Inana, in a final exultation of the goddess's powers. Toward the end of the text, we find a line that is reminiscent of the *Exaltation:* "My lady, your might is proclaimed; may your heart return to me" (l. 270). While Enheduana's motives for praying to Inana in the *Hymn* remain unclear, the line implies that she again fears that she has incurred Inana's wrath and so has set about exalting her.

Queen of vast heart,
wild lady, proudest
among the Anuna.
Outstanding in all
lands, great daughter
of Nanna, eminent
among the Igigi.
Lady of glory, who
reaps the powers of
heaven and earth,
rival to mighty An.
It is she who rules
the gods, she who
seals their verdicts,
as the Anuna crawl   5
beneath her mighty
words. Even An does
not understand her
ways; he dares not go
against her orders.
She overturns what
she has done; nobody
can know her course.
She has brought the
mighty powers to
perfection, she has
seized the shepherd's
staff and become their
great leader. She is
a mighty chain that
holds down the gods;
her splendor shrouds   10
the mountains and

silences the roads.
At her deep roars,
the gods of the land
are filled with fear.
At her howling cry,
the Anuna tremble
like lonely reeds. At
her booming blare,
they all hide together.
Without Inana, An
can reach no decisions,
Enlil can fix no fates.
Who can challenge a
queen who raises her
head higher than the
mountaintops? When
she speaks, cities turn   15
to ruins—homes for
ghosts—and temples
become deserts. When
her fury makes people
shake, the fever and
panic they feel are
like the fetters of a
demon. She whirls
chaos and confusion
at those who disobey
her, hurrying havoc,
hastening the flood,
dressed in a dreadful
gleam. Her joy is to   20
speed up conflict
and combat: ever

restless, she straps
on her sandals. She
splits the blazing,
furious storm, the
whirlwind billows
around her as if
it were a dress.[5]
Her touches bring
despair: the south
wind . . . . . .
. . . .
Sitting on leashed
lions, Inana rips
apart those who
feel no fear of her.
Like a leopard of
the mountains, she
bursts onto the road

. . . .
. . . .

Queen, huge aurochs!
Fierce in her might,
no one turns to fight
her . . . .
leader of the Igigi.
She is a pit for the
wayward, a trap for
the wicked, a snare
for the enemy. Her
venom strikes like
the storm . . . .

. . . .
. . . .

25

. her fury is a flood
that no one can face.
A mighty stream . .   30
. . . .
. . . and humbles
whomever she scorns.
The queen is an eagle
that leaves no man
alive . . . . . .
. . Inana, hawk of
the gods, shreds up
the sheepfold. In
the town at which
she frowns, fields

. . . .
the fields that the
queen . . . . .
its furrows . . .
. . . . . . An   35
may oppose her
. . . .
does not . . . .
set on fire . . .
on the upland . .
the queen . . . .
. . . Inana . . .
. . . .
. . . .
. . . queen . . .
. . . battle . . .
. hurrying conflict
. . . .
. . . .

and sings a song, a
song of the fate that 40
is fixed for . . . .
weeping—the food
and drink of death.
Inana is the mistress
of weeping—the food
and drink of death:
those who eat it do
not last, those to
whom she feeds it
burn with bile, in
their mouths . . .
. . . . In
her happy heart,
she sings the song
of death in battle:
singing the song
in her heart, she
washes her weapons 45
with blood and guts

. . . .

. . . .

hatches crush heads,
spears eat flesh, and
axes are drenched in
blood . . . . . .
she pours blood and
strews death on their
offerings. On the vast,
silent plain, the bright
daylight is darkened:
she turns the midday

heaven into a starry
sky. People look at
each other in anger,
they look for a fight:
their noise disturbs   50
the plain, their shouts
weigh on wasteland
and meadow. Her
cry is a storm: skins
crawl throughout
the lands. No one
can withstand her
frenzied attack:
who will dare to
defy her? No one
can gaze at her
frenzied assault:
she hurries havoc!
She is a raging,   55
rushing flood that
sweeps across the
land and leaves
nothing behind.
She, the queen,
is a plow that
breaks hard soil,
leaving . . . .
. . . . . Those
who praise her keep
their heads bowed,
their feet . . . .
. . . . Her
vast heart bids her do

as she does. Only she,
the queen, does these
things. Eminent in the
assembly, enthroned
in power, noblemen
to her right and left!
She humbles great   60
mountains, leaving
them as rubble . .
. . . .
She splits up the
mountain ranges,
from east to west,
. . . . . Inana,
triumphant, breaks
down walls of stone:
the hardest stone she
will crush like clay;
for her they turn to
tallow. In the hand
of this proud queen
is a knife: its sheen
shrouds the land. In   65
the depths of the sea,
all fish are caught in
her trawling net, not
even bottom dwellers
are left in the abyss.
Like a clever fowler,
she will let no bird
escape her snare. Her
. . . . place . . .
unjust word . . . .

. . . .
. . . .
. . . . . the plans
of heaven and earth.
Her words . . . .

. . . .
. . . . An.
She confounds the
assembly of the great
gods with her advice,
nobody knows why.

. . . .
. . . .
. . . .
. . . .
. . . .
. . . .

Queen, leopard of
the Anuna, full of
pride, given control,
. . . fight . . . .

. . . .
. . . Inana . . .

. . . .
. . . young woman
. . . queen's palace
. . . . she receives
. . . . . . heart
. . . . . . charm
. . rejected woman
. . . . evil

. . . .

. . . . . country
. . . .
. . . . . . great
. . . .
. . roaming through
the square of the town
. . . .
. . . in the house,
the spouse looked at
the child. She set a   80
great burden on their
body, blessed them,
and named them the
pilipili.[6] She snapped
a spear and gave it
to them, as if they
were men. On the
. . . she imposed
tribulation. . . .
. . their pride . .
. . . . . . She
opens the doors to
the house of wisdom
and reveals what lies
within. Those who   85
do not fear her net
will soon be caught
in its mesh. The man
she once called on,
she now has no care
for: she goes to the
woman, snaps the
weapon, and gives

her the spear. On
the reed pipers,
the ecstatics, and
the reed women,
she imposes her
tribulations, she
makes them weep
and wail for her.
The mystics and
the **pilipili** whom
she transformed,
the **kurĝara** and
the **saĝ-ursaĝ** . .

. . . .
dirges and songs .

. . . .
. . . . . . They   90
exhaust themselves
with tears and tears,
lamentations . . .

. . . .
Daily tears . . . .
your heart . . . .
. . . . knows no
calm. Lovely lady of
heaven . . . . . .
. . . . tears

. . . .
In the heavens . .

. . . .
. . . .
. . . .
On your breast . .   95

. . . .
. . . .
. . no one can rival.
Only you are truly
great. Your name
is known, heaven
and earth . . . .
. . . You rival An
and Enlil, enthroned
in power! Seated in
shrine or sanctuary,
you are superb. In
your stride, you are
magnificent. The
goddess of grain
. . mighty throne
. . . .
The god of storms

100

. . . roars from
the sky . . . . .
. . . . His
heavy clouds . . .
. . . .
. . . . . . When
the great powers of
heaven and earth .
. . . .
Inana, your triumph
is a terrifying thing.
The heart . . . .
. . . . . . The
Anuna bent down,
bowed before you,

as you emerged
from the heavens
riding on seven
great lions. Even
An was scared of
your dominion; he
dreaded your home,
so he gave you his
own home, that he
would no longer
shiver in fear: "I
entrust to you the
mighty rituals of
kings and the great
rites of the gods."[7]
And the great gods
did kneel to kiss the
earth—even mighty
mountains bowed
before you, those
lands of lapis and
red carnelian. Only
Ebih would not bless
you, this mountain
did not bow down
before you.[8] So like
thunder was your
wrathful carnage,
like the tempest
you destroyed it.
Lady! An and Enlil
you have surpassed,
. . . .

105

110

. . . You! When
you are not there,
no fate can be fixed,
no clever counsel
can find favor.

To run, to flee, to   115
calm, and to quiet
are yours, Inana.
To roam, to rush,
to rival, to rise,
and to throw down
are yours, Inana.
To set out on path
or road, to rest at
a place of peace, to
help a tired friend
are yours, Inana.
To maintain the
tracks and trails,
to split the earth
and make it firm
are yours, Inana.
To destroy and
to create, to plant
and to pluck out
are yours, Inana.
To turn men into   120
women, to turn
women into men
are yours, Inana.
Desire and lust,
to gain goods, to

have a rich home
are yours, Inana.
Profit, absence,
poverty, wealth
are yours, Inana.
Gains and riches,
losses and debts
are yours, Inana.
To see, show, and
scrutinize, to find
fault and set right
are yours, Inana.
To know power,   125
pride, guardian
gods, and a place
to pray—these
are yours, Inana.
To change . . .
. . . .
. . . .
. . . .

Calamity . . .
. . . .
. . . .
. . . .
. . . .
. . . .
. . . .
. . . .
. . . .
. . . .
. . . .
. . . .

. . . .   130
. . . .
. . . .
. . . .
. . . .
. . . .
. . . .
are yours, Inana.
. . . .
. . . .
. mercy and pity
are yours, Inana.
. . . .
. . . .
. . . .
are yours, Inana.
The heart . . .
. . quake . . .
. . shiver . .
are yours, Inana.
To marry . . .   135
good things, to
love and to please
are yours, Inana.
To be happy and
to be haughty, to
. . . .
are yours, Inana.
To neglect and to
protect, to arise
and kneel down
are yours, Inana.
To make a family

and build a home
for the women, to
fill it with goods,
to kiss the lips of
the newborn child
are yours, Inana.
To step, to stride,
to strive, to arrive
are yours, Inana.
To turn brutes   140
into weaklings
and to make the
powerful puny
are yours, Inana.
To reverse peaks
and plains, to raise
up and to reduce
are yours, Inana.
To assign and allot
the crown, throne,
and staff of kings
are yours, Inana.
. . . .
. . . .
. . . .
. . . .
. . . .
. . . .
. . . .
. . . .
. . . .   145
. . . .
. . . .

. . . .
. . . .
. . . .
. . . .
. . . .
. . . .
. . . .
. . . .
. . . .
. . . .
. . . .
. . . .
. . . .
. . . .
. . . .
. . . .
. . . .
. . . .
. . . .
. . . .   150
. . . .
. . . .
. . . .
. . . .
. . . .
. . . .
. . . .
. . . .
. . . .
. . . .
. . . .
. . . .
. . . .
. . . .
. . . .
. . . .
. . . .

. . . .
. . . .
. . . .
. . . .

To make small or
majestic, weak or
huge, to withhold
and to give freely
are yours, Inana.
To bestow the
rituals of kings
and gods, to obey
and to mislead,
to speak slander,
to lie, to gaud,
and to overstate
are yours, Inana.
Rejoinders, truths,
falsehoods, sneers,
harassment, scorn
and provocation,
laughter, fame and
insignificance, evil,
gloom, grief, glory,
light and darkness,
trembling, terror,
anguish, splendor
and frightful light,
triumph, military
leadership, shivers,
sleeplessness and
restlessness, gifts
and submission,

155

160

. . . .
battle cries, strife,
dissent, conflict,
war, the speeding
of combat, . . .
. . . .
omniscience, to
make a nest next
to . . . . .
. make firm for
the future . . .
the desert . . .
vipers . . . .
drive to desertion
and foil one's foes
. . . .
. . . .
. . . .
are yours, Inana.
The throw of the
dice . . . . .
. . . .
. . . . . . To
gather the exiled
and bring them
home . . . . .
. . . .
. . . .
. . . . receive
. . . .
. . . .
. . . .
are yours, Inana.

165

170

. . . .
. . . .
. . . .
. . . . runners.
When your mouth   175
opens,⁹ . . . . .
turns into . . . .
. . . When your
eyes gaze, the blind
do not listen to the
sighted; when your
eyes rage, the bright
light turns to gloom,
midday to midnight.
When your love for
a land has run its
course, you crush
it, and the earth
shakes, for nothing
can resist your rule.
Your rule is mighty,
who can oppose it?
You are the ruler of
heaven and earth.
Inana, palaces . .   180
. . . . gift
. . . all the people
. . . . submission.
When your name is
spoken, it is greater
than the mountains,
An cannot compete
with . . . . . .

When your mind is
deep in thought, all
the gods . . . .
You alone are great.
All the gods of earth
and heaven: you are
like a huge aurochs
among them. When
you raise your eyes,
they fall silent, they
wait for your words.
When you make a   185
place your home,
the Anuna come
to chant prayers.
When your light

. . . .
. . . . . life.
When your name
is being praised—
let it go on forever!
Where is your name
not extolled? . .

. . . .
. . . .
. . . .
. . . .
. . . .
. . . .
. . . .
. . . .
. . . .   190
. . . .

. . . .
. . . .
. . . .
. . . .
. . . .
. . . .
. . . .
. . . .
. . . .
. . . .
. . . .
. . . .
. . . .
. . . .
. . . .
. . . .
. . . .
. . . .   195
. . . .
. . . .
. . . .
. . . .
. . . .
. . . .
. . . . . Your
song is sadness, it
is grief. . . .
. . . . No one
can understand the
changes that take
place in your mind,
but the fury they

lead to is crushing.
Your changefulness
is . . . . . . An
does not go against
your orders. In the   200
gods' great gathering,
with An and Enlil,
the wise bestow the
. . . . to
the woman. With
one voice, An and
Enlil . . . . . .
You seize the land
in your hand. When
you speak, An does
not retort. You say
"Let it be!" and great
An does not oppose
you: your "Let it be"
comes to be. You
decree destruction,
destruction comes:
when you deliver   205
your retort in the
assembly, An and
Enlil do nothing.
When you make
your decision, it
is indelible from
heaven and earth.
If you say: "Let this
land be," no one can
destroy it. If you say:

"Destroy this land,"
no one can let it be.
Your godhood is a
downpour of light
from holy heaven,
like the rays of the
moon and the sun.
Your beacon lights
every corner of the
heavens, it brings
brightness to all
that was dark. Men
and women walk
in single file before
you, to display what
the day has brought.
All the people pass
before your watchful
eyes, as under the
rays of the sun. No
one dares approach
your precious powers:
the powers pass before
your watchful eyes.
You rule to perfection
in heaven and earth,
holding all things in
your hand: Queen!
You are mighty, no
one can pass ahead
of you. You share a
holy home with great
An.[10] Is there any god

210

215

like you? You reap the
harvest of heaven and
earth. You are mighty,
your name is sacred,
you alone are mighty.

I am Enheduana, the
high priestess,[11] I am
the . . . . . .
Nanna . . . . .
. . . .
. . . .
. . . .
. . . .
. . . .
. . . .
. . . .
. . . .
. . . .
. . . .
. . . .
. . . .
. . . .
. . . .
. . . .
. . . .
. . . .
. . . .
. . . .
. . . .
. . . .
. . . .

220

225

. . . .
. . . .
. . . .
. . . .
. . . .
. . . .
. . . .
. . . .
. . . .
. . . .
. . . .
. . . .
. . . .
. . . .
. . . .
. . . .
. . . .
. . . .
. . . .
. . . .
. . . .   240
. . . .
. . . .
. . . .
. . . .
. . . .
. . . .
. . . .
. . . .
. . . .
. . . .
. . . .
Advice . . . .
. . . .

. . . .

. . . .

Grief, evil . . .

. . . .

. . . . woe . .

. . . .

My lady, when .   245
. . . . . pity
. . compassion.
I am yours! This
will always be so.
May your mind
be kind toward
me. When your
heart . . . . .

. . . .

. . pity. May this
song be recited
before you! This
is my offering to
you: to proclaim
your great divinity
across the land. I   250
know your great
burden from my
own body. Grief
and evil keep my
eyes open, the pain
spills out. But pity,
compassion, care,
mercy, and grace
are also yours, as
is the flooding of

rivers, the breaking
of hard soil, the dark
turning into light.

My lady, across the
lands I will magnify
your majesty, I will
praise your path's   255
supremacy. You!
Who can compete
with your divinity?
Who can rival your
rituals? May great An,
whom you love, beg
for mercy from you.
May the great gods
appease your mind.
May this throne   260
of lapis lazuli that
is suitable for your
sovereignty say to
you, "Enter!" May
the seat of your
magnificence say
to you, "Sit!" May
your holy bed say
to you, "Rest!" In
that place where
the sun rises . .
your . . . . . .
. . . .
. . They proclaim
your supremacy.

You are the queen
of . . . . .
Across all heaven,   265
An and Enlil have
granted you your
destiny: ascendancy
in the assembly of
the gods. You, who
are fit to rule, fix the
fates of queens and
ladies. Queen! You
are mighty, you are
magnificent! Inana,
you are mighty, you
are magnificent! My   270
lady, your might
is proclaimed; may
your heart return
to me! There is no
deed that can rival
yours—so let me
extol your might.
Youthful Inana,   274
how sweet it is to
sing your praise.

THE TEMPLE HYMNS

THE LONGEST WORK ATTRIBUTED TO ENHEDUANA
is a collection of poems known as *The Temple Hymns*, an anthology
of forty-two hymns to the temples of Sumer. As with other Sume-
rian poems, it was known by its opening words, in this case **eunir**,
"House of the Ziqqurat." The poems in the collection celebrate
the greatness of the temples, the gods who live there, and the
cities in which they stand. The hymns in the collection are quite
brief, between seven and twenty-three lines each, and offer nug-
gets of compact praise, as if they were beads on a hymnic string.

The first hymn goes to the main temple in Eridu, at the south-
ern edge of the Sumerian world: it leads off because Eridu was
thought to be the oldest city, where the god Ea founded the first
human settlement. The following five hymns are all dedicated to
temples in Nippur, which lay at the center of the Sumerian heart-
land. Nippur held a special place in Sumerian cosmology because
it housed the temple of Enlil, the king of the gods. After opening
with these key locations, the sequence of hymns moves to the
southeast, with Kesh and Ur, and zigzags along a vaguely north-
western line. Finally, it reaches Akkad, the city of Sargon and his
empire. The last hymn goes to Eresh, a city that has not yet been
identified. Eresh was placed last because it held a temple to the
goddess of learning, Nisaba; the entire collection thus concludes
with praise of writing itself. In the last lines, it is announced that
the collection was compiled by Enheduana.

The hymns all begin with a direct invocation of the temple
or holy site, addressing it by name and describing its features
in highly metaphorical language. The hymns then turn to the

deity who lives in the temple, typically marking the shift with the phrase "Your lord/lady is . . ." (Sumerian **nun-zu**). The hymns end with the same refrain, stating that the deity "has built a home in your holy court, and has taken his/her seat upon your throne." The hymns are very repetitive: there is a core set of terms—such as **ni**$_2$, "awe," **nun**, "lord, lady, noble," or **uru**$_{16}$, "towering, soaring"—that recur with great frequency. Metaphors, contrasts, phrases, and even whole lines are repeated.[1] This uniformity of both language and poetic structure serves to weave the collection together, turning what would otherwise be a motley collage of praise poems into a coherent composition.

The philologist Monica Phillips, who has undertaken to produce a new edition of the *Temple Hymns*, argues that the collection as a whole revolves around the power of names and unfurls the metaphorical significance of each temple's name.[2] The temples were known as the "house" (Sumerian **e**$_2$) of the god in question, and were named accordingly: House of Heaven (E-ana), Shining House (E-babbar), Mighty House (E-mah), and so on. As such, the names all contained a key metaphor that could be explored and expanded, like a musical theme being turned into a song. For example, Enlil's temple in Nippur is the E-kur, "House of the Mountain," and so the hymn to that temple (hymn 2) is a cluster of mountainous metaphors. But the associations are often much subtler and frequently based on links at the level of writing or sound. The hymn to Ea's temple, the E-Abzu (House of the Deep Sea, hymn 1), begins by invoking the ziqqurat of that temple, the E-unir (House of the Ziqqurat). The name E-unir is written with the sign U$_6$, which taken on its own refers to a plant, and the following lines are indeed full of plants and sprouts. Readers looking for an account of the architectural features of Sumerian temples will be disappointed: the hymns approach their subject first and foremost through metaphors and poetic associations.

Most of the hymns invoke their temple by more than one name. In some cases, this is because the temple had a primary name as well as an epithet: for example, hymn 3 is addressed to Ninlil's temple E-kiur (House of the Leveled Land), but this temple was also called E-Tummal (House of Tummal). In some cases, the alternative names refer to a part of the temple: hymn 5 is about Ninurta's temple E-shumesha (the meaning of this name is unclear), but it begins by invoking a shrine within that temple, the E-meurana (House That Harvests the Powers of Heaven). Finally, some alternative names may simply refer to different temples of the same deity: hymn 6 concerns the Dusangdili (Singular Hill) and the Gaduda (House That Is Home to a Hill), which may have been separate sanctuaries to the goddess Shuziana, both located in the sacred Gagimah district in Nippur.[3] At times, the hymns blur the distinction between temple and city. Especially in the case of smaller cities, such as Kesh or Kuara, the hymn seems to invoke the city as a whole, treating it as one big sacred site dedicated to the local deity. Finally, the hymns also use multiple names for one deity—Ea is also called Nudimmud, Enlil is also called Nunamnir, Nanna is also called Ashimbabbar—but I have not used these alternative names in my translation.

A striking feature of the *Temple Hymns* is how many of the hymns concern deities and cities that are otherwise little known. The religious and political landscape of ancient Iraq was constantly shifting: the *Temple Hymns* preserve a snapshot of that landscape, but deities that were important in the Old Akkadian period had become irrelevant a mere century later. The most telling example is Ilaba (hymn 41), city god of Akkad and patron deity of Sargon's empire, who faded into almost total obscurity after the fall of that empire. The main gods—Ea, Enlil, Nanna, Utu, Ninhursanga, Ishkur, Nergal, Nisaba, Dumuzi, and Inana—retained their positions over the centuries, though even major deities were subject to change: Ningirsu and Ninurta were later merged into one figure, as were Baba and Gula. But many smaller gods were quietly demoted, even if they did not disappear completely. Gods such as Ningublaga and cities such as Urum would have seemed esoteric even to the scribes of the Old Babylonian period. Already then, the *Temple Hymns* may have held what we call "historical interest": the collection did not match contemporary reality but instead provided a glimpse of what the Sumerian world had looked like in previous centuries.

1. E-ABZU, THE TEMPLE OF EA IN ERIDU

Eridu was considered to be the oldest of the Sumerian cities. Ea was the god of wisdom and creativity, and he resided in the Deep Sea, or Abzu, a mythical underground lake from which fertile freshwater was thought to rise, nourishing the fields and feeding the land.[4]

House of the Ziqqurat. You sprouted up with heaven and
    earth.
Great hall of Eridu, you are the foundation of heaven and
    earth.
Deep Sea. Shrine that was built for its lord.
House of the Holy Hill, where people eat pure plants
and drink water from the sacred canals of its lord.   5
This land, this sacred place, is kept clean with soap.

Deep Sea. Your drums are part of the cosmic powers.
Your great . . . wall has been brought to perfection.
From the entire residence in which the god lives
—this great building, this beautiful building—light is
    kept out.   10

Your house is bound in place, its prayers are unrivaled.
Your lord, the great lord, has fixed the sacred crown
inside your sacred court. Eridu, city where the great
    crown lies,
where thornbushes sprout, where holy bushes grow
    among priests.

Shrine of the Deep Sea. Your place, your great place!   15
Yours is the place where they call upon the Sun God.
Yours is the oven that is full of food, of basketfuls of bread.

Yours is the ziqqurat, the shrine that touches heaven.
Yours is the oven that is as large as a huge hall.

Your lord is the lord of heaven and earth . . . does not
   change.   20
. . . . . spoken, the creator . . . . . pondering,
. . . . the lord Enki
has built a home in your holy court, House of Deep
   Waters, and has taken his seat upon your throne.

Twenty-three lines. House of Enki in Eridu.

2. E-KUR, THE TEMPLE OF ENLIL IN NIPPUR

Enlil was the king of the gods, and the city of Nippur, in which his
main temple stood, was the religious center of ancient Iraq. Here
and in the following hymns, Enlil is sometimes referred to by his
epithet Great Mountain.

House of the Mountain. Shrine where fates are fixed.   25
Foundation of . . . . . . high-raised ziqqurat,
. . . . home of Enlil.
To your right lies Sumer, to your left Akkad.[5] House of Enlil!
In your heart, there is quiet. In your court, the fates are fixed.

The beam above your door is the peak of a mountaintop,   30
the pilasters at your sides are proud pinnacles.
Your top is the top of a . . . your noble court.
Your roots toil with heaven and earth.[6]

Your lord is the great lord Enlil, the good king,
the king who rules all sides of heaven, the king who fixes fates. 35

Shrine of Nippur: Enlil, the Great Mountain,
has built a home in your holy court, and has taken his seat
    upon your throne.

Thirteen lines. House of Enlil in Nippur.

3. E-KIUR, THE TEMPLE OF NINLIL IN NIPPUR

Ninlil was Enlil's wife. Her worship was centered in Tummal, a
sanctuary south of Nippur, which was renowned as an ancient site
that had been rebuilt by legendary kings over millennia. Ninlil's
shrine in Nippur, the Leveled Land (E-kiur), was also called House
of Tummal after this sanctuary.[7]

Tummal. You were selected for the great noble powers, you
    spread awe and the tingling of fear.
Strong foundation, whose purifying rituals span the
    Deep Sea.   40

Ancient city! You are a marshland kept green by old reeds
    and new shoots.
Inside you stands a mountain of plenty and abundance.
For the New Year's festival, you are wreathed in wonder,
and the great queen of the Leveled Land stands as Enlil's
    equal.

Your lady, Mother Ninlil, the beloved wife of Enlil,   45
has built a home in your holy court, House of Tummal,
    and has taken her seat upon your throne.

Eight lines. House of Ninlil in Nippur.

4. E-MELEMHUSH, THE TEMPLE
OF NUSKA IN NIPPUR

Nuska was Enlil's servant and minister. The River Ordeal was a
religious ritual used to test suspected criminals whose guilt could
not be determined by normal means, usually because they were
accused of sorcery: they would be plunged into the rushing waters
and declared innocent if they survived.

House of Furious Splendor. Wrapped in a great, frightful
    light.
Mighty shrine, the noble powers were assigned to you in
    heaven.
Treasury of Enlil, you were founded to house the ancient
    powers. Lordship befits you.   50
You lift your head in majesty, giving guidance to the
    House of the Mountain.
Your rampart is like a horn. Your house . . . . a court
    with heaven.

In the River Ordeal, where the mighty suits are settled,
    your verdicts
give new birth to the righteous and coil gloom around
    wicked hearts.
Your great place, suited for the sacred rituals and the
    purifying priests: 55
King Enlil has filled it with food.

Your lord is the lord who counsels Enlil, who is worthy of
    the Mighty Shrine,
the demon of the House of the Mountain: the noble
    Nuska

has built a home in your holy court, House of Enlil, and has
   taken his seat upon your throne.

Twelve lines. House of Nuska in Nippur.   60

5. E-SHUMESHA, THE TEMPLE
OF NINURTA IN NIPPUR

Ninurta, a warrior god famous for his battles against monstrous
opponents, was the son of Enlil and Ninlil.

House That Harvests the Powers of Heaven. Built upon a
   mighty land.
The true powers that the hero . . . throne . . . grow.
The strength of battle, the mace of youth, armed with
   arrows.
Towering, bustling building: your foundation is everlasting.

You were founded by an ancient king. Your verdicts are
   part of the powers of your lord.   65
Holy earthwork that would fill a mountain. You raise
   your head high among kings.
Huge house. Like sunlight, the flow of your wonder extends
   across the land.
House of . . . Powers.[8] Enlil has infused your name with
   furious splendor.

Your lord is the great . . . the warrior whose strength is
   unmatched.
Enlil's great commander, the ruler who rivals heaven and
   earth.   70

. . . seal bearer of Father Enlil, who perfects the great
powers.
. . . . vanguard of Father Enlil.

The leader, the lion, who was born to the Great Mountain,
who destroys the wicked lands: Lord Ninurta
has built a home in your holy court, House of . . . Powers,
and has taken his seat upon your throne.   75

Fifteen lines. House of Ninurta in Nippur.

6. GAGIMAH, THE TEMPLE OF SHUZIANA IN NIPPUR

The Gagimah was a section of the religious district in Nippur
reserved for women and sacred to Shuziana, Enlil's second wife.

House That Is Home to a Hill. Raising your head . . .
Crown of the uplands. Holy place, sacred place!
House. Your foundation is a mighty pillar of dominion.
Your queen is a singular woman. She keeps the throne
room full,   80
House of the Singular Hill, and your sacred court rejoices
in her rule.

Your lady is the wisest, she holds back her anger.
The powerful daughter, who thrives by Enlil's side:
Shuziana, second wife to Father Enlil,
has built a home in your holy court, House of the Singular
Hill, and has taken her seat upon your throne.   85

Nine lines. House of Shuziana in the Gagimah.

7. E-KESH, THE TEMPLE OF
NINHURSANGA IN KESH

Ninhursanga was the goddess of birth and motherhood. She was known by many names, including Ninmah, Mama, and Nintu, the latter of which is here translated as "Lady of Birth."

Towering Kesh. You are the image of heaven and earth.
Like the mighty viper of the desert, you spread fear.
House of Ninhursanga, you stand on a land of wrath.
Glorious Kesh: your heart is deep, your form is huge.   90
Great lion . . . the upland, roaming through the wild.

Great mountain, brought here by holy incantations.
Your heart is dusk, moonlight cannot enter you.
The Lady of Birth has given you beauty.
House of Kesh: your brickwork is your birthing.
Your terrace is a crown of lapis lazuli: your frame is
    your creation.[9]   95

Your lady is the lady who imposes silence. The great good
    queen of heaven.
When she speaks, heaven shakes. When she opens her
    mouth, storms roar.
Ninhursanga, Enlil's sister,
has built a home in your holy court, House of Kesh, and
    has taken her seat upon your throne.

Thirteen lines. House of Ninhursanga in Kesh.   100

8. E-KISHNUGAL, THE TEMPLE OF NANNA IN UR

It was at the E-kishnugal temple that the historical Enheduana
served as high priestess. Nanna is often linked to cattle, because
the crescent moon was likened to a pair of horns. Ur lay in the
south of ancient Iraq, next to a vast expanse of marshlands that
was associated with the Abzu.

Ur. Bull standing in the canebrake.
House of Alabaster.[10] Calf of a great cow . . . holy heaven.
Your oxen rest by the door to your nest.[11]
Ur. You are a basket filled with food, feeding all the lands.

Shrine, most sacred place in heaven and earth.   105
House of Nanna. Your front is a king, your rear is a throne,
your feast is a song, and your great holy halls are the sacred
    drums.
You shine with the light of righteous rule, of precious fates.

Home of high priestesses.[12] Noble shrine of holy powers.
    The sun . . .
House of Alabaster, your shimmering moonlight shines
    over the country,   110
your dazzling daylight spreads across the land.

House. Your court is a mighty serpent, a marshland of
    snakes.
Your foundation reaches down to the fifty Deep Seas,
    the seven Deep Waters.
Shrine. You see into the heart of the gods.

Your lord is the lord who delivers decisions, he is the
    crown of vast heaven.   115

The lord of heaven, Nanna,
has built a home in your holy court, shrine of Ur, and has
   taken his seat upon your throne.

Seventeen lines. House of Nanna in Ur.

9. E-HURSANG, THE TEMPLE OF SHULGI IN UR

This hymn is identified in the postscript as a later addition to the
collection. King Shulgi was worshipped as a god, perhaps even
during his lifetime, and a temple in his honor was built in Ur.[13]

House of the Mighty Name. Peak rising into heaven.
Your holy base and your great foundation are precious
   destinies.   120
Your heart is full of noble powers. Beaming, shining light.
Shrine. Behind you lies beautiful heaven, before you
   endless humankind.
You bind the land together and make of it a single track.

Mighty river, flowing out . . . gathering . . . the cosmic
   powers.
Your roots spread fear. Righteous mountain, sprouting
   from a vast plain.   125
A mighty home of majesty, of all the noble powers.
. . . . shouting.
House of joy. Your court delights the settled people.

House. Your lord, Shulgi, has made your dominion great.
The perfect, magnificent . . . the great, soaring tempest,   130
he who is adorned with cosmic powers, who settles suits:
House of the Peak! Shulgi of heaven

has built a home in your holy court, and has taken his
    seat upon your throne.

Fifteen lines. Addition. Shulgi's House of the Peak in Ur.

10. E-KUARA, THE TEMPLE OF
ASARLUHI IN KUARA

Asarluhi, the god of magic and incantations, was Enki's son.

City. Like grain, you grew from the Deep Sea.   135
You took your cosmic powers from the cloud-covered
    steppe.
Kuara, you are the foundation for a worthy hall.
Your lord does not hold back his gifts. He stands as a
    wonder to behold.
The Seven Sages[14] have made your house great, from
    depth to peak.

Your lord is the precious lord, the precious Asarluhi,   140
the hero born to be a noble lord. He is a leopard who
    catches those who take flight.
Like the strike of the storm, he strikes the rebel land,
pouring cruel words upon it until it submits.
Asarluhi, son of the Deep Sea,
has built a home in your holy court, House of Kuara, and
    has taken his seat upon your throne.   145

Eleven lines. House of Asarluhi in Kuara.

11. GABURA, THE TEMPLE OF
NINGUBLAGA IN KIABRIG

Ningublaga was Nanna's son. Like his father, he is associated with
cattle; this hymn suggests that he was also linked to rainfall and
possibly to magic.

House of All the Perfect Oxen, whose lord is seated on
    sacred agate.
The mighty portal looms for the noble prince.
Its fine, first-rate oil is holy and well made.
Chamber of Jars, sacred stall, whose cows graze on licorice.   150

Your lord is a great wild bull, an elephant delighting in his
    might,
an aurochs adorned with horns, delighting in his splendid
    light.[15]
Speaking in a strange tongue, this sorcerer gathers clouds
    in the sky.
The storm roars in the sky: he grants the storm that beats
    the earth.
Ningublaga, son of Nanna,   155
has built a home in your holy court, Kiabrig, and has taken
    his seat upon your throne.

Ten lines. House of Ningublaga in Kiabrig.

12. KARZIDA, THE TEMPLE OF NANNA IN GAESH

Nanna had a temple in the small city of Gaesh, not far from
Ur, where his main temple stood (see hymn 8).

Shrine. Great chapel that lies by the cow stalls.
Small, shining city of Nanna.
Righteous Wharf. Inside you is a tall tower, founded on a
    base that is holy and pure.   160
Shrine. The home of high priestesses stands upon a sacred
    spot.
Your door is made of copper—strong stuff. It stands upon
    a mighty place.
Loud and lordly cow stall, you raise your horns as if you
    were a bull.

Your lord is the ruler of heaven, standing in joy,
at midday   165
Righteous Wharf! Nanna
has built a home in your holy court, and has taken his seat
    upon your throne.

Ten lines. House of Nanna in Gaesh.

13. E-BABBAR, THE TEMPLE OF UTU IN LARSA

Utu, the sun god, had two main temples, both named E-babbar,
"Shining House," one in Larsa and one in Sippar. Kulaba was a
district in the neighboring city of Uruk; the hymn is thus claim-
ing that the splendor of Utu's temple was visible from many miles
away.

House that came from heaven, pouring light on Kulaba,
shrine of the Shining House. Shining bull,   170
lifting your neck to Utu . . . in heaven.
Your brilliance is furious, like the stamping of hooves.
    It is holy and lustrous.

. . . . a beard of lapis lazuli.

Your lord is the soaring sunlight, the ruler . . . righteous
    voice.
He lights up the horizon, he lights up the zenith of heaven.   175
Utu, lord of the Shining House,
has built a home in your holy court, House of Larsa, and
    has taken his seat upon your throne.

Nine lines. House of Utu in Larsa.

14. E-GIDA, THE TEMPLE OF NINAZU IN ENEGIR

Ninazu was a god of the underworld and the son of Ereshkigal, the
queen of the dead. It was traditional to offer libations—sacrifices
of beer, wine, honey, and other liquids—to the spirits of one's
ancestors, by pouring them into pipes that would lead down to
the realm of the dead.

Enegir. Great channel of offerings, channel to the land of
    Ereshkigal,
the underworld of Sumer, where all humans gather.[16]   180
House of the Vault. Your shadow shrouds the lords of the land.

Your lord is the seed of a great king. Priest of the mighty
    underworld, born to Ereshkigal.
He plays the lord-voiced lyre, sweet as the sound of a calf.
Ninazu, to whom the people pray,
has built a home in your holy court, House of Enegir, and
    has taken his seat upon your throne.   185

Seven lines. House of Ninazu in Enegir.

15. E-GISHBANDA, THE TEMPLE OF
NINGISHZIDA IN GISHBANDA

Ningishzida was Ninazu's son, and like his father he was associated with the underworld. He was also linked with agriculture and plants.

Ancient land. Small mountain, wrought with skill.
Chamber. Place of terror, lying in a meadow,
site of fear, whose ways no man can fathom.
Gishbanda. You are a chain, a snare, a shackle of the
    mighty underworld that no foot escapes.   190
The frame of your building is raised up, jutting out like
    a trap,
but sunlight shines inside you, and ample gifts are handed
    out there.

Your lord is a lord who stretches out his holy hand, sacred
    in heaven.
On the back of Lord Ningishzida falls abundant, joyful hair.[17]
Gishbanda! Ningishzida   195
has built a home in your holy court, and has taken his seat
    upon your throne.

Ten lines. House of Ningishzida in Gishbanda.

16. E-ANA, THE TEMPLE OF INANA IN URUK

Inana's main temple was in Uruk; as related in Enheduana's *Hymn,* the goddess shared this temple with An, though the present hymn does not mention that. Kulaba was a sacred district in

Uruk, sometimes used as a byname for the city as a whole. The
phrase "Steadfast Chapel" (**niĝin ĝara**) was an epithet for various
temples dedicated to Inana.

Home to the mighty powers of Kulaba. Your court lets the
    great shrines grow,
fresh green fruit that is filled with pleasure and delight.
Shrine built for a bull. You were brought down from
    heaven's heart.   200
House of Heaven, house of seven corners, of the seven
    flames that are raised high at dead of night,
gazing on the seven desires.[18]

Your lady is the holy horizon.
Your queen is Inana, who . . . .
She orders gems for the women and covers the men's head
    with a cloth.   205
She is a crown of glittering desire, she is the basilisk of the
    Steadfast Chapel.
The sovereign of heaven and earth, Inana,
has built a home in your holy court, House of Heaven, and
    has taken her seat upon your throne.

Eleven lines. House of Inana in Uruk.

17. E-MUSH, THE TEMPLE OF DUMUZI IN BADTIBIRA

Dumuzi was the god of shepherds and Inana's lover. After Inana's
ill-fated attempt at invading the underworld, she consigned Du-
muzi to death so that she herself could be brought back to life.

House where gleaming herbs are strewn upon a bed of
    flowers.   210
Holy bedroom of Inana:
this place soothes the Lady of the Wild.
In the House of the Court, the sacred brickwork is full
    of flowers, the clay is set . . .
To the countless ewes of the upland
and to the shepherd, O House of the Underworld, your
    vault gives shelter.[19]   215

Your lord is a lion prowling through the wild. The jewel
    of the holy woman,[20]
whose breast is sacred and delightful. The lord, the holy
    husband of Inana,
Dumuzi, ruler of the House of the Court,
has built a home in your holy court, Badtibira, and has
    taken his seat upon your throne.

Ten lines. House of Dumuzi in Badtibira.   220

18. E-AKKIL, THE TEMPLE OF
NINSHUBUR IN AKKIL

Ninshubur was Inana's assistant and steward. She was instrumental in bringing Inana back to life after her foray into the underworld by lamenting her death and so rallying Ea to rescue her. Akkil, the city where Ninshubur was worshipped, literally means "lament."

House of Mighty Eyes. From your heart flows wealth.
House. Your vault is a mountain of abundance,

and your sweet smell is a mountain of grapevines.
Your righteous steward is foremost in heaven.

House. Your lady is a leader among gods, 225
the righteous steward of the House of Heaven, who holds
    the holy scepter.
Ninshubur, righteous steward of the House of Heaven,
has built a home in your holy court, House of Akkil, and
    has taken her seat upon your throne.

Eight lines. House of Ninshubur in Akkil.

19. E-MURUM, THE TEMPLE OF
NINGIRIM IN MURUM

The goddess Ningirim was associated with magic and incanta-
tions, as the few surviving lines of this hymn attest.

City. Founded on the Deep Sea's throne, built for priests. 230
House where they speak the spells of heaven and earth.
. . . .
. . . .
. . . .
. . . . 235
purifying waters . . . . holy heaven and sacred earth.
Ningirim, queen of the shining purifying waters,
has built a home in your holy court, House of Murum,
    and has taken her seat upon your throne.

Nine lines. House of Ningirim in Murum.

POEMS

20. E-NINNU, THE TEMPLE OF
NINGIRSU IN LAGASH

Ningirsu was the son of Enlil and a warrior god. He was later
identified with Ninurta (for whom see hymn 5); his defeat of the
Thunder Bird (Anzu) using the Myriad-Mowing Mace (Shar-ur) is
best known from an epic where he appears as Ninurta.[21] The "Sa-
cred City" refers to the neighboring city of Girsu, where Ningirsu
was also worshipped: his name literally means "Lord of Girsu."
The full name of the E-ninnu temple was "House of Fifty Shining
Anzu Birds," presumably because it contained fifty images of the
enemy that Ningirsu vanquished.

House of Fifty. Righteous might of Lagash, vanguard
    of Sumer. 240
Thunder Bird gazing on the mountains,
Myriad-Mowing Mace of Ningirsu . . . all the lands.
Battle strength, wrathful storm that drowns the people,
infusing the great Anuna with strength for the fight.
Brickwork on whose holy hill the destinies are fixed,
    you are like a beautiful peak. 245
Your canal . . . . . . blow against each other.
You are the gate to the Sacred City.
Beer is poured out into the beautiful bowls of holy An,
    they are laid out beneath the open sky.

All that comes into you will be without equal,
all that leaves you will be without end. 250
. . . . furious front, house of splendor.
King Ningirsu's place of judgment,
source of awe and tingling fear,
where the Anuna gather to drink your mighty beer.

Your lord is a raging wind, razing cities and rebel lands.   255
Your ruler is an angry aurochs flaunting his strength,
    an angry lion smashing skulls.
Hero. As lords do, he works out battle plans,
as kings do, he seizes victory.

Strong one, mighty champion of battle, lord without rival.
The son of Enlil, the lord Ningirsu,   260
has built a home in your holy court, House of Fifty, and
    has taken his seat upon your throne.

Twenty-two lines. House of Ningirsu in Lagash.

21. E-TARSIRSIR, THE TEMPLE OF BABA IN GIRSU

Baba (whose name can also be read Bau) was Ningirsu's wife. In
later periods, she was merged with Gula, the goddess of healing
and medicine. On the River Ordeal, see hymn 4. The "Sacred City"
(Iriku) was the temple district in Girsu.

Sacred City. Shrine of holy An, from which sprang the
    human seed. Blessed with a good name.
Within you is the River Ordeal that brightens the righteous.
House That Spreads Guidance. Holy treasury, forever full of
    lapis lazuli.   265
House That Heaps Up . . . . from which powers and
    verdicts spring. Honored by heroes.

Your lady is the lady of mercy, mother of all lands.
Queen, great healer of humanity: in this city, she fixes fates.
The firstborn of An, the young Mother Baba,

has built a home in your holy court, Sacred City, and has
    taken her seat upon your throne.   270

Eight lines. House of Baba in the Sacred City.

22. E-SIRARA, THE TEMPLE OF
NANSHE IN SIRARA

Nanshe was Enki's daughter; she was associated with the sea.
Sirara was a temple district in the area ruled by the city of
Lagash.

House. Sacred cow . . . .
Beaming city, dressed for its lady in shining colors.
Sirara, great and noble place.
The walls of your shrine   275

Your lady is Nanshe: a mighty storm, a massive flood.
She was born on the shore of the sea,
she laughs on the foam of the sea,
she plays with waves and water.
. . . . Nanshe, lady of . . .   280
has built a home in your holy court, House of Sirara, and
    has taken her seat upon your throne.

Ten lines. The house of Nanshe in Sirara.

23. E-ABSHAGALA, THE TEMPLE
OF NINMARKI IN GUABA

Ninmarki was Nanshe's daughter and like her mother associated
with the sea. Guaba—whose name means "bank of the sea"—was
a port city in the Lagash area.

House That Spans the Sea's Midst. Built upon a sacred land.
Guaba, steadfast storehouse, from you all things are born.
Holy shrine. You are a sacred cow, for you all things endure. 285

Your lady is Ninmarki, the mighty steward . . .
Strong . . . . of Father Enlil,
Lord Enlil seeks her guidance . . . .
Born . . . the swell of the sea . . . .
Like her father . . . overseeing the sacred sea. 290
House of Guaba! Holy Ninmarki
has built a home in your holy court, and has taken her
    seat upon your throne.

Ten lines. House of Ninmarki in Guaba.

24. E-KINIRSHA, THE TEMPLE
OF DUMUZI-ABZU IN KINIRSHA

Little is known about the goddess Dumuzi-Abzu (whose name
literally means "righteous child of the Abzu"), and her relation to
Dumuzi is unclear. The name of the city is likewise uncertain: the
signs could also be read Kinunir.

House of Kinirsha. Worthy of its queen.
. . . raising the ziqqurat like a beautiful peak.   295
House . . . where the noble voice of joy resounds.

House. Your lady is a storm. She sits astride a lion . . .
She is exalted in sacred songs, in call and response, and
    she herself sings with a mighty voice.
Daughter of a righteous aurochs, nursed at her mother's
    sacred breast.
Shrine of Kinirsha! Dumuzi-Abzu   300
has built a home in your holy court, and has taken her
    seat upon your throne.

Seven lines.[22] House of Dumuzi-Abzu in Kinirsha.

25. E-MAH, THE TEMPLE OF SHARA IN UMMA

Shara was Inana's son, but it is unclear who his father was (no
mention is made of Dumuzi), and Inana is not generally portrayed
as a motherly figure.

House of Beautiful Bowls. Built by An,
towering hall, carrying out the right orders.
. . . . abundance in the sea's midst.   305
In the holy . . . prayers are spoken, and hymns of joy
    are sung.
Mighty House, home of Shara. The righteous man
has made it grow in opulence for you.

Your house is the Mighty House. Your lord is the holy
    woman's noble son.

. . . . a place of peace and plenty.   310
His hair hangs loose, his eyes are oxlike.
Shara, who . . . all things good, the son who secures
     the powers for his mother,
has built a home in your holy court, Mighty House, and
     has taken his seat upon your throne.

Eleven lines. House of Shara in Umma.

26. E-SHERZIGURU, THE TEMPLE OF INANA IN ZABALAM

Deities like Inana, who had major temples in several cities, often
developed various local identifications, so that one could speak of
Inana of Uruk (hymn 16), Inana of Zabalam, and Inana of Akkad
(hymn 40). These local forms could take on distinct characteristics
and traditions of worship.

House Wrapped in Radiance. Adorned with agate,   315
great wonder. You are the sacred chapel of Inana,
garlanded all over with powers, righteous powers.
Zabalam, shrine of the shimmering mountain, shrine
     that . . . at dawn,
where ecstasy resounds.
In her ecstasy, the holy woman gave you a great hall.   320

Your queen is Inana. . . . the singular woman,
a basilisk taunting the man who . . . . .
Brightly beaming, bearing down on rebel lands,
and bringing beauty to the firmament at dusk.[23]
The great daughter of holy Nanna, Inana,   325

has built a home in your holy court, House of Zabalam,
and has taken her seat upon your throne.

Twelve lines. House of Inana in Zabalam.

27. E-UGALGALA, THE TEMPLE
OF ISHKUR IN KARKARA

Ishkur was the storm god, and this unfortunately fragmentary
hymn seems to have emphasized both his destructive side, as the
death-dealing tempest, and his positive side, as the life-giving
rain.

House. Like a mighty lion, you are wrapped in dread.
Each day you deliver shrewd verdicts to the uplands.
House of Ishkur. Your front is wealth, your rear is joy,   330
the base on which you stand is a horned bull, a great
    lion.
Sacred staff. You are heaven's breast, giving rain to grain
    and flax.
The pilasters of your house jut out like aurochs horns.
. . . . foundation, your walls rise high,
. . . . heavy clouds,   335
. . . . snake,
. . . . moonlight.
. . . . Ishkur, a devastating flood,
. . . . . the southern and the seven northern winds,
. . . . the north wind blows,   340
. . . . running,
. . . splits . . . mountain, diorite, stones . . .

. . . .

. . . .
. . . .   345
. . . . the seed of the land . . . . . .
. . . . . watchman of the waterways, in heaven and
   earth,
. . . . living beings and the plentiful people,
. . . . Ishkur
has built a home in your holy court, House of Karkara,
   and has taken his seat upon your throne.   350

Twenty-three lines. House of Ishkur in Karkara.

28. UNKNOWN TEMPLE

Too little of this hymn is preserved to determine which temple,
city, or god it invokes.

. . . . bolt of An . . . .
. . . .
. . . . heaven and earth . . . . . .
. . . . Enki   355
. . . .
. . . .
. . . .
. . . .
. . . .   360
has built a home in your holy court, ... and
   has taken her[24] seat upon your throne.

Ten lines . . . .

29. E-MAH, THE TEMPLE OF
NINHURSANGA AND ASGHI IN ADAB

The hymn is addressed to Ninhursanga, the mother goddess, whose main temple, also named E-mah, stood in Kesh (see hymn 7). She shared the temple in Adab with her son Ashgi, about whom little is known. Adab lay next to the Iturungal, a major irrigation canal diverting water from the Euphrates.

. . . .
. . . .
. . . .   365
An has . . . your holy court . . . .
Mighty House, home of all! Worthy of its queen.
Your front is wrapped in mighty awe. Your heart is strewn
    with frightful light.
The Lady of Birth has fixed your fate, together with Enlil
    and Enki.

House of Joy . . . . life of humanity.   370
From heaven's heart, An has given you mighty powers.
Your sacred sanctuary and sturdy shrine:
Ninhursanga has founded their fortune in Kesh.

House of great powers. The rituals of purity shine bright
    on your holy platform.
Adab, house that lies by the canal: Asghi, god of Adab,   375
has built a home in your holy court, House of Adab,
    and has taken his seat upon your throne.

Fifteen lines. House of Ninhursanga in Adab.

30. E-GALMAH, THE TEMPLE
OF NINISINA IN ISIN

Ninisina—whose name means "Queen of Isin"—was a local form
of Gula, the goddess of healing. The "Steadfast Chapel" is not the
same as the epithet used for Inana's temples (see hymn 16) but a
part of Ninisina's temple.

Isin. City founded by An, built in an empty land,
whose front soars up, whose heart is finely wrought,   380
whose cosmic powers were fixed by An.

Sacred dais beloved by Enlil,
where An and Enlil determine destinies,
where the great gods dine.
Source of awe and tingling fear,   385
where the Anuna gather to drink your mighty beer.

Your lady is the mother, the holy woman wreathed in
     agate,
who cares for the Steadfast Chapel of this sacred place.
She holds the great gems of her holy women,
she has set aright the breasts of the seven priestesses.[25]   390
The seven ecstasies resound for her.

Your queen, the great healer of the land,
Ninisina, daughter of An,
has built a home in your holy court, House of Isin, and
     has taken her seat upon your throne.

Sixteen lines. House of Ninisina in Isin.   395

31. KUNSATU, THE TEMPLE OF
NUMUSHDA IN KAZALLU

Numushda was Nanna's son and may have been a god of storms.

Kazallu. Your crown lies in the heart of heaven.
Splendor . . . . stand in wonder.

Your lord is the son of an aurochs . . . born to a bull.
Mighty. . . . iridescent eyes, lion-toothed lord,
who catches calves with his claws,   400
who catches . . . .
who catches . . . .
. . . . giving strength to . . . .
Threshold of the Peak! The great lord Numushda
has built a home in your holy court, Kazallu, and has
    taken his seat upon your throne.   405

Ten lines. House of Numushda in Kazallu.

32. E-IGIKALAMA, THE TEMPLE OF
LUGAL-MARADA IN MARADA

The name of this god means "King of Marada." He was a local
form of Ninurta, for whom see hymns 5 and 20.

House That Is the Land's Eye. Your foundation is sound.
Sprouting mountain, you stand wide upon the earth.
. . . . the enemy land.
. . . .   410
. . . .

. . . .
. . . .
has built a home in your holy court, Marada, and has
    taken his seat upon your throne.

Eight lines. House of Lugal-Marada in Marada.   415

33. E-DIMGALKALAMA, THE TEMPLE
OF ISHTARAN IN DER

Der stood on the eastern border of the Sumerian heartland, and
its god Ishtaran was charged with enforcing respect for borders
and treaties. He was often portrayed as a snake. Urash was the
goddess of the earth.

Der. You who give great verdicts . . . .
On your gate, which is filled with awe and frightful light,
is a relief of a basilisk and a great serpent intertwined.

Your lord is the captain of the gods,
mighty words and clever counsel suit him.   420
Son of Urash, skilled in the great powers of dominion.
Ishtaran . . . king of heaven,
has built a home in your holy court, House of the Land's
    Great Bond, and has taken his seat upon your throne.

Eight lines. House of Ishtaran in Der.

34. E-SIKIL, THE TEMPLE OF
NINAZU IN ESHNUNNA

Ninazu seems to have had two roles: he was worshipped in Enegir
as a god of the underworld and a son of Ereshkigal (see hymn 14),
and in Eshnunna as a warrior god, son of Enlil and Ninlil. They
may have been originally separate deities who were linked be-
cause of their shared name (which literally means "Lord Healer").

Holy House, whose sacred powers are foremost in the land,   425
whose name stands tall and proud. Mighty home of a hero,
sacred house of Ninazu, hallowed house of great powers.
House, your powers are holy, your rituals shine bright.
The hero finds calm in your chamber,
Ninazu dines on your dais.   430

Your king is the great lord, the son of Enlil.
Prowling proud, the lion pours poison on the enemy,[26]
he rises like the wind against the foreign lands,
he snarls like a basilisk against the rebels' walls.

He is a storm that shrouds the disobedient, stomping his
     feet on his foes.   435
When he runs, no wicked man escapes,
when he wins, rebel cities are destroyed,
when he frowns, their people are cast into dust.

House. Your lord is a great lion. The enemy hangs from his
     hand.
Your king is a towering, terrifying storm, he is the wrath
     of war.   440
Like a . . . . . in combat, a shield on his mighty arm.
He is a net that holds the vast people, no enemy escapes it.

When this great lord steps forth, his majesty is unmatched.
Righteous seed, born to the Great Mountain and to Ninlil.
Holy House! Your king, the hero Ninazu,   445
has built a home in your holy court, Eshnunna, and has
    taken his seat upon your throne.

Twenty-two lines. House of Ninazu in Eshnunna.

35. E-DUBA, THE TEMPLE OF ZABABA IN KISH

Kish was seen as the center of political power, just as Nippur was
the center of religious worship: it was said that kingship had de-
scended from heaven to Kish. Its god Zababa was a patron of war
and the husband of Inana in one of her many guises, Inana of Kish
(for Inana's various identifications, see hymn 26).

House, built amid abundance.[27] Kish, you raise your head
    among the noble powers.
Steadfast city, your great foundation cannot be undone.
You stand upon a huge cloud, preeminent in heaven.   450
Your heart is a weapon, a club covered in . . . . . .
On your right, mountains shake, on your left, enemies
    wither.

Your lord is mighty and magnificent, a great storm that
    overwhelms the earth, spreading vast and terrifying
    awe.
House of the Granary! Your king, the hero Zababa
has built a home in your holy court, House of Kish, and
    has taken his seat upon your throne.   455

Eight lines. House of Zababa in Kish.

36. MESLAM, THE TEMPLE OF NERGAL IN KUTHA

Nergal was the god of premature death, disease, and disaster, and the city of Kutha (also known as Gudua or Kutû) was traditionally associated with rituals for the dead. The name of Nergal's temple was Meslam.

House that binds the land together.
Ox. Noble strength . . . among the gods.
Aurochs spreading fear, bull sowing grief.
Kutha. Your harbor is deep, it drinks the river.   460
Your heart is finely wrought, your weapon is a . . . mace,
    assigned to you in heaven.
Your holy court glistens, encircling the Meslam.

Your lord is the fierce god,[28] king of the Meslam,
furious god of the underworld, king of the darkening day.
Nergal, who comes forth from the Meslam,[29]   465
has built a home in your holy court, and has taken his seat
    upon your throne.

Ten lines. House of Nergal in Kutha.

37. E-ABLUA, THE TEMPLE OF NANNA IN URUM

This hymn again highlights the association between the Moon God and cattle (see hymns 8 and 12).

Towering Urum,[30] where Nanna settles suits.
House of Teeming Cattle, huge stall:
Nanna is your herdsman.   470

House, my king! Your scepter reaches heaven.
. . . . moonlight . . . joy . . .
. . . . daylight . . . may . . .

Your lord is the lord of holy joy. . . .
who steps forth on the night sky that glitters like lapis
    lazuli, joy of . . . honored by heroes.   475
He lights up the land . . . Nanna
has built a home in your holy court, House of Urum, and
    has taken his seat upon your throne.

Ten lines. House of Nanna in Urum.

38. E-BABBAR, THE TEMPLE OF UTU IN SIPPAR

The second of the Sun God's major temples stood in Sippar, in the
north (for the temple in Larsa, see hymn 13).

Sippar. Throne where Utu takes his daily seat.
House of the Heavenly Lord: you are a star, a crown born
    to Ningal.   480
House of Utu. Your lord is . . . of everything, filling up
    heaven and earth.
When this lord sleeps, the people sleep,
when this lord rises, the people rise.
Bull . . . the people bow to him.

For Utu the herds graze.   485
For him the humans bathe.
For him the land . . . .
He doles out great powers—your shrine is a flood.

At sunrise his verdicts are revealed. In the soaring
    daylight a beard hangs from his chin;
in the dead of night a crown is tied to his head.[31]   490
Utu, king of the Shining House,
has built a home in your holy court, House of Sippar, and
    has taken his seat upon your throne.

Fourteen lines. House of Utu in Sippar.

39. E-HURSANG, THE TEMPLE OF NINHURSANGA

This is the third and final hymn to Ninhursanga, which like the
previous two (7 and 29) dwells on her role as the goddess of birth.
The name of the city in which this temple stood is unknown: it is
written with the cuneiform signs HI.ZA, but we do not know how
those signs are to be read.

House of the Peak. Like a tree, you are beautiful in fruit,
. . . . your heart is abundance.   495
Where the fates are fixed—there you will be, fixing fates.
May the crown bring delight to your court.
Your roots are like a mighty coiling serpent—
may daylight shine on your sacred foundation.

The mother, the Lady of Birth, queen of creation,   500
does her work within your dark place.
She fastens the crown on the newborn king;
on the newborn lord she lays the wreath that she holds in
    her hand.
The midwife of heaven and earth, Ninhursanga,

has built a home in your holy court, House of . . . .
　　and has taken her seat upon your throne.　　　　　　505

Twelve lines. House of Ninhursanga in . . . .

40. E-ULMASH, THE TEMPLE OF INANA IN AKKAD

Ulmash was a district in Akkad that was sacred to Inana. The two previous hymns to Inana (16 and 26) bring out her association with sensuality and delight, but this hymn focuses on her warlike character—and, implicitly, on her support for the Akkadian kings in their military exploits.

Ulmash. North . . . of the land.
Furious lion that batters bulls,
net spread out to catch the enemy.
You impose silence on the rebel land,　　　　　　510
pouring cruel words upon it until it submits.
House of Inana, made of silver and lapis lazuli, treasury
　　built of gold.

Your lady is a waterbird, the holy woman of the Steadfast
　　Chapel.
She wears war, jubilant and beautiful, she lays out the
　　seven maces,
washes her weapons for battle,　　　　　　515
opens the door of battle and . . . .
The clever goddess of heaven, Inana,
has built a home in your holy court, House of Ulmash,
　　and has taken her seat upon your throne.

Twelve lines. House of Inana in Ulmash.

41. E-AKKAD, THE TEMPLE OF ILABA IN AKKAD

Together with Inana, Ilaba was the city god of Akkad, and like her he was associated with warfare.

House. Righteous strength. Battle-ax that fells rebels,   520
then digs up their green meadows.

. . . .
. . . .

Your lord is the hero who . . . .
He defeats everyone in battle, playing   525
Ilaba, god of Akkad,
has built a home in your holy court, House of Akkad, and
    has taken his seat upon your throne.

Eight lines. House of Ilaba in Akkad.

42. E-ZAGIN, THE TEMPLE OF NISABA IN ERESH

The collection ends with a celebration of writing itself. Nisaba (whose name can also be read Nidaba) was the patron of scribes, scholarship, mathematics, and measurement. It is perhaps unsurprising that this hymn also displays some of the most cryptic writing in the collection. The text is fully preserved, but several lines resist interpretation, no doubt because they contain as yet uncracked wordplays; these are indicated by the ellipsis points that also mark missing text.

House of Stars. House of Lapis Lazuli, sparkling bright, you
    open the way to all the lands.
. . . . are set in the shrine.   530

Eresh. Each month, the ancient lords raise their head
    for you.
On the hill, soap . . . .
The great goddess Nisaba[32]
has brought the great powers from heaven, adding to your
    powers.
. . . .   535

Righteous woman of unmatched mind.
Soothing . . . and opening her mouth,
consulting a tablet of lapis lazuli,
giving guidance to all the lands.
Righteous woman, cleansing soap, born to the upright
    stylus.[33]   540
She measures the heavens and outlines the earth:
All praise Nisaba.[34]

The weaver of the tablet was Enheduana.
My king! Something has been born which had not been
    born before.

Fourteen lines. House of Nisaba in Eresh.   545

FRAGMENTARY HYMNS

TWO SHORT, FRAGMENTARY HYMNS CONTAIN THE name Enheduana.[1] The first is told in Enheduana's own voice, but it seems to have been written after her death, as it refers to a temple in Ur, the "House Whose Base Is Clad in Awe" (E-temen-ni-guru), which was built in a later period, so it was probably written in Enheduana's name by another poet. It was clearly composed in dialogue with Enheduana's other works, as shown by its many allusions to the *Exaltation:* it was probably intended to elaborate on and expand the poetical corpus attributed to Enheduana.

The first hymn is the better preserved of the two, and it is identified in a colophon (a short note at the end of the tablet) as a **balbale**, a genre of hymns that was performed by two groups of singers, who would alternate in call-and-response fashion. It is mainly addressed to the E-kishnugal, Nanna's temple, though it also calls on Nanna himself, his wife, Ningal, and the city of Ur. Indeed, it can be hard to tell whether a line such as "You dole out kingship" refers to the temple, the city, or the god. After the initial hymn, Enheduana introduces herself, describing how she correctly performed the duties of the high priestess, and highlighting two duties in particular: the purifying ritual known as šuluh, and the preparation of bread and beer for the god.[2] It ends with a celebration of Ningal.

The second hymn describes Enheduana in the third person. It is far more fragmentary, but as best we can tell it invokes Nanna and praises Enheduana's suitability as his high priestess. It is intriguing because it is the earliest preserved literary text that mentions Enheduana's name: it dates to the Third Dynasty of Ur, and is thus two centuries older than the manuscripts of the other hymns. However, so little is left of it that it is difficult to say much about it: the reference to Enheduana bringing prayers to the Deep Sea is particularly puzzling. Portions of three columns of text have survived, but we do not know how much of the poem is missing.

FIRST HYMN

House that rises with the sun over Sumer,[3]
House of Alabaster,[4] of the resplendent rituals,
House of Nanna, I will sing of your greatness!
Shrine of Ur, I will raise up your name,
you that rose from a sacred mountain's holy heart.   5

The wisdom of heaven and earth is in Ur—
it is a worthy home for the House Whose Base Is Clad
    in Awe.
You dole out kingship with An,
the lands all praise your greatness.
Far and wide, I will raise up your name!   10

I have perfected the priestess's rituals,[5]
I have prepared a home in Ur.
Your name is sweet, the lord proclaims it,
and your holy words are pleasant to An.
I am Enheduana. I have made you excel in the heavens![6]   15

I have perfected the rituals of the temple,
. . . the powers of the priestess
. . . passing through the temple
Nanna . . . .
. . . .   20
. . . .
The song . . . .
I will sing your holy song.

The lord . . . .
Knowledge   25
The great powers . . . .

An and Enlil . . . .
Ningal . . . .
Excelling . . . .
Nanna   30
Like the sweet moonlight . . . .
In the temple, my delight . . . .
An and Enlil . . . .
Mother Ningal, wrapped in charm . . .
High priestess of Nanna[7]   35
Enheduana . . . .
My king . . . .
His great powers . . . .
This holy song I will sing far and wide
Your name   40
I am Enheduana, I have made you excel in the heavens!

Your joy . . . .
. . . .
. . . . . who knows your rituals,
. . . . perform it,   45
. . . build for you in the holy . . .
. . . . does not go into the bedroom,
she grinds grain for you in her holy basket.[8]
Your miller does not rest in her sanctuary,
she does not let water touch your ground groats,   50
and the malt is kept from spoiling.

Palace of Nanna—what does anyone know of you?
. . . . of the priests.
The basket of offerings must be brought,
the hymns of joy must be sung,[9]
the temple must be kept good, the temple must be kept firm, 55
the holy purifying rituals must be perfected.

Ningal! I am Enheduana,
I will make your heart happy again!
Spouse of Nanna, let me praise you,
wife of Nanna, let me raise up your name!   60

SECOND HYMN
First Column

. . . .
. . . . . . the position of priestess
Your . . . Nanna, for you to dwell
the shrine, your delight: the Ekishnugal.

. . . .

Second Column

. . . .
. . . . pleasant
she has praised you,
she is beaming,
the high priestess chosen for the holy powers,   5'
Enheduana,
may she bring your prayer to the Deep Sea.
She who is worthy of Nanna,
my bliss . . . . . .

. . . .

Third Column

. . . .
water . . . .
the priestess . . . .

the priestess . . word . . . . 5'
She who is worthy of Nanna,[10]
the priestess . . . future . . . .
Heaven and earth, the priestess . . .

. . . .

ESSAYS

ENHEDUANA'S WORLD

I WAS ABOUT A YEAR INTO MY UNIVERSITY STUD-
ies when I first heard the name "Enheduana." I learned about
her in an introductory course on cuneiform literature, and when
we were asked to write a term paper on a topic of our choosing,
I chose Enheduana. That was ten years ago; she has followed me
ever since. I have written about her, I have lectured about her, she
was the topic of my thesis, and I published a Danish translation
of the *Exaltation*. She has shaped my career by making me realize
what it is I like to do: I like to find overlooked stories and bring
them to life (I call it "historical dumpster-diving"). If my writing
about Enheduana seems at times overexcited, this is because I am
still at heart that nineteen-year-old boy who cannot quite believe
what he has come across. I do think that our understanding of
Enheduana should be tempered by academic reserve and that we
should bear in mind just how much about her we do not know,
how much depends on uncertain reconstructions. But I would be
lying if I said that Enheduana's poems do not thrill me. This book
is by no means the final word on Enheduana; on the contrary, I
hope that it can be the beginning of a broader, deeper engagement
with her work. There is so much about Enheduana we have yet to
understand, and smarter minds than mine will make new sense of
her legacy. In the meantime, I want to set out what I believe we
can, with varying degrees of certainty, say about Enheduana and
the poems attributed to her.

DAUGHTER OF SARGON

Enheduana lived through one of the most turbulent periods in the history of the ancient Near East. She did not simply witness this turbulence—her family was at the heart of it. For some five hundred years before her birth, southern Iraq had been dotted by dozens of independent city-states, including Ur, Uruk, Nippur, Kish, Lagash, Umma, and Sippar. These cities were caught in a web of conflicts, peace pacts, and exchanges of goods and ideas, but each was its own political entity. They had different systems of government, local deities, customs, and traditions, and sometimes even their own ways of counting and measuring. Then came Enheduana's father, Sargon of Akkad. He united the cities under one rule, creating the first known empire. He expanded his rule in all directions, and soon it stretched from the mountains of Iran to the shores of the Mediterranean. Sargon and his successors worked hard to bring the conquered cities into line, standardizing their rule and administration, bulldozing their way through any local differences they encountered. But the opposition was immense: the nobles of the once independent cities deeply resented their new overlords from Akkad, and they revolted at any given chance.[1]

At some unknown point in his royal career, Sargon made Enheduana high priestess of Ur. Both their names are titles they assumed on taking office: "Sargon" means "Steadfast King," while "Enheduana" translates as "High priestess (en) who is the ornament (hedu) of heaven (ana)." The word en also means "ruler" or "lord," and its double meaning is evocative of the high priestess's position: she essentially acted as the ruler of her temple. The temples were institutions of great power in ancient Iraq, wielding a huge cultural cachet and employing a small army of personnel, from the farmers who tilled their fields to the priests who sang their hymns. We know little about the exact role of a high priestess in this period, and it may have been a purely symbolic position.

But we have reason to believe that it was also an administrative office, giving the high priestess control over her temple's vast holdings of land and wealth.[2] As the head of Ur's largest temple, Enheduana may have held both the reins of its economy and the political authority it bestowed. And as Sargon's daughter, she probably acted as the de facto representative of the empire in its southern region. Though we know little about her life, these facts alone suggest that she was an extremely influential figure, and she may well have been the single most powerful woman of her day. But her position was also beset by many challenges, which must have taken great verve and nerve to navigate.

The revolt depicted in the *Exaltation* would have been a fact of life in the empire. Two of Sargon's sons—Enheduana's brothers—ascended to the throne only to be killed in court conspiracies.[3] The first, Rimush, ruled for nine years, and he probably died childless, since the throne passed to his younger brother Manishtushu, who was in turn killed after fifteen years in power.[4] But Manishtushu's son and successor, Naram-Sîn, was a different kind of king. Naram-Sîn expanded the empire, quashed revolts, ruled for four decades, and eventually declared himself a living god. This was an unprecedented claim in ancient Iraq.[5] Kings had always been thought to have a close connection with the gods, but Naram-Sîn was the first, as far as we know, to claim that he himself was a god made flesh. Under Naram-Sîn's rule, the empire founded by Sargon reached its political and cultural climax. A stele now in the Louvre shows him trampling on a pile of dead enemies. He is bare-chested and crowned with horns—the traditional sign of divinity in Sumerian and Babylonian art.[6] But Naram-Sîn was also a profoundly unpopular king: in what historians call the Great Revolt, he had to suppress nine uprisings in a single year. According to one source, though it is a late and dubious one, the uprising in Ur was led by a man named Lugal-Ane, the same name that appears in the *Exaltation*.[7] If this source can be trusted, and if the *Exaltation* was written by Enheduana herself—both huge ifs—it would place the events of the poem during the reign of Naram-Sîn. As we can safely assume that Enheduana was personally installed as high priestess by Sargon (it was a tradition for kings to make their daughters high priestesses), it would mean that she had served at the temple of Ur for at least twenty-five and perhaps as many as fifty years by the time of the Great Revolt, and the *Exaltation* would thus be the drama of a mature or even elderly poet.[8] But as always with Enheduana, such an attempt at reconstructing the reality behind the text is uncertain at best.

After Naram-Sîn's death, the empire began to unravel, and his son Shar-kali-sharri was the last of the dynasty, a dynasty that wound up ruling for a little over a century. Today, scholars refer to this slice of history as the Old Akkadian period, after the version of the Akkadian language that was spoken at the time. The Old Akkadian Empire was a brief but magnificent bubble: it spread across the known world, changed everything, and then collapsed. Life during this period must have been full of thrilling innovations. Sargon's campaigns expanded the Sumerian cities' sense of the world, bringing back people, stories, and rare objects from previously unknown lands, through both violent conquest and peaceful trade. Precious metals flowed in from the mines of what is now Afghanistan, trade ships sailed to the Indus Valley, Akkadian soldiers made their way into the highlands of Anatolia, and some of the period's art shows the influence of Egyptian styles. The world in which Enheduana lived must have felt larger than ever. Ur was a port city, lying on the banks of the Persian Gulf. (The coastline has since shifted, and its remains now lie some 150 miles, or 250 kilometers, inland.) Its docks bustled with exciting and exotic wares, such as lapis lazuli, ivory, carnelian, cat's eye, jasper, diorite, and serpentine, not to mention the products that have not survived in the archaeological record: textiles, perfumes, wines, and foreign foodstuffs.

The Old Akkadian Empire brimmed with wealth, plundered or traded from faraway lands, and these riches were transformed by the court's artisans into objects of luxury. The art of this period is some of the finest in ancient Near Eastern history. Technical breakthroughs in glassblowing and metalworking allowed Sargon and his sons to grace their palaces with elaborate bronze statues and bowls of faience.[9] Of course, this surge of wealth was not equally distributed: it mainly went to Sargon's family and their immediate retinue. Loyalty to the new empire was rewarded with luxurious gifts and prestigious posts. It was not only Enheduana who was placed by her father in a position of power. Naram-Sîn installed his son Nabi-Ulmash as governor of the city of Tutub and made his daughters Tutanabshum and Shumshani high priestesses, the first in Nippur, the second in Sippar. He also installed his daughter Enmenana as high priestess in Ur and so Enheduana's successor.[10] To many at the time, this wave of social change—with wealth and power tightly concentrated around the royal family—must have felt unbearable, which would help explain the political instability of the time.

Everything was changing, including the language people spoke. The region was bilingual, with Akkadian and Sumerian being spoken side by side. Akkadian is a Semitic language, like Arabic or Hebrew, while Sumerian is what linguists call an *isolate:* it is unrelated to any other known language. Sumerian was more prevalent in the South, including around Ur, while Akkadian was more prevalent in the North, home of Sargon and his family—the language was named after the city from which they ruled, Akkad. Sargon's state was the first to use Akkadian in its administration, setting in motion a shift that would eventually culminate in the death of Sumerian as a native language. Though the demise of Sumerian was still far away in Enheduana's time, the new empire had disturbed the linguistic balance that had prevailed for centuries, tipping the scales in favor of Akkadian.[11] It is tempting to think that Enheduana, like the rest of her family, spoke Akkadian as her mother tongue. If true, it would be all the more impressive that her hymns are written in a beautiful and highly refined Sumerian.

Not just spoken language was changing. So too was the writing system. Cuneiform, which had been invented about a thousand years earlier, in the late fourth millennium BCE, seems to have been developed by a Sumerian-speaking people, but during Naram-Sîn's reign, it was adapted to better represent Akkadian, while also gaining a sleeker and more elegant look. The new signs looked less like the objects they were based on and more like abstract symbols. They were also turned ninety degrees counterclockwise, perhaps to make them easier to write. Cuneiform was most often written by pressing a stylus made of reed into a hand-sized tablet of wet clay. The stereotype of ancient writing is that it was made by chiseling letters onto bulky slabs of stone, but reality was quite different. Clay is a wonderfully versatile material on which to write. It is cheap and easy to find: you can literally pick it up from the ground and shape it into any form you like. And clay is, above all else, durable. Books printed on paper are unlikely to last more than a few decades or a few centuries at most. But clay tablets made during Sargon's reign survive to this day. Much of what we know about the period we know because its scribes wrote on clay. The rest of our knowledge comes from the close study of objects that were brought to light through archaeological excavations—including the occasional dazzling discovery.

PRIESTESS OF THE MOON

Among the graves that archaeologists uncovered at Ur was the seemingly unremarkable PG 503 ("PG" stands for "personal grave"). The body of the man buried in it had not been preserved, but excavators found the grave goods that had been entombed with him. These objects, which are now kept in the Penn Museum in Philadelphia, include a silver ring, earrings and anklets of bronze, four jars of copper, razors and other blades, an ax, and what is known as a cylinder seal.[12] A cylinder seal was a small, richly decorated object that was generally worn around the neck and used on documents as a form of identification, much like a signature today. To approve a contract, the signer would roll the cylinder over the clay document: the decorative relief left a unique pattern that served as proof of identity. (Ancient lawsuits attest to the vexing problem of lost or stolen cylinder seals, leading to the ancient equivalent of identity theft.)[13] During Enheduana's lifetime, the decoration of cylinder seals reached new artistic heights. The imperial elite wanted to celebrate their power with lavish jewelry, and the seals of this period are tiny works of gorgeous sculpture. What makes the cylinder seal found in PG 503 noteworthy is not its artistic design, however, but its inscription, which identifies the bearer as "Enheduana, daughter of Sargon of Akkad: Ilum-palil is her hairdresser."[14] In English, we differentiate between barbers and hairdressers, but the Sumerian **kinda** would style hair for both men and women. The hairstyles found on statues from the Old Akkadian period are highly elaborate, and the **kinda** would have had frequent access to members of the nobility, making it a high-standing profession. Ilum-palil served as Enheduana's personal **kinda**, so if he was buried with the tools he used while alive—another big if—then the razors and blades found in PG 503 would have cut Enheduana's hair.[15]

The story of Ilum-palil's razor is a perfect example of how much and how little we know about Enheduana. Since she lived so long ago, it seems incredible that we should know anything at all—and indeed, we know neither where or when she was born nor the year in which she died. But we do have the grave goods of her hairdresser. Through similar finds of cylinder seals, we also know that the person who supervised Enheduana's estate was called Adda, and that she had a scribe named Sagadu and one whose name ended in "-kitushdu" (part of his seal has been lost).[16] Further, the ax found in Ilum-palil's grave tells a story of its own. It is a kind of ax that would have been out of fashion in Enheduana's time—some three centuries out of fashion. The excavator of Ur, Leonard Woolley, speculated that people in Enheduana's time might have unearthed artefacts that were already then ancient, prizing them as precious relics.[17] Ilum-palil was buried with such an artefact: Might Enheduana's hairdresser have been a lover of antiquities? Once again, we have flashes of knowledge about the past, but to give them the flesh of stories, we must rely on conjecture and guesswork. Either way, the ax reminds us that though Enheduana's time now seems impossibly remote, even then people could look back on a much older history. The deep past is nothing new.

When she arrived in Ur, Enheduana moved into a building that was as old as Ilum-palil's ax: the ĝipar (Akkadian gipāru).[18] It had stood in the city for three centuries, housing successive generations of high priestesses: Enheduana was joining a long lineage of women, though she was doing so as a foreign invader. The ĝipar stood in the temple area that rose high in the heart of Ur, separated from the surrounding cityscape by a large wall. The center of this holy precinct was the temple of Nanna, which was flanked by smaller temples and shrines to other deities. The cemetery in which Ilum-palil was buried lay in the eastern corner of the area, while the ĝipar was in its western corner, next to the main temple. The temple area was extensively rebuilt about a century after Enheduana's death, and little remains of the building that she would have known. The later version of the ĝipar was massive for its time—a square brick building of about 65,000 square feet (6,000 square meters), a little larger than the U.S. White House.

In Enheduana's time, it would have been smaller, but the basic architectural layout was probably the same.[19] Like most buildings in ancient Iraq (and in many modern Middle Eastern countries), it was organized around a series of open-air courts. Surrounding these courts were rooms of various sizes, including living quarters for the high priestess and select members of her staff. There were also storerooms, a large kitchen, and a dining room for ceremonial meals. The ĝipar may have had several stories, but since archaeological excavations in Iraq usually recover only the ground plan of a building, we do not know for sure. Inside the priestess's residence was a shrine dedicated to the king who installed her, and Enheduana would have performed prayers and rituals on Sargon's behalf.

The later version of the ĝipar was divided by a central corridor into two halves, one of which held the residence of the high priestess, the other a shrine for the goddess Ningal, Nanna's wife. The shrine to Ningal may have been a separate building in Enheduana's time, but it would still have stood close to the ĝipar, for one simple reason: Enheduana would sometimes act as Ningal's earthly embodiment. As shown by the philologist Joan Goodnick Westenholz, the high priestess of Nanna "may be understood as Ningal on earth."[20] This is not to say that Enheduana was seen as a living deity; rather, in some ceremonial contexts she would have ritually personified Ningal, becoming a kind of living cult statue for the goddess. It therefore made sense for her and Ningal's homes to be so closely connected. The archaeologist Penelope Weadock has further argued that Ningal's shrine held a bed on which the high priestess would perform a ritual known as the Sacred Marriage, in which the god would lie with his human wife, but the exact nature and even the existence of this ritual are contested among scholars.[21] If the temple did celebrate the bond between the Moon God and his priestess, it was probably a symbolic affair, not an actual physical union.

As the symbolic wife of the god they served, the high priest-esses were not allowed to marry or bear children: this was a fundamental requirement of their role.[22] They had to abstain from what would, for most women at the time, be the defining event of their lives, childbirth. In a patriarchal world where women were defined as first the daughters of one man, then the wives of an-other, then the mothers of a third, high priestesses stood out. They were wives of gods and mothers to none. This did not mean that they were like nuns in the Christian sense: there is at least one reference to a high priestess engaging in anal sex to avoid preg-nancy, and sex, in Sumerian culture, was not viewed as inherently sinful.[23] The ban was against procreation, not pleasure, but it is difficult to overstate the symbolic importance of childlessness in the Sumerian worldview. Children were expected to ensure that their parents were not forgotten after their death, and when a person passed away, his or her children would bring offerings of food and beer, ensuring their parent's well-being in the afterlife.

Since the high priestesses had no children, they instead had to rely on their successors to care for their spirits. When a high priestess died, she was buried in a part of the ĝipar known as "the place of the fateful day of the ancient priestesses," the "fateful day" being a euphemism for death.[24] It was common practice in the ancient Near East to bury the dead under the floors of the family house, and the same logic applied to the ĝipar. The priestesses formed a kind of extended family, a community across time, so they too were buried inside the building where they had lived. Centuries of women inhabited the same space, each of them con-tinuing the work of her predecessors while ensuring their welfare in the underworld. The large kitchen that prepared ritual meals for Ningal and dinner for the living priestess also cooked offer-ings for the dead beneath the floorboards. Enheduana would have looked after the well-being of those who came before her and ex-pected those who came after her to do the same in their turn. And they did: the high priestesses who succeeded Enheduana were still revering her memory three centuries later.

THE DISK OF ENHEDUANA

Inside the ĝipar, archaeologists uncovered a disk. On one side of it is a relief showing a woman overseeing a ritual, on the other is an inscription identifying that woman as Enheduana. The Disk of Enheduana, as it is known, is a cylinder made of limestone, ten inches wide and three inches thick (twenty-five and seven centimeters, respectively).[25] While the inscription is heavily damaged, it was copied out by later scribes onto a clay tablet, and so it can be restored as follows: "Enheduana, priestess of Nanna, spouse of Nanna, daughter of Sargon, the king of the world, built an altar in the temple of Inana-Zaza at Ur and named it Altar, the Table of Heaven." These few words contain several key pieces of information. They tell us that Enheduana was seen as the human embodiment of Ningal and hence as the "spouse of Nanna," that she presented herself as high priestess and royal princess—in that order!—and finally, that she had a personal devotion to Inana (who is here named in one of her many guises, Inana-Zaza, probably corresponding to the goddess Ashtar).[26] It was not unusual for a woman employed as the priestess of one god (here Nanna) to have a personal devotion to another (here Inana). To be a priestess did not imply, as it does today, a particularly strong faith in the deity one served. Priests and priestesses were responsible for maintaining the worship of the gods, but this was a question of resource management as much as personal vocation. In Enheduana's case, she would have had good reasons for devoting herself to Inana, who was the patron deity of the Old Akkadian Empire—a later Babylonian scholar described this period as "the reign of Ishtar."[27] The deep-felt love for Inana that one finds in the *Exaltation* and

Hymn has a clear political overtone, and the disk shows that the historical Enheduana really did share in this devotion.

The relief cuts across the disk to form a horizontal band, showing four figures standing in front of an altar. The disk was broken and had to be heavily restored; Leonard Woolley described it as "a sadly-battered alabaster disc" in his account of the excavation at Ur.[28] The left side of the disk is completely missing, but it is thought to have shown a ziqqurat.[29] The altar stands in front of this temple, and a nude male priest pours an offering onto it, probably beer or sesame oil. Behind him stands Enheduana, wearing a flounced garment and a tall hat, with one lock of plaited hair falling over her ear. She assumes a ritual posture, with her left arm bent horizontally at waist level and her right arm upturned, so that she touches her nose with her hand, in a Sumerian gesture of reverence that was literally called "to place the hand at the nose" (**kiri**$_3$ **šu ĝal**$_2$). Enheduana is followed by two, probably male, figures, one of whom is carrying a vessel, but they are difficult to make out on the fragmentary relief.[30] Enheduana is clearly the central figure in the composition, and the largest of the four, marking her out as the most important person in the visual scheme.

The relief gives us a glimpse of an activity that would have preoccupied Enheduana for much of her working life: the overseeing of rituals. Rituals were of fundamental importance to Sumerian and Babylonian culture, as they served to maintain proper relations between gods and humans, keeping the former happy and the latter from harm. The regular offerings of food, incense, beer, and praise that priests and priestesses lavished on their deities were the grease that kept the wheels of the universe spinning. The Sacred Marriage between Nanna and his high priestess may or may not have actually taken place outside literary imagination, but the disk shows us a far more common and in many ways more important ritual: the presentation of food for the gods.[31] The inscription on the back reveals that the disk was carved to com-

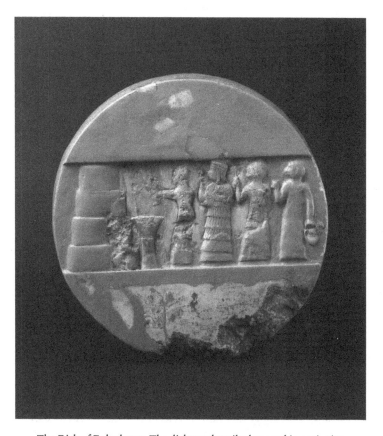

The Disk of Enheduana. The disk was heavily damaged in antiquity, and much of the relief—including the ziqqurat on the left side—was restored by archaeologists. Courtesy of the Penn Museum, image no. 150424 and object no. B16665.

memorate Enheduana's construction of a new altar for Inana, and as its name makes clear—"Altar, the Table of Heaven"—it was essentially a dining table on which the goddess's feast would be laid. The first of the fragmentary hymns that mention Enheduana's name also describes the grinding of groats, noting that the temple personnel worked ceaselessly to prepare food and beer for Nanna: "Your miller does not rest in her sanctuary" (l. 49).

The ritual offerings served to maintain order and cultural continuity. In fact, the position of the high priestess in itself marked a continuity with the past. It was once thought that Sargon had been the first king to install his daughter as high priestess, thereby inventing the position. But as shown by the art historian Irene Winter, older reliefs and plaques reveal that the office had existed for centuries.[32] Far from inventing something new, Sargon was honoring an established convention and so displaying his respect for the traditions of the cities he had conquered. Winter argues that the disk serves two functions at once. It emphasizes a similarity in style to older depictions of high priestesses, and it identifies the priestess by name in a way previous plaques had not. Earlier representations were not engraved with the priestess's name, but on this disk Enheduana is both named and singled out as Sargon's daughter. This combination of continuity and contrast reveals a key aspect of Enheduana's political position. She was installed in an ancient office by a new kind of ruler, and she had to portray herself as both a keeper of tradition and an enforcer of change.

The disk was found in the remains of the ĝipar, but the archaeological context suggests that it was left there not in Enheduana's own time but three centuries later.[33] After the collapse of the Old Akkadian Empire, King Ur-Namma founded a state known as the Third Dynasty of Ur (often abbreviated Ur III). Under his rule, the ĝipar in which Enheduana had lived was razed and rebuilt. But when the Third Dynasty of Ur fell in its turn, around 2000 BCE, the ĝipar was destroyed by soldiers from the land of Elam, a longstanding rival of the Sumerian cities lying in what is now western Iran. The soldiers raided the sacred precinct of Ur, smashing the relics they found there and plundering the tombs of the high priestesses. Some seventy years later, the ĝipar was rebuilt once more, and it is in this archaeological layer—the one from *after* the Elamite raid—that the disk was found. Next to it lay a small statue of Enanatuma.[34]

Enanatuma was the daughter of King Ishme-Dagan and another high priestess of Ur, and in many ways, she was a woman no less impressive than Enheduana, though her feat was one of architecture, not poetry. Enanatuma rebuilt the ĝipar as it had been before the Elamites destroyed it, following the old architectural plan but using sturdier building materials and so restoring the defaced temple to new glory.[35] The version of the ĝipar that was most fully excavated by archaeologists (the one whose dimensions match those of the White House) was the one completed under Enanatuma. The bricks of the building were stamped with her name, to ensure that her feat would be remembered forever. Such was her reputation that when Ur was conquered by her father's rival, King Gungunum of Larsa, Gungunum did not have her deposed but allowed her to serve out her term as high priestess.[36] It also seems that Enanatuma skirted the rule that high priestesses were not allowed to have children: a cylinder seal gives the name of Enanatuma's son, showing that the ban could be circumvented.[37]

Enanatuma had a clear objective in rebuilding the ĝipar and following the plans of the old building. After the fall of the Third Dynasty of Ur, the cities of southern Iraq were thrown into a cycle of conflict, with each king attempting to conquer the other cities and declare himself the rightful successor to the old emperors. Everyone wanted to be the next Sargon or the next Ur-Namma. Enanatuma's father, Ishme-Dagan, likewise sought to follow in the footsteps of these legendary rulers, and part of his strategy was to install his daughter as high priestess in Ur, just as his predecessors had done. Enanatuma worked hard to forge connections with the past, repairing the temple that Ur-Namma had built and linking herself with Enheduana.[38] The Disk of Enheduana and the statue of Enanatuma were found next to each other, and this is probably because they were laid next to each other as part of

Enanatuma's quest to present herself as Enheduana's successor and equal. The disk had been broken into five pieces, perhaps during the Elamite raid, where many objects in the ĝipar had been wrecked. But the tablet onto which the inscription was copied can be dated to after that date. Someone must have carefully reassembled the damaged disk, copied the inscription, and laid it next to Enanatuma's statue. The archaeologist Rhonda McHale-Moore argues that Enanatuma purposely buried these objects beneath the new ĝipar to form a symbolic foundation for her new temple.[39]

The story of how the disk was treated and treasured after Enheduana's death also tells us something important about the object itself. Today we intuitively see an image that depicts a human being as that person's *portrait*. Looking at the disk, we imagine that it captures some of Enheduana's likeness—the shape of her face, perhaps, or the style of her hair. We judge these kinds of images by their verisimilitude, the degree to which they mimic the real world, and we assume that there is a fundamental difference between art and reality, portrait and person. But according to the art historian Zainab Bahrani, images were viewed differently in the ancient Near East. The aim of an image like the ones on the disk was not to represent a person but to bring that person into existence.[40]

In the Sumerian and Babylonian cultures, people were thought to exist in several ways at once: through their bodies, their names, their children, the stories told about them, and the images that depicted them.[41] (Likewise, the gods were thought to be present in the world in more than one way. The Moon God, for example, existed as a series of statues inside his various temples, as a character in myths and legends, and as the shining orb that could be seen crossing the night sky.) As a result, it is not quite right to think of reliefs like the disk in terms of representation and resemblance. What mattered was not that the image looked exactly like the person it depicted, but that it gave that person a new medium of being. The disk was not Enheduana's representation but her *presence*, standing in for her as a kind of avatar in stone. This explains why it was reassembled and copied after it had been destroyed. For Enanatuma, the disk was not a curious holdover from an age-old past but a heavily charged religious artefact that in a very real sense carried with it some of Enheduana's essence.

Enanatuma's time was marked by constant strife between small states, all of which wanted to fill the power vacuum left behind by the Third Dynasty of Ur. About a century later, this struggle was decisively resolved in favor of Babylon, a previously minor city brought to greatness by King Hammurabi. Hammurabi's reign marked the beginning of an age known as the Old Babylonian period (ca. 1800–1600 BCE), named, like the Old Akkadian period, after the version of the Akkadian language that was spoken at the time. It was during this period that Enheduana's second life began, as her poems came to be widely read and studied in the Old Babylonian schools. The students were made to copy tablet after tablet of Enheduana's poems, and it is thanks to this system of education that her works have survived to this day.

ENHEDUANA AT SCHOOL

Babylonian school began in early puberty, but what is really remarkable is the reason we know this. A clay tablet containing a basic school exercise of the kind that students would be given early in their education was found with a set of teeth marks in its upper right corner. The student, whoever this was, must have tried to take a bite out of the tablet after finishing the exercise.[42] We can only speculate as to why. Since students at this level were still learning how to write, which in cuneiform is done by pressing a reed stylus into wet clay, this student must have been thinking about the imprints that solids leave on surfaces, and perhaps it was only natural to experiment by biting it. Or the student may have been thinking about death. According to Babylonian belief, shades in the underworld were condemned to "eat dust and live on clay." Perhaps our unnamed student was nagged by fears of the afterlife, and thought to test how bad it would be.[43] Either way, the tablet has proved helpful to modern scholars. Based on the shape and size of the bite marks, philologists were able to determine the age of the student: he or she had reached early pubescence, and this gives us a clue as to when Old Babylonian schoolchildren began their studies.[44]

The Old Babylonian schools were known as **edubba**, "houses where tablets are given out."[45] The students memorized the tablets and made copies of them, creating thousands of texts for philologists to study, and allowing us to reconstruct the curriculum in great detail. The students began by learning how to mold clay into tablets and write out simple signs. They then expanded their repertoire and learned the intricacies of cuneiform, in which every sign can carry many meanings, referring to both single sounds and whole words. The students learned long lists of signs, names, and technical terms, as well as sample sentences and increasingly complex grammatical patterns. They were then made to write out model letters and contracts, a foretaste of the work that many of them would go on to do. (Not everyone was equally keen: one student erased the model letter he or she had been writing and drew a goat and a fish in its place.)[46] The students were also given mathematical exercises, learning how to count and calculate at an advanced level: a famous mathematical tablet from the Old Babylonian period shows that the scribes were familiar with Pythagoras's theorem some twelve hundred years before the man after whom it is named was born.[47] A particularly important element of the school system was Sumerian grammar. The shift that had been set in motion when Sargon made Akkadian the language of state had led, sometime around 2000, to the death of

Sumerian.[48] That did not mean that the language disappeared, only that it ceased to be anybody's mother tongue: now it had to be learned. Though Sumerian had fallen out of favor among the general population, it continued to hold great cultural prestige. Much like Latin in Europe and Sanskrit in India, it would go on to serve as the medium of religious worship and erudite scholarship for the next two thousand years—scholars were still writing texts in Sumerian in the first century BCE.

In the Old Babylonian schools, Sumerian became an object of intense study. After learning the basics of cuneiform writing, mathematics, Sumerian grammar, and long lists of technical terms, advanced students would move on to a second tier of education. This tier consisted of the classics of Sumerian poetry, which the students first learned by heart and then wrote down in manuscripts for their teacher to inspect. Among the poems studied in this advanced stage of education were Enheduana's hymns—which were presumably some of the most difficult texts the students would encounter during their education. Sumerian would have been a challenge to Akkadian-speaking students at the best of times, but few texts stretch and strain the expressive range of the language quite as much as Enheduana's poems.

But why was so much effort channeled into the learning of a dead language? One reason was that Sumerian continued to be used in religious rituals. The best preserved of the Old Babylonian **edubba** is a building in the city of Nippur, which was at this time the religious center of the Babylonian world: Nippur's main temple was the home of Enlil, king of the gods.[49] The school building was in many respects like any other home of this period, a small house of some 480 square feet (45 square meters), organized around a central courtyard and perhaps two stories tall.[50] Were it not for the roughly thirteen hundred school tablets that archaeologists discovered there, it would have been all but undistinguishable from any other Nippurian home. But the school tablets were everywhere. When the students had finished writing their exercises, the tablets were wiped clean and reused, chucked away, or, even better, recycled. Discarded tablets doubled as handy bricks, and some school exercises had been built into the floors, walls, and furniture of the house. (Archaeologists also found a board game—an indication, one hopes, that school life allowed for the occasional break.)[51] But the most revealing aspect of this building is its location. It lies a mere 275 yards (250 meters) from the E-kur, "House of the Mountain," the main temple of Enlil. At the time, this was the most prestigious religious institution in the cuneiform world. The house probably belonged to a priest at that temple who worked as a teacher on the side, taking on students in his home. Many of his students must have wanted nothing more than to follow in his footsteps, and that was their reason for learning Sumerian: to perform the hymns and ritual recitations that would please the gods. And who better to learn from than Enheduana, the famous high priestess whose hymn had swayed the heart of Inana herself? Among the exercise tablets found in the Nippurian school were thirty-six copies of the *Exaltation* and nine of the *Hymn*, the largest single trove of Enheduana-related manuscripts yet found.[52]

The other main career path open to Old Babylonian students was the civil service of the burgeoning state. For the students who went in that direction, the appeal of Sumerian was less direct. They did not expect to use the language in their daily lives, but it gave them something equally important: cultural capital, a familiarity with learned matters that made them seem cultivated and so worth hiring.[53] To know Sumerian was to be part of an elite group of educated scribes who shared a pool of references that only they knew. Think of the path that today leads from public schools like Eton through the learning of Latin to the top of the British political system. Just as successive prime ministers have been made to sweat over Virgil, so were Babylonian would-be courtiers made to parse the *Exaltation*.[54] Of course, Enheduana's poems were not the only texts read in school—the corpus of Sumerian poetry is large and varied—but they did become remarkably popular, leading the philologist Annette Zgoll to dub the *Exaltation* "the world's first best seller."[55]

One reason for the popularity of Enheduana's poems is that they embodied a nostalgia for what Babylonian scribes regarded as a golden age. They saw the Old Akkadian Empire as a time of larger-than-life conquest and drama. With that nostalgia came the inevitable distortion, as the memory of the Old Akkadian period was reshaped to fit contemporary needs. The two main kings of the empire, Sargon and Naram-Sîn, became in this view opposing archetypes. Sargon was remembered as the paragon of kingship—a sly general and self-made monarch, the son of a gardener who rose to rule the world.[56] Naram-Sîn, meanwhile, was remembered as a hubristic and tragic king who ignored the gods' counsel and was therefore stricken by misfortune, leading to the collapse of his empire. The story of how he defeated nine revolts in one year was turned on its head, as he was instead said to have *lost* nine battles in one year.[57] Enheduana's poems were likewise subjected to historical mythmaking. She belonged to the same lost world that the students remembered fondly and—perhaps—contrasted with the political disarray they saw around them.

The longing for better times must have been especially salient during the 1740s, a turbulent period that followed the relative stability imposed by Hammurabi.[58] Under Hammurabi's successor, King Samsu-iluna, there had been a general uprising among the cities to the south of Babylon, including Ur and Nippur, but the rebellion had been mercilessly crushed. The following years saw the gradual decline of the southern cities: their economy dwindled, their inhabitants left, and their royal patronage was withdrawn. The great majority of the school texts unearthed by archaeologists were written in the shadow of this social decay. Since these texts are so essential for our knowledge of Sumerian poetry, a sinister pall seems to hang over the entire corpus. Summarizing the events of the 1740s, the philologist Nicole Brisch concludes, "This is the historical background for the Sumerian literary texts as preserved. The Nippur texts offer us a glimpse into a school curriculum *after* the rebellion."⁵⁹

What might Enheduana's poems have meant in this time of social crisis? What feelings did the *Exaltation* spark in the scholars of a crumbling city? We will never know, but we can certainly guess. It would be only natural for the scribes to reminisce about the days when the cities of Sumer were (so they thought) united and strong, and the *Temple Hymns* in particular project an image of the Sumerian-speaking world as an ordered, coherent whole—not the mess of local, conflicting affiliations it actually was. It is also possible that as the scholars watched Nippur decline around them, they doubled down on what it was best known for. The city's claim to fame had always been as a center of religious worship and first-rate scholarship, and the scholars seem to have focused with renewed intensity on the study of Sumerian language and literature, perhaps in one last push to save their city's reputation. If that was the case, Enheduana's meaning for them would have been similar to what we call a "cultural heritage": a precious, precarious remnant of the past that affirmed their own sense of identity and importance.⁶⁰

But who knows? Babylonian scholars were individuals too, and they would have approached Enheduana's poems with their own perspectives and reflections, just as modern readers do. One piece of evidence suggesting that their interest went beyond antiquarianism to focus also on the literary quality of the poems is an Akkadian translation of the *Hymn*. It was not uncommon for scholars of the Old Babylonian period to produce Akkadian translations of Sumerian texts, often in an interlinear format, in which each line of Sumerian was followed by a line of Akkadian.[61] The translation of the *Hymn* is fragmentarily preserved, but because our knowledge of Akkadian is much more solidly established than our knowledge of Sumerian, we sometimes have to rely on the translation to make sense of the original. But the meaning of the two is not always identical, and the Akkadian version is no mere crib. For example, in the list of Inana's domains we find the line I translate as "To see, show, and scrutinize, to find fault and set right are yours, Inana" (l. 124). The Sumerian text here has a play on words, in the sequence **igi ĝar igi ĝar-ĝar igi bar**, which can be literally translated as, "to see, to stare (?), to look."[62] The Akkadian translation re-creates this threefold repetition with the phrase *taklimtum takirtum tašertum,* "to reveal, to choose (?), to check," using words that are rare in Akkadian and not an exact match for the Sumerian. The translator must have felt that it was more important to render the wordplay than to convey the precise meaning of the original, probably assuming that the reader would have been able to decode the Sumerian as well.

Likewise, the phrase I translate as "to neglect and to protect" (l. 137) forms a striking pair in Sumerian, **gum₂-gum₂ ĝar ĝar-ĝar**. The meaning of these words is obscure, so we must rely on the Akkadian rendition, *temkû teknû,* "to neglect and to care for." The Akkadian at least makes sense, but it is no straightforward gloss either, since it clearly translates the Sumerian pun for pun: *temkû teknû* is a no less striking sequence of words. In turn, my translation seeks to re-create these sound games by rhyming *neglect* with *protect,* but that leaves the modern reader with an echo of an echo of the original poem, with each link in the chain focused on form at least as much as on content.[63]

Another telling example of a deeper engagement with Enheduana's poetry is its influence on Akkadian compositions. A hymn known as *Lob der Ishtar,* "Song of Ishtar" (also called

Ishtar-Louvre, after the manuscript's current location in the Louvre Museum), appears to be directly influenced by Enheduana's *Hymn* in its praise of Ishtar, Inana's Akkadian counterpart.[64] The poem takes over the *Hymn*'s telltale celebration of the goddess's paradoxical nature, listing her contradictory qualities and repeating the phrase "is yours, Ishtar" (i 15–60). The passage that follows this list is also reminiscent of the *Hymn*, as it describes how Ishtar created a group of gender-subverting performers to serve in her rituals: women carrying weapons and men wearing female dress (ii 1–20), just like the **pilipili, kurĝara,** and **saĝ-ursaĝ** in the *Hymn.* As the poem exclaims, "Their behavior has been reversed, their appearance has been transformed" (ii 1).[65]

Nor is this the only example of Enheduana's *Hymn* influencing later texts. A particularly important genre for ancient scribes was the lexical list; these lists were long enumerations of Sumerian words, sometimes with Akkadian translations. The lexical lists were a core part of the school curriculum: the students would improve their Sumerian vocabulary by copying out seemingly endless sequences of words and signs. Given Enheduana's central place in the school curriculum, it is not surprising to find that there are echoes of her texts in the lexical lists: rare words from the *Hymn* turn up with striking frequency in the lexical list *Izi,* and a passage from the lexical list *Erimhush* is closely based on the *Hymn*'s list of Inana's attributes.[66]

Examples like these reveal the popularity of Enheduana's poems in the Old Babylonian schools, showing that the students and scholars of this period saw Enheduana as a literary figure worthy of close study and emulation. And as best we can tell, the ancient scholars accepted her authorship of these texts as a matter of course. But if the ancient scribes were convinced by her authorship, why do modern philologists doubt it?

WAS SHE THE AUTHOR?

In the *Temple Hymns*, Enheduana is mentioned in a postscript to the last of the forty-two hymns, which states, "The weaver of the tablet was Enheduana. My king! Something has been born which had not been born before" (ll. 543–44).[67] The metaphor of authorship as an act of weaving went on to become a tremendously popular trope throughout literary history. It is found in countless cultures, periods, and contexts, and it is probably the single most commonly used description of how texts are made. It is embedded in the English word *text*, which shares its origins with the word *textile*—literally, a text is something woven.[68] In the *Temple Hymns*, this image is combined with another key metaphor for literary creation: that of the poem being born, of the text coming into being for the first time.

Fascinating as it may be, this authorial claim raises more doubt than it dispels. Crucially, we would like to know how accurate it is. Five hundred years separate the Old Babylonian manuscripts of this and the other poems from Enheduana's lifetime, raising the difficult question I discussed in the introduction: Were the poems written by Enheduana herself, surviving in some oral or now lost written form until they reached the Old Babylonian schools? Or were they composed after her death, in her name, using real historical information but recasting it in a partly fictional form? Philologists have yet to reach any kind of consensus on this question.[69] I argued in the Introduction that the debate has detracted from other, more important analyses of Enheduana's poems, but in the interest of fairness, I here lay out the arguments for and against the historicity of her authorship.

There are two manuscripts of Enheduana's poems that date to the Third Dynasty of Ur, substantially closer to her lifetime than the Old Babylonian copies, but neither adds much to the debate. One is the second fragmentary hymn, the one that mentions

Enheduana but seems not to be told in her voice—and which is too fragmentary to give us much information anyway. The other is a manuscript of the *Temple Hymns*, showing that the composition did exist during the twenty-first century BCE, but not that it was attributed to Enheduana, since the manuscript is fragmentary and the crucial final lines are missing.[70] The postscript could theoretically have been added later, attributing an originally anonymous composition to Enheduana after her fame as an author had become established. Conversely, there is nothing inherently suspicious about the fact that Enheduana's poems are found mainly in Old Babylonian manuscripts: we have only a tiny trickle of literary texts from the third millennium, and most Sumerian poetry survives only in Old Babylonian copies. In that respect, Enheduana's poems are entirely typical. But the problem is that we have no way of working backward from the written manuscripts. We can tell roughly how old a given manuscript is (by examining the archaeological context or, failing that, the form of the script), but we cannot always tell whether the text written on it was composed the day before or five centuries earlier.

An interesting parallel is the *Kesh Temple Hymn*, which was also known only from Old Babylonian school copies until a set of manuscripts turned up from the Fara period, around 2500 BCE—making it one of the oldest-known poems not just in Sumerian but in any language.[71] These early manuscripts contain much the same text as the Old Babylonian ones, allowing for minor adjustments in grammar and style, so it was clearly possible for literary texts to pass largely unchanged through the centuries until reaching the Old Babylonian schools. The same may have happened to Enheduana, but one can just as easily find counterexamples. Another set of texts studied in the Old Babylonian period was the "correspondence of the kings of Ur": these texts purport to be copies of real letters exchanged between kings and dignitaries in the dramatic final days of the Third Dynasty of Ur, as the empire was collapsing. But philologists have shown that the letters were in fact written (or at least heavily redacted) long after that time. They are not real letters, but a retrospective reimagining of the events leading up to the fall of the empire.[72] That could also be the case with Enheduana.

One argument holds that it does not matter whether the poems can be dated to the Old Akkadian period: it is unlikely that Enheduana composed them anyway, because the norm was for kings and rulers to commission hymns and autobiographical accounts that they could pass off as their own.[73] According to this argument, even if the hymns could be dated to Enheduana's lifetime, they would be better attributed to her scribes than to the priestess herself. I do not much care for this idea. The hymns written in the names of later kings are very different; they are adulatory and often full of clichés—a far cry from the soul-searching, poetically pathbreaking hymns attributed to Enheduana. It is of course possible that several scribes assisted in the making of the texts, but that would not lessen the scope of Enheduana's accomplishment. When Enanatuma rebuilt the ĝipar, she did not carry the bricks herself but supervised a larger operation, yet we still credit her with the architectural feat: the same might be true of Enheduana's authorship. And as noted by the philologist Brigitte Lion, Enheduana's literary reputation proves that in the Old Babylonian period a woman could be *thought* of as an accomplished poet, which is in itself telling for how women were perceived at the time.[74]

However, this does not solve the central problem. Can the poems be dated to Enheduana's lifetime or not? Looking only at their content, we find no anachronism in the *Exaltation* or the *Hymn* that would make an Old Akkadian date impossible, no mention of tools or technologies that were invented later. The *Temple Hymns*, however, presents a murkier picture. At least one of the hymns is a later addition and is explicitly described as such in the text:

hymn 9 celebrates a temple built by Shulgi, a king of the Third Dynasty of Ur, and it is noted as being an "addition" (*taḫḫum*) to the collection (l. 134). This does not speak against Enheduana's authorship; on the contrary, it suggests that by Shulgi's time the collection already existed and was held in so high an esteem that the king himself would want his name and temple added to it. But other hymns in the collection also celebrate temples that seem to have been built after Enheduana's death. These are not acknowledged as later additions, suggesting that the text was at least revised in the following centuries.[75] And yet the structure of the *Temple Hymns* does suit the political ideology of the Old Akkadian Empire remarkably well, especially since it culminates with two temples in Akkad, giving that city a privileged position in the text. The god Ilaba (from hymn 41) almost completely disappeared after the fall of the Old Akkadian Empire, evidence that the creation of the *Temple Hymns* must at least have begun during Enheduana's lifetime.

Likewise, the first of the fragmentary hymns refers to the "House Whose Base Is Clad in Awe" (E-temen-ni-guru), a temple that seems to have been built by Ur-Namma in the twenty-first century BCE. But if this hymn was written after Enheduana's death, it must also have been written after the *Exaltation*, since it engages closely with this poetic predecessor, using phrases and formulas taken from that better-known hymn.[76] One gets the impression that the fragmentary hymn was written as a response to the *Exaltation*, using the same language to address Nanna rather than Inana. If that is true, it would mean that Enheduana's literary persona stimulated later poets to mimic her works and contribute to her legend. However, it does not tell us whether that poetic persona was first created by Enheduana herself or by someone writing in her name.

The weightiest argument against Enheduana's authorship is the language of the poems. Many of the phrases used in the texts do not match the version of the Sumerian language that was used during the Old Akkadian period. But once more, the matter is far from clear-cut. The Old Babylonian scribes did not necessarily copy the texts precisely as they had come down to them: the notion of intellectual property was still millennia away, and the scribes felt free to adjust the texts as they saw fit. They revised the poems to make them easier to understand, updating obsolete expressions, changing archaic spellings, or correcting what they saw as errors but which were in fact the remnants of an older form of Sumerian.[77] The scribes learned the poems by heart, which would make it all the more important for the texts to be at least intelligible.[78] This flux in transmission kept the poems alive, but it also makes it much harder for modern scholars to date them.

This brings me to a more general point: authorship in Babylonia was not the same as it is today. Any attempt to establish the historical truth of Enheduana's authorship will inevitably be an anachronistic project, as we try to hold ancient poetry up to a modern standard. The notion of authorship had only just been invented in the Old Babylonian period, and it carried different connotations from those it does today. For example, some of the *Temple Hymns* have precise parallels in a much older collection of hymns found in the city of Abu Salabikh. Like the *Kesh Temple Hymn*, these poems date to the Fara period, some two centuries before Enheduana's lifetime.[79] Specific lines from the Abu Salabikh hymns can also be found in the *Temple Hymns*, and there are also more general stylistic similarities between them. So, with some of the *Temple Hymns* being older than Enheduana and some having been added later, what sense does it make to attribute the collection to her? And how can the text claim that Enheduana created something new—something that "had not been born before"—if she was actually reusing existing verses and literary forms?

An answer can be found in the metaphor of weaving. Today we think of original creation as making new verses out of thin air, but that is not the model of authorship that we find in the ancient world. Before the eighteenth century CE, a mere three centuries ago, authorship was most often thought to consist in taking a preexisting tale, text, or tradition and shaping it into a new form. That is, authorship was thought of as weaving old threads into new textiles: the material being reshaped may have had a long history, but the poet would arrange it according to an individual design, and therein lay the author's contribution.[80] Likewise, Enheduana was credited with the creation of something new in the sense that she had arranged the traditional temple hymns in an updated and more complete format. When this pattern had been created, others could add to it, working within its structure, just as Shulgi did. As long as these later contributors respected the warp and weft of the collection, the text could still be attributed to Enheduana. The same is true of the more personal poems, such as the *Exaltation*. When later scribes copied and amended the text, they were working within a literary fabric that they attributed to Enheduana. They were helping to distribute and, in a sense, *create* her authorship, by carrying it across time and reshaping it for their time. It was not only the texts that were being reworked: the memory of Enheduana was also transformed when the scribes modified her poems. In that respect, the cultural image of an author is like a classical portrait—it may show a single person, but it was often painted by more hands than one. Authors, editors, singers, and scribes all participate in the making of the author's image, by transmitting and transforming it. That is not just the case with Enheduana—that is the nature of authorship as such.[81]

The translator Ranjit Hoskote makes a similar point about another female religious writer whose authorship is philologically suspect—namely, the Kashmiri poet Lal Ded. Hoskote refers to the tradition of scribes and singers who circulated Lal Ded's collection of poems—sometimes adding to it, sometimes revising it—as a *contributory lineage*.[82] He likens the process to open-source software: once it is released into the world, other users can tweak and expand it, and by so doing, they keep it relevant. The author surrenders control over the text and gains its renewal in return. Just as with Enheduana, Lal Ded *emerges* from a textual tradition that she played only one part in creating. As Hoskote puts it, Lal Ded "is a play of versions, not an absolute entity," and it makes no sense to insist that the author should "stand before and apart from the text, resident in a biographical persona that scholars construct from scanty data." Lal Ded is better said to "breathe within the text, through the flow of the poems attributed to her, vigorously and often meticulously produced in her name."[83] In the case of Enheduana, one can compare this contributory lineage to the succession of high priestesses in Ur, each of whom honored and fed the women who had gone before her. As readers, we too are part of this process. Each time we read, retell, or perform her poems, we step into this contributory lineage, reviving and subtly revising the figure of Enheduana.

THE HONEYED MOUTH

WHAT DOES IT MEAN TO READ A POEM? AND WHAT exactly is going on when we try to explain what we felt and thought as we read it, what ideas and associations were forced into our minds, how we responded to its rhythm and structure? To carry out a literary reading—that is, to set down an account of how a poem might be understood—is a curious affair. No reading can capture every aspect of the text, no matter how simple the text or how long the reading: apart from anything else, a reading is typically produced by one person, and others would highlight different aspects of the text. But neither is a reading a random response, like an answer to a Rorschach test. The best readings are sophisticated arguments that build up their case through detailed scrutiny: connecting lines from different ends of the poems, highlighting hidden ambiguities, placing words in their original context, or tracing how the text was transformed over time. Clearly, then, literary readings must exist in some murky space between the subjective and the objective, never fully one or the other. That is the situation confronting not just academic critics but all readers of poetry, who react to the text in ways that are individual but not random, personal but still part of a social sphere that shapes how they read.[1]

Literary readings, it seems to me, are reductions of the irreducible. The complexity and changeability of poetic texts means that they will always defy a definitive description, but when we set down our reading, we single out an aspect of that complexity that seems to us particularly important. Every line in the *Exaltation* is a meld of meaning and music, each of them ringing with its own echoes and allusions; and the structure of the text draws the lines into an incalculably intricate web of words, whose effects on the reader cannot have been fully predicted by their author—whoever that was. What critics do, faced with this overflow of sense and sensation, is pick out a strand that runs across the text and seems in some way revealing of the whole. This is what I attempt to do in this essay, as I lay out my thoughts about Enheduana's poems. But as with all readings, mine too is a reduction of the irreducible—a particular perspective on the texts, highlighting some aspects at the expense of others. Literary readings are social creatures; they crave the company of other interpretations.

VOICES INTERTWINED

The *Exaltation* is a key text for the emergence of authorship, not just because it was attributed to Enheduana, but also because her authorship is so memorably described within the text itself.[2] It could easily have been the case that the first known poem by a named author had nothing to say about authorship. Suppose that, of Enheduana's poems, only the *Temple Hymns* had survived: it would still be a landmark in literary history, but it would be less significant, because Enheduana is mentioned only in the final lines of the final hymn. The *Exaltation*, by contrast, gives us a vivid account of how poets make poems, and of what happens when texts are released into the world. In so doing, the *Exaltation* makes a crucial claim about authorship—namely, that it is born out of dialogue. The poet is not shown as an isolated figure who scribbles away in a candlelit chamber, or meanders alone in a far-off meadow when inspiration strikes, or recites her song while the audience listens in silence. Enheduana becomes an author by conversing with Inana and by engaging other people in her poetic creation, including the lamenter who repeats her words and the scribes who copy them out.

Consider how the "I" of the poem is introduced into the text. In the opening hymn to Inana, the first-person pronoun appears only in the repeated phrase "my lady," placing Enheduana in a position of devoted submission to Inana. The first time she acts as an independent subject is in the phrase "I will sing you a sacred song" (l. 63), but even here the "I" is still defined by its relation to Inana—her invocation of Inana. Enheduana speaks to Inana and in so doing gains a place for herself in the poem, finally declaring, "For you, I stepped into my holy home" (l. 66): here it is as if Enheduana has come into herself, though still in the service of Inana. Only then is she ready to announce her identity: "I am Enheduana, I am the high priestess" (l. 67). In other words, Enheduana's poetic voice arises out of a bond with the goddess she invokes. The "I-you" relation comes first, and the "I" is created out of that relation.[3] First speech, then the speaker. And because of the primary importance that the text attributes to relations and dialogue, the various voices of the poem come to be bound together in a complex web of speech and response. Enheduana is always speaking with a view to how her words will influence others. She speaks to Inana in the hope that the goddess will speak out on her behalf, adjudicating her case against Lugal-Ane. Her monologue is an attempt to sway Inana's words and ensure that those words will have the desired effect by elevating Inana's position of power.

The *Exaltation* may be a long monologue, but it is a monologue shaped by an acute awareness of the words of others. At one point, Enheduana turns to Nanna and instructs him to tell An about her situation (l. 75).[4] Since An was the grandfather of the gods, his words carried a special authority, and so Enheduana asks Nanna to intercede with An on her behalf. In turn, she suggests that An would then give Inana the order to destroy Lugal-Ane, in a chain of speech leading from one god to the next: from Enheduana to Nanna to An to Inana. That is the way words acquire power—by connecting with other words. The dialogue between the gods, the chain of increasingly authoritative speech, is the only way Enheduana can hope to influence events on earth. Enheduana also says to Inana, "You give orders by the holy order of An" (l. 15), meaning that Inana's orders carry An's seal of approval, but also showing that the power of words is always dependent on other words: Inana speaks power because An spoke his approval. In this constant interplay of voices, even silence can come to sound like speech. Later in the poem, Enheduana tells Inana that "Nanna has said nothing, so he has left it up to you" (l. 134). Enheduana is here arguing that since the Moon God has failed to resolve her case, he has effectively passed the matter on to Inana, leaving it for her to decide. In other words, Enheduana's speech refers to Nanna's lack of speech and reinterprets that silence as a kind of speech—specifically, as an invitation for Inana to speak!

In short, in the *Exaltation*, all words carry the quality of dialogue, by referring to and depending on the words of others. Enheduana's speech to Inana is particularly shaped by the hope that the goddess will speak back and rule in her favor, and nowhere is that clearer than in a line from the very end of the poem, "What she said to her holy woman was magnificent" (l. 151), which in a literal translation would read: "Her speech to her **nugig** was magnificent." The **nugig** were originally wetnurses or midwives, but the word came to be used more broadly for high-status women affiliated with a temple and was sometimes used interchangeably with other words for priestesses.[5] It also served as an epithet for goddesses, as earlier in the *Exaltation*, where Inana is called "the **nugig** of An" (l. 3, which I translate as the "holy woman of An"). In the *Temple Hymns*, **nugig** refers to the goddess Ninisina and to her human priestesses within the same stanza (ll. 387 and 389, respectively), showing that the word could apply to both.[6] It might then also apply to Enheduana herself, who was indeed a high-status woman affiliated with a temple. As a result, we can read the line "Her speech to her **nugig** was magnificent" in two different ways at once: as saying that Inana's ruling in favor of her holy woman Enheduana was magnificent and as saying that Enheduana's hymn to her holy woman Inana was magnificent.[7] We can flip back and forth in our mind between these possibilities, which are like an optical illusion: now one figure and now the other steps forward as the subject of the speaking. The ambiguity implies that the two women have all but merged into one in this final scene, exalting each other with the power of their words: Enheduana glorifies Inana, Inana reinstates Enheduana. Their speech binds them together and elevates them together.[8]

This interlacing of words also shapes the way authorship is depicted in the climax of the text (ll. 136–42):

Queen, beloved of
heaven! I will sing
of your fury. I have
piled up the coals, I
have purified myself.
The Holy Inn awaits
you. Will your heart
not have mercy on
me? The pain filled
me, overwhelmed me.
Queen, lady! For you,
I have given birth to
it: what I sang to you
at dead of night, let
a lamenter repeat at
midday.

Enheduana shows herself composing the *Exaltation* during a nighttime encounter with Inana in a temple called the "Holy

Inn"—a name that is itself suggestive of revelry, sensuality, and altered states. The text almost bursts out of the poet, as Enheduana describes herself being filled, overfilled by emotion before giving birth to the poem. Inana's identification as **nugig**, which as noted above originally meant midwife or wetnurse, lurks in the background of this scene, as the goddess is made the recipient of the newborn text. And indeed, Inana's presence is crucial for the creation of the poem: Enheduana does not compose the text alone but in an intimate dialogue with the goddess.

To understand the logic of these lines, it helps to consider another passage that uses the same phrase, "dead of night" (Sumerian $\hat{g}i_6$ u_3-na). When describing the rebellious city devastated by Inana, Enheduana tells us (ll. 54–57):

Something
is wrong with the
wombs of the city.
The woman there
no longer speaks
beautiful words to
her spouse—in the
dead of night, she
will not converse
with him. She does
not show him what
shines inside her.

These lines balance beautifully between sex and speech, making one a precondition for the other: without conversation there can be no intercourse, and therefore no childbirth. The woman and her spouse have become estranged from each other, so their words, sex, and pregnancy all fail. The repetition of the phrase "dead of night" carries that logic over to the moment when

Enheduana composes her poem, making the two scenes mirror images. The rebellious woman is a foil for Enheduana's successful authorship, showing by contrast what the making of beautiful words entails. Enheduana does speak beautiful words to Inana, she does converse with the goddess, she does show Inana what shines inside her, and this is what allows her to give birth to the poem we have been reading. Authorship, according to the *Exaltation*, is not something one can do alone: it requires conversation.

Enheduana's description of her own authorship centers around the line "for you, I have given birth to it," in Sumerian **ma-ra-du$_2$**. It is a powerful evocation of what it means to become an author, especially considering the ban on birth imposed on the high priestesses. The text becomes a sort of substitute child, created in a moment of intimacy and pain, and borne forth almost by its own will: Enheduana can no more stop the words welling up inside her than she could stop a baby ready to be born. But matters are more complicated than that. The *Exaltation* as we have it now exists in a series of school copies, and this particular line survives on sixteen manuscripts. However, these manuscripts present the crucial line differently. Some use the sign **du$_2$**, "to give birth," but others use the sign **du$_3$**, "to create," or **du$_{11}$**, "to speak," or **du$_8$**, "to release." So which is it? Did Enheduana compose her poem by metaphorically birthing it, making it, speaking it, or freeing it? Once more, the ambiguity is probably intentional, as each of the four meanings makes sense in the context. Authorship is an act of creation, recitation, delivery, and release all rolled into one. What better way of communicating the nature of authorship than by allowing different scribes to represent it differently?

Two of these meanings, to release and to give birth, imply a separation between the author and the newly created text. When the poet has completed her work, she passes it on to others, like a mother handing her baby to a wetnurse. We have seen the role played by scribes in distributing and sometimes reshaping the newborn poem, but within the narrative of the *Exaltation* itself, the person who stands ready to receive the text is the lamentation priest, or **gala**: "What I sang to you at dead of night, let a lamenter repeat at midday." It is at this very moment that Enheduana is transformed from "I" to "her." After the lamenter begins to perform the text, Enheduana is referred to in the third person. She has stepped out of her own poem, allowing the lamenter to circulate it for her, and that is the moment she becomes an author. A writer who does not share her words is no author at all; it is only when others read, repeat, hear, sing, or copy a text that their creator can claim authorship. Becoming an author is to surrender one's words to the care and craft of others. It requires conversation and collaboration, not as a mere practicality but as a foundational necessity.

As a result, the voice within the poem becomes a rather complicated thing, and it can be surprisingly difficult to tell who is speaking in the text at any one time. Take the couplet "My honey-mouth is full of froth, my soothing words are turned to dust" (ll. 72–73). Who speaks these lines? On the one hand, they describe Enheduana's loss of eloquence; on the other, they do so in eloquent terms, adorned with well-crafted metaphors and poetic symmetry. So the lines are spoken by Enheduana the character, who is describing how words fail her; but they are also spoken by Enheduana the narrator, who has regained her eloquence and looks back on this moment of crisis. And according to the end of the poem, the lines are in fact being spoken by the lamenter, who is reciting the text on the day after Enheduana composed it. But in reality, the lines come to us through a series of manuscripts, which were written by a multitude of students who copied the words of their teacher, and did so in slightly different ways. We may say that ultimately the couplet was created by the historical Enheduana, but there is always the possibility that it was composed by someone else writing in her name. The first-person pronoun of the

Exaltation thus seems to refer to a bewildering number of people, all of whom come together to create the text.[9] Authorship, in the *Exaltation*, is born from an intertwining of many voices.

One last topic bears consideration. I have spoken of the "voice" of the poem, which raises the question of whether the hymns were oral or written. In all likelihood, they were both. The poems come to us in a written form only, but that is simply because performances do not survive in the archaeological record. After all, the *Exaltation* refers to itself as a song performed by a lamenter, and it is possible that Old Babylonian students learned to recite the texts in some way or another—perhaps musically, perhaps ritually, perhaps accompanied by instruments. We have no sure-fire evidence of this, but the philologist Paul Delnero has shown that several Old Babylonian manuscripts display odd spellings indicating that they were meant to be performed, and not just memorized and copied.[10] At the same time, the texts were also meant to be appreciated as written artefacts—a deliberate arrangement not just of sounds but of signs as well. In the *Exaltation*, the lines I translate as "raging rainfall of fire" and "you give orders by the holy order of An" (ll. 13, 15) both contain a play on words that only works in cuneiform writing: the same sign is written three times in a row, denoting a sequence of different sounds.[11] When the line is recited, the sign's multiple meanings have to be resolved into distinct words, so the pun is no longer apparent. Clearly, then, the writing of the text also mattered. But once the students had finished writing their copy and having it checked by their teacher, the tablet they had produced was considered worthless. School manuscripts were thrown away, reused by new students, or even repurposed as bricks. This was not the case for all cuneiform manuscripts—many were treated with great reverence and care[12]—but in the **edubba** schools, the written form of the text was not a goal in itself: the manuscripts were side products of a pedagogical exercise. When the students left school, they would carry the poems with them not in a suitcase of tablets but stored away in their minds.

POWER AND CHAOS

Enheduana's hymns are poems of power. The theme of power recurs time and again in the texts, perhaps unsurprisingly, given that they were attributed to the daughter of an emperor. Even if the poems were composed after Enheduana's death, the theme of power would have remained central to their Old Babylonian reception, as the scribes of the crumbling cities recalled the might of Sargon and his dynasty. And it is no less relevant today: the poems' exploration of power is part of what makes them so compelling to modern eyes. The kinds of power treated in the poems—of words, kings, natural forces, gods over humans, and some gods over others—make these hymns more than mere panegyrics. The recurring question of who controls what infuses the texts with violence, conflict, and unresolved tensions.

As noted in the Introduction, a central term in Enheduana's treatment of power is the **me**, a concept that continues to puzzle Sumerologists.[13] The word literally means "to be" or "to exist," but it is used as a noun. It is clear from literary and religious texts that the **me** were seen as the province of the gods: they would hold the **me** in their hands and derive their power from them. In *Inana's Descent to the Underworld,* Inana is tricked by her sister Ereshkigal into leaving behind the **me** that adorn her body at the entrance to the underworld. Without the **me**, Inana is stripped of her powers, leaving her defenseless against Ereshkigal's attacks: it is by wielding the **me** that Inana can impose her awe-inspiring terror. It would seem, then, that **me** refers to the fundamental elements of existence—"that which is"—and that the gods controlled the cosmos by exerting power over these elements.

But the **me** is an even trickier concept than that. When the Babylonian scholars translated the word into Akkadian, they rendered it as *parṣu*, "ritual." This is not necessarily to be understood as a religious ritual of the kind performed in the temples. In this context, *parṣu* may refer more generally to something that was done again and again to sustain human society: institutions such as kingship, agriculture, metalworking, craftmanship, and sex, which were all seen as **me**. These **me** were not just cosmological elements that merely existed, like hydrogen or gravity, but activities that had to be performed repeatedly for civilization to survive—in other words, a kind of ritual on a culture-wide level. Sometimes individual objects are said to have their own **me**, in which case the **me** should probably be thought of as the destiny or cosmic role of that object. As the philologist Gertrude Farber concludes in her study of the **me**: "All spheres of civilization and culture—be it the institutions of state or religion, spiritual or emotional values, social conditions, professions, offices, or any object or tool—are permeated by the 'divine powers' [the **me**], which are designed and executed by the gods."[14]

Inana and Enki tells of how Inana stole a trove of **me** from the trickster god Enki by drinking him into a stupor and loading his **me** onto her boat.[15] The **me** that Inana absconds with include, among many others, joy and justice, honesty and lies, rebellion, kindness, awe and reverent silence, wisdom, the scribal arts, shepherdship, leadership, leathercraft and metalwork, the kindling and dousing of fire, the making of families, strife and triumph, old age, weapons, various priestly offices, sex and blowjobs ("the kissing of the penis"), singing and musical instruments. All these were **me**—that is, practices which formed the fabric of the human world. Note especially how the **me** are treated in the story: as physical objects that Inana can load onto her boat while Enki sleeps, almost like shipping crates. The **me** themselves seem to be silent and inert, but owning them bestows cosmic power.[16] That is what makes them so odd. They are both objects and rituals, powers and practices, elements and destinies.

In *Inana and Enki*, Inana does not necessarily get away with all the **me** that exist. Notably absent from the list are aspects of life such as medicine and disease, which were controlled by other gods. The list we find in this text is probably not a comprehensive enumeration of all the **me**, but only a catalogue of those that Inana stole from Enki. This is what makes the claim we find in the *Exaltation*, that Inana controls *every* **me**—that she is **nin me šara**, "queen of all the **me**"—so startling. It amounts to saying that every aspect of existence, every part and province of the human world, belongs to Inana, and that all the other gods had their domains delegated to them by Inana. In the Introduction, I noted that Enheduana does not merely assume Inana's cosmic supremacy; she seeks to bring it about through the poem. She explicitly states that Inana was born as a "second-rate ruler" (l. 114), and that the goddess can now claim universal rulership by stepping into the power vacuum left by Nanna's silence. The idea that Inana was in need of empowerment does not reflect historical fact: it should be seen as a poetic device in which Enheduana claims that Inana was not held in high enough regard, and therefore she could take it upon herself to do the exalting.[17] The narrative does not just praise Inana's power; it actively seeks to make her the "queen of all the **me**."

No less significant is the opening line of the *Hymn*, **innin ša gura**, "Queen of vast heart." Again, we must understand these words in their Sumerian context. Today when we say that someone is big-hearted, we mean that the person is kind and compassionate, but those are not the first qualities that spring to mind when we think of Inana. For the Sumerians, the heart was the center not just of emotion but of thinking and reasoning as well. The heart was the expanse within each person through which moods and ideas flowed, eventually coalescing into a decision.

When Inana is said to have a vast heart, it means that her mind is so large that it can contain contradictory schemes and impulses, that she is changeable and erratic, and that the plane on which her decision making unfolds is so grand that no human being can hope to comprehend it. As the *Hymn* puts it, "She overturns what she has done; nobody can know her course" (l. 7). But this unpredictability does not make Inana a fickle or weak-minded ruler. On the contrary, it is the foundation of her power.

Behind the bustle and bombast of the *Hymn*, the text presents a clear-headed account of what power really is. It makes two fundamental claims about Inana. The first is that she controls everything: Inana is shown changing all that there is to change, reversing genders, turning midday into midnight, razing mountains, empowering the weak and crushing the strong, destroying and creating at will. The second is that Inana is not controlled by anyone: no one can comprehend her vast heart, no one can understand or predict her decisions, no one can keep her in check or impose any kind of order on her actions. And this asymmetry of control is the essence of a particular kind of power—one that is indistinguishable from chaos. We tend to think of control and disorder as opposite forces: the power of the state versus the bedlam of anarchy. But that need not be the case. The *Hymn* displays a keen insight into the nature of power, a perspective later laid out at length by the philosopher Friedrich Nietzsche: the essence of power is not order but freedom from the order of others. In their most extreme form, power and chaos coalesce. And this is the kind of power that Inana is given in the *Hymn*.

In the final section of the *Hymn*, beginning with line 254, the text begins to repeat the syllable **nam** with striking insistence. The syllable appears fifteen times in twenty lines. In Sumerian, **nam** is used to build abstract nouns, so, for example, **lugal** means "king" and **nam-lugal** means "kingship." The repetition of **nam** at the conclusion of the *Hymn* marks a shift in the kind of power that is attributed to Inana. Now we see that she rules over the underlying patterns of existence as well as individual persons and events. She controls not just kings and gods but royalty and divinity; she is not just great, she holds the concept of greatness within her. This repetition of **nam** reaches a climax in the line "You, who are fit to rule, fix the fates of queens and ladies," which in a phonemic transcription would read, **innin nin-ene nam nammatare nam-nina tuma** (l. 267).[18] The significance of the line is that Inana herself rules as queen, **nin**, and in turn gives "queenship," **nam-nina**, to other women, thus ruling the very abstraction of rulership. In short, Inana has power over power. That is the culmination of the *Hymn*'s poetic program: since no one else can control or even understand Inana, and since she can transform everyone and everything at will, she rules supreme in every way.

Reading a line like this, we may be tempted to celebrate Enheduana as a proto-feminist, a poet of female empowerment and **nam-nina**. But the power we find in Enheduana's poems is also, and more importantly, the power of empire. Inana was the patron deity of the Old Akkadian Empire: to extol her might was also to extol the might of Sargon and Naram-Sîn. In the *Exaltation*, Inana's power is fleshed out through the grueling account of how she destroys the rebel city. Any revolt against Inana—and implicitly, against the empire—is mercilessly put down, foreshadowing what will happen to Lugal-Ane when Inana finally takes action against him. The *Exaltation* and the *Hymn* were not conceived as feminist statements, for feminism was still thousands of years in the future. In their historical context, they celebrate female rulership only within a specific and rather unappetizing political framework: imperial subjugation.

Perhaps the clearest example of the imperial logic that undergirds these poems is a text that at first glance seems the least political of Enheduana's works: the *Temple Hymns*. This poem too is about power, but it makes its claim through the way it is structured, not its explicit content. One of the most important facts about this collection is that it *is* a collection. Before Sargon's conquests, the cities of Sumer were independent states, culturally interrelated but politically independent. In the *Temple Hymns*, the cities are brought together into a single composition, yielding a kind of hymnic imperialism. As noted above, the collection draws on older texts, combining existing hymns into a new anthology. In this process, the hymns were standardized and made to conform to a specific format. The hymns are highly repetitious, following the same poetic structure and drawing on a relatively small set of key terms. They all begin with an invocation of the temple's name, then turn to the deity with the phrase **nunzu**, "Your lord/ lady is ...," and end with the same closing formula ("... has taken his/her seat upon your throne"). Just as Sargon and Naram-Sîn sought to impose consistent standards of administration and accounting on the cities they had conquered, so the *Temple Hymns* imposes a poetic uniformity on the previously disparate hymns.[19]

Some hymns even repeat whole lines found elsewhere in the collection. Take the following phrase: "Source of awe and tingling fear, where the Anuna gather to drink your mighty beer." The phrase occurs in the hymn to Ningirsu's temple in Lagash (hymn 20, ll. 253–54) and in the hymn to Gula's temple in Isin (hymn 30, ll. 385–86). But Lagash and Isin were different cities, and like all the other Sumerian cities they vied with each other in their quest for political supremacy. The link that the *Temple Hymns* establishes between them by using the same phrase to describe their temples is a textual illusion aimed at establishing an overarching unity between the cities. Through this and similar poetic effects, the *Temple Hymns* turns the miscellany of Sumerian cities into one homogenous entity.[20] If the collection really was compiled in Enheduana's lifetime, it would have carried a clear message: Enheduana was doing poetically what Sargon had done politically; she was achieving with words what he had achieved with swords. This agenda is reflected in the sequence of temples, which begins with Eridu and Nippur, the traditional centers of Sumerian culture, and then zigzags through Sumer before reaching Akkad. The cities are arranged in an order that culminates, as if by logical necessity, in the imperial city that ruled them.

Even if the *Temple Hymns* was a later composition, or perhaps an originally anonymous composition that was later attributed to Enheduana, it would have carried this or a similar connotation for the Old Babylonian students. To them the Sumerian-speaking world of Enheduana's time was dead and distant, and the *Temple Hymns* gave them a literary roadmap through this ancient landscape, arranging it into a coherent collection. The text would have allowed them to reimagine what was in fact a motley gathering of city-states as a stable, united region—something that it never fully became, even at the height of the Old Akkadian Empire. The scribes could then measure the success of the state under which they lived against this notion of a once-united Sumer. As shown by the philologist Niek Veldhuis and others, this was a persistent ideological goal of the Old Babylonian curriculum: to reimagine the Sumerian world as a single political entity, rather than as a medley of city-states.[21] This goal is most fully realized in the *Temple Hymns*, which turns a sequence of individual poems into a literary entity. For the Old Babylonian students, the appeal of the text was no doubt increased by the fact that after celebrating Akkad, the *Temple Hymns* adds one last city: Eresh, home of Nisaba, the goddess of writing. Akkad may have fallen, but the power of writing lived on.[22]

NATURE, WAR, EXILE

When Enheduana describes Inana's power, she repeatedly turns to the natural world for metaphors and similes. And because Inana is described as holding a kind of power that transcends rules and undoes order, the images that are taken from the natural world are often images of terrifying destruction. The natural world that lies outside human settlements is not depicted as a rustic, romantic setting of idyllic peace, or as a place of potential resources to be extracted by human ingenuity. The land outside the cities is a dangerous, awe-inspiring world into which humans fare at their own risk. With few exceptions, nature appears in Enheduana's poems in one of two guises: as a source of destruction, in the form of storms, floods, fires, thorns, lions, leopards, eagles, and the like; or as a target of destruction, as when Enheduana flees like a swallow or the Anuna gods flutter like bats and tremble like reeds. Tellingly, Inana is compared both to wild animals, such as a swooping hawk, and to a clever hunter who catches all birds in her net: she is part of nature and part of its slaughter. Particularly hair-raising is the comparison between Inana and the aurochs, the magnificent but now extinct breed of wild oxen that walked the plains of ancient Iraq, weighing up to fifteen hundred pounds (around seven hundred kilograms), crowned with horns up to thirty inches (around seventy-five centimeters) long, and spreading fear wherever they went.

At the same time, the poems also blur the distinction between the natural and the human worlds. The *Exaltation* and the *Hymn* do so by reminding the reader that humans have no safe refuge from the forces of nature even within their own homes: if the people displease Inana, their city gates will burst into flame, and storms will level the land. But the *Temple Hymns* takes a different approach, highlighting not just the destructiveness of the natural forces but also their grandeur. The temples are all described with metaphors drawn from the natural world: they rise like mountains, gore like bulls, or feed their people like fragrant grasslands. It is as if these buildings, which were the centers and pinnacles of the ancient cities, have been folded back into the natural landscape.

The hymnic vision of the text fills the cities with wild animals, exuberant plant life, and huge mountains, imbuing the temples with the force of natural processes. The otherwise static buildings are made to move: the temples do not just stand, they emerge from the ground like a bull brandishing its horns; they are not just kept clean, they shine like the dawning sun. The line between the human-built structures and the surrounding environment is, for a moment, erased.

This description of nature as a place of disturbance and destruction may have a basis in historical fact. It is possible that Enheduana lived through a period of sudden climate change that would have wrought havoc on the seasonal cycles. Geologists have uncovered evidence of what is called, rather blandly, the "4.2-kiloyear event": a climatic event of uncertain nature that happened around forty-two hundred years ago, during the Old Akkadian period. Whatever triggered it, the event led to droughts all over the world, and while it is unclear whether its consequences were truly global, ancient Iraq was certainly affected by it: a dip in rainfall and river levels led to farmlands becoming unusable, which in turn led to famines and mass migrations. Some archaeologists have argued that these changes in climate led to the collapse of the Old Akkadian Empire.[23] But neither the onset of the geological event nor Enheduana's lifetime can be dated with any kind of precision: while they are in the same centurial ballpark, we do not know whether Enheduana would have witnessed these disturbances firsthand, or whether they would have influenced the texts attributed to her. If the poems were composed at a later date, this would make it more likely that their bleak view of nature was shaped by the 4.2-kiloyear event, since its aftereffects lasted for centuries.

What the historical Enheduana certainly did witness is another source of terror depicted in the poems: war. It is not only floods and storms that can bring destruction; humans are perfectly capable of doing so themselves. As with the natural world, the poems' description of war is double-edged. There can be no doubt that the narrator exults in warfare, particularly when it leads to the crushing defeat of those who rebel against Inana and the empire. But war is not treated as a source of honor, a test in which men may prove their worth and build up fame, as is the case in many other ancient (and, indeed, modern) accounts of warfare. Instead, Enheduana's depiction of war seems oddly impersonal. It is as if the machinery of murder is powered by its own innate will, a will to which humans are merely subjected: "Hatches crush heads, spears eat flesh, and axes are drenched in blood" (*Hymn*, l. 46).[24] Soldiers appear not as the heroes or even the agents of battle, only as its victims. In a particularly touching scene, the *Exaltation* describes the troops that are led away in chains as the wind blows where the soldiers once danced (ll. 49–50). In Enheduana's poems, war is unheroic. If the texts celebrate war, they do so in the same way they celebrate hurricanes and flash floods: as a powerhouse of chaos that no human can control.

In ancient literature, Inana is mainly shown in one of two guises. In some texts, she is an alluring and unmarried young woman, wrapped in charm and ready to be seduced by the shepherd god Dumuzi. In others, she is the terrifying goddess of war, leading the charge against the enemy. It is in this second role that Enheduana depicts her: the Inana of these poems is almost exclusively the warlike Inana. But even in that role, the goddess displays her inbuilt duality. A recurrent trope in ancient descriptions of Inana (and especially of her Akkadian counterpart, Ishtar) is that she mixes the lethal world of war, battles, and slaughter with the lighthearted world of games, dance, and song. War is to her a toy, conflict a source of grim pleasure. We find this disconcerting mix of mirth and cruelty in the *Hymn*, where it is said of Inana that "in her happy heart, she sings the song of death in battle: singing the song in her heart, she washes her weapons with blood and guts" (ll. 43–45). These lighthearted metaphors do not lessen the horrors of war, with which ancient readers would have been tragically familiar. Rather, they help serve to make war inglorious by revealing the absurdity that lies at its heart. In place of ordered battle lines and heroic conduct, we find war depicted as revelry and frenzy, no more predictable than the throw of dice or the whirling of dance.

Enheduana's depiction of warfare is all too relevant to modern Iraq, which has endured four decades of fruitless and mismanaged wars, the brunt of which has been borne by its civilian population. The remains of ancient Ur now lie within the Tallil Air Base, also known as Camp Adder, a military airport originally built by Saddam Hussein and later used by the U.S. occupation forces in Iraq. Between the tremors caused by landing fighter jets, the wartime tourism of the soldiers stationed at the base who would stroll around the site and pick up souvenirs to take back home, and the looting carried out by desperate Iraqi citizens whose livelihoods have been destroyed, the damage to the site has been enormous. This is a particularly tragic chapter in the long history of Enheduana's city, and it shows no sign of ending. War is as unheroic today as it was four thousand years ago.

Closely related to the pain of war is that of exile. Enheduana is forced out of her city and depicts herself wasting away "in this land of lies," roving through "the thorns of foreign lands" (*Exaltation*, ll. 101, 106). The pain of uprooting is again all too relevant to modern Iraqis, many of whom have been forced out of their country by war, persecution, and poverty. The poet Dunya Mikhail, who was born in Baghdad and now lives in the United States, speaks of relating to Enheduana as a fellow exile. (She also speaks of relating to Enheduana as a fellow practical-minded woman, and admiring her sensible choices: when one god does not answer her prayers, she turns to one who will.) "Exile," says Mikhail, "carries two codes," because the exiled are forever caught between two languages, two places, two moments in time: home and here. Mikhail connects the duality that is so forcefully expressed in Enheduana's hymns with her own displacement: "As an immigrant, I myself have that duality of existence." Though no human can fully embody the paradox of Inana's being, Mikhail argues that immigrants come closer than most.[25]

In turn, by reading literature and especially ancient literature, we can gain a sense of what the double-coded duality feels like. "A new poem opens a space of discovery for me, and then it invites others to come into that space and add their own meaning to it," Mikhail says. "It's like immigration. The readers immigrate to our poem, and then gradually, they begin to associate it with some experience that may be familiar or unfamiliar to them." Rather than treating the ancient poem as an exiled stranger arriving in the present, Mikhail turns readers into immigrants who must struggle to make sense of a world utterly alien to them, leaving them dazzled and disoriented. While we should not think that by reading Enheduana's poems we will know what it is like to live in exile, Mikhail's relation to Enheduana holds up the possibility for new connections across the many-layered codes of time, space, and language, revealing the full range of displacements that Enheduana's poems set in motion.

GRIEF AND GENDER

In Enheduana's hymn, natural disasters and warfare seem always to be looming overhead, and the only human response is to weep and wail. But this grim picture of the world does not necessarily correspond to what ancient readers and writers actually thought. Rather, we can think of it as a strategic stance that was meant to soothe the hearts of the gods, and so prevent the very dangers that are described in the text. This strategy underlies the ancient practice of ritual lamentation, a form of religious performance that was common throughout the history of the ancient Near East. Ritual laments are central for understanding Enheduana's poetry, as allusions to those rituals appear time and again in the *Hymn* and the *Exaltation.*

Briefly put, the logic of lamentation was that the gods might impose terrible disasters on the human population simply to prove how powerful they were. To avert this, the priests and priestesses would show the gods that they appreciated their terrifying powers by ritually grieving over the devastation that the gods might choose to impose, making a future show of force unnecessary. As Paul Delnero has put it, these laments were performed "neither as a cause of grief, nor as a means of generating it, but instead to prevent catastrophes from occurring."[26] When the gods had their powers recognized through laments, they were expected to cease their devastation. That expectation is made clear in the *Exaltation* when Enheduana says to Inana, "When they sing their lamentations, my queen, then sail your boat of sorrow to another shore" (ll. 97–98). The lament is here clearly meant to stop the destruction being lamented: Inana is imposing sorrow simply because she enjoys having her strength recognized by humans, so when they do acknowledge it through laments, she should impose her sorrow on another land instead. Paradoxically, the lamenters' lavish display of submission was a way for humans to gain a measure of control over the gods.

References to ritual laments are scattered throughout the *Exaltation.* Enheduana says that she will weep to please Inana: "I will let my tears stream free to soften your heart, as if they were beer" (ll. 82–83)—the implication being that Inana finds human grief intoxicating. "For your captive spouse and your captive child, your fury grows ever greater" (ll. 142–43) also seems to be a deliberate allusion to the genre of ritual lamentation.[27] Another allusion comes in the line "With the harps of the temple, they strike the beat of a sorrowful song" (l. 33). The word I translate as "harp of the temple" is **balaĝ**, a musical instrument that would accompany the laments (it was originally a stringed instrument but later transmogrified into a large kettledrum).[28] But of all the references to lamenting in the *Exaltation*, the most important comes when Enheduana describes how she composed the text: "What I sang to you at dead of night, let a lamenter repeat at midday" (ll. 140–41). The word "lamenter" is in Sumerian **gala**, a group of priests whose main duty it was to sing the laments. Since the *Exaltation* is to be performed by a **gala**, one wonders if the whole text can be understood as a lamentation, comparable in nature to the ritual songs that these priests would recite as part of their duties. The comparison is certainly illuminating: after all, the *Exaltation* does spend a considerable time elevating Inana by describing the horrors she inflicts on the human population, and Enheduana's description of the agony she suffered in exile can likewise be understood through the lens of laments—her pain is proof of Inana's power. But it would be simplistic to claim that the *Exaltation* is a ritual lament and nothing else. The poem mixes several styles, using the logic of laments in one line and the logic of court cases in the next. The text cannot be pinned down as one or the other; it freely takes from other genres what it can use to advance its main cause, the elevation of Inana.

The mention of the **gala** highlights another key aspect of Enheduana's poems: gender, and especially the subversion of gender. The ritual laments were performed in a special dialect of the Sumerian language called Emesal (literally, "thin tongue"), which in literary texts is spoken only by goddesses.[29] It is therefore thought to have been a ritual literary language associated with the female gender, but the main performers of lamentations, the **gala**, were otherwise treated as men. They bear male names and take male roles in society. Some Sumerian texts suggest that the **gala** had a socially ambiguous position, and they are sometimes linked to homoerotic activities.[30] The evidence is scant, and it changes substantially from one century to the next: after the Old Babylonian period, all evidence of the **gala**'s nonnormative gender presentation disappears, and they are treated like any other type of male priest. But in earlier periods, the **gala** were sometimes connected with gender-subverting behavior, acting as men in some contexts and as gender-ambiguous figures in others.[31]

The evidence for activities that sought to actively subvert established gender norms is much clearer when we turn to another and much more motley class of ritual performers. These included the **kurĝara**, the **saĝ-ursaĝ**, and the **pilipili**, as well as several other groups who were associated with the worship of Inana and who performed rituals in which they upended the usual conventions of gender. Ancient texts describe processions in honor of Inana in which the participants would wear female clothes on one side of their body and male clothes on the other. They would brandish weapons, which were the traditional signs of masculinity, as well as weaving instruments, such as spindles and distaffs, the traditional signs of femininity.[32] By mixing and juxtaposing the standard symbols of gender, they would introduce an element of confusion and capriciousness into the conventions of gendered behavior: if the same person could wear both female and male clothes, viewers were led to ponder the nature of gender itself. It is highly likely that the various groups, such as the **kurĝara** and the **saĝ-ursaĝ**, would subvert gender norms in different ways: some were perhaps individuals who generally appeared to be female but performed stereotypically male actions, others the reverse, but because of the limitations of our sources, it is difficult to reconstruct the differences between them.[33] Either way, these groups were all engaged in a playful scrambling of what was thought to be typically male and typically female. As the *Lob der Ishtar* puts it, "Their ways are different, their work is strange" (l. ii 17).[34] Ultimately, these ritual activities were meant to exalt Inana's supremacy: part of the awe that clung to the goddess was her power to change the sex of anyone at any time, and the ritual performers embodied that power in their own persons.

The *Hymn* celebrates these figures, and Enheduana dwells especially on the **pilipili**, describing how Inana created their identity by imposing a "burden" on their bodies. (The word **šer$_7$-da** can also mean "punishment" or "transgression.")[35] Inana then blessed them, named them, and gave them a snapped spear "as if they were a man" (ll. 80–81). The passage implies that they were generally seen as women and that they announced their distance from normative gender by carrying a broken emblem of maleness. However, the text identifies them not with one gender or the other but with the transition between genders, referring to them as "the changed **pilipili**" (l. 88). Together with the reed pipers, the **kurĝara**, the **saĝ-ursaĝ**, and the ecstatics, they are depicted as ritual lamenters: Inana "makes them weep and wail for her," so that they "exhaust themselves with tears and tears" (ll. 87, 90). The text is not implying that they led miserable lives which made them grieve for what Inana had done to them. Rather, their tears are once again to be understood as a celebration of Inana. Since their norm-breaking bodies were thought to represent the goddess's ability to transform anyone at will, they performed ritual lamentations to remind people that there was nothing Inana could not do.

While the autobiographical section of the *Hymn* is largely missing, what little remains presents us with an intriguing parallel. Enheduana says to Inana, "I know your great burden from my own body. Grief and evil keep my eyes open, the pain spills out" (ll. 250–51). The metaphor of a burden on the body and the constant lamentations that follow from it closely mirror the description of the **pilipili** earlier in the text. The parallel implies some kind of link between Enheduana and the **pilipili**, though the nature of that link remains unclear. It would be unwise to take the equation too far: though Enheduana's hymns do share many features with the lamentations, we should not conclude that she herself was a **pilipili**. Rather, she may be pointing to a more general similarity between herself and the ritual lamenters, perhaps simply through the sorrow they both endure.[36] But it is also undeniably true that as high priestess, Enheduana would have deviated from the conventional views of womanhood. As noted above, a central requirement for the high priestesses was that they should abstain from childbirth. The priestesses stood out among the women of their time, as they were bound not to the household of their father, husband, or child but to that of the deity they served.

The main characters of the poem, Inana and Enheduana, certainly do not correspond to the ideal of femininity that was widespread at the time. Nanna's wife, Ningal, would be a more typical representative of Sumerian womanhood, precisely because we hear so little about her. Women were expected to look after the house, cook, clean, weave, wash, manage the domestic expenses, and look after the children. They were supposed to be healthy, humble, caring, quiet, and attractive to look at.[37] They were certainly not supposed to interfere in the affairs of men, such as politics and warfare. Tellingly, the Babylonian epic *Gilgamesh* contrasts the "work of women," meaning sex, with the "work of men," meaning war.[38] But Inana flouts all these restrictions by meddling in the warrior's melee and daring to speak in the assembly of the gods—the ultimate site of political power. However, if Inana can push through these gendered boundaries, it is precisely because she is the divine embodiment of subversion. She breaks the rules that hold for others and by breaking them makes them visible. The tacit rules that govern society are clearest when they are being transgressed: mythical rule breakers like Inana actually play a useful social role by setting up an example of what not to do. Inana was seen as a counter-ideal from which human women were expected to distance themselves, not as an empowering figure for others to emulate.[39]

That being said, women in ancient Iraq were not entirely powerless either. They enjoyed rights and protections that women in ancient Athens would have envied. In the Old Babylonian period at least, women from better-off families were allowed to own and sell property, initiate divorce proceedings, engage in contracts, and in some cases learn how to read and write.[40] For the privileged few, the temples could be a path to power and prosperity: the *nadītu* women of the Old Babylonian period are a celebrated example of priestesses who engaged in shrewd economic investments.[41] However, after the Old Babylonian period, the situation for the women of ancient Iraq deteriorated. Talk of a "Sumerian matriarchy" has often been overblown by popular writers, but there is no denying that in the third and early second millennium women generally held more power than in later periods of cuneiform history. Around the middle of the second millennium BCE, a cultural shift took place that we have yet to fully understand. Priestesses lost most of the status they had previously enjoyed, and female deities were pushed to the side.[42] Female scribes are not common in Old Babylonian texts, but they do appear; in the first millennium, they are all but nonexistent. In the Old Babylonian period the divine patron of writing was the goddess Nisaba; in later periods she was replaced by the god Nabû. In the Old Babylonian epic *Atra-hasis*, humanity is created by the god Ea and the goddess Belet-ili working together; in the later epic *Enuma Elish*, humanity is created by two male gods, Ea and his son Marduk, after the latter's defeat and dismemberment of the goddess Tiamat.[43] We have yet to understand how this "great gender gap" in cuneiform culture came about, but its consequences were profound. As an author, Enheduana was a lone figure in the Old Babylonian period: no other work of literature was attributed to a named individual. In the first millennium, a new wave of authorship emerged, as literary texts that had once circulated anonymously were attributed to famous scholars of ages past. *Gilgamesh*, for example, was composed over many centuries by a long lineage of poets and performers, but around the eighth century BCE it was reinterpreted as the work of a single man, Sîn-leqi-unnenni (who may or may not have existed). But crucially, all the literary authors of the first millennium BCE were men, and Enheduana had been entirely forgotten.[44]

After the end of the Old Babylonian period, a new educational program came into use, one less focused on Sumerian literature. Many of the classics from the Old Babylonian period were left out of this new curriculum, including Enheduana's poems. The last preserved copy of the *Hymn* dates to around the fourteenth century BCE; after that, we find no mention of Enheduana or her works. She would have been completely erased from history—had it not been for the serendipitous rediscovery of her poems.

THE PRIESTESS RETURNS

"IT IS AN ODD QUESTION, 'WHO WAS THE FIRST author?,'" as Andrew Bennett writes in his introduction to the theory of authorship, noting that the question "is itself immersed in what we might call an authorcentric or *auteurist* ideology."[1] Literary critics have for more than fifty years been pushing against this "authorcentric" ideology, which Bennett explains as the view that "literary culture is invariably based around isolated individuals, around the solitary figure of the genius."[2] Against this view, critics have argued that prose and poetry are not the product of "original" creators who pluck their verses out of thin air but are made and remade through networks of collaboration, as authors borrow each other's words, create new texts within existing traditions, and rely on long chains of editors, scribes, and other intermediaries to reach their readers. In short, authors are embedded in and depend upon communities of words and people. To ask, "Who was the first author?" would seem to go against that critical tide by assuming that behind every concept stands a singular creator—that even authorship was authored.

That might be so in the abstract, but as I explored in the previous essay, it is not actually the case. The *Exaltation* gives us a very different account of authorship by portraying the text as emerging from dialogue and collaboration, as scribes and singers come together to create the text in a complicated interplay of voices. Time and again in this book it has become clear that Enheduana's story is also the story of those who came after her. The story of the building in which she lived is also the story of the later high priestesses; the story of the disk that carries her name is also the story of Enanatuma, her successor in Ur; the story of her poems is also the story of the Old Babylonian scribes who copied, memorized, and translated them. Far from reinforcing an authorcentric myth, the history of Enheduana can help us rebut it by showing that literature can survive only within the communities that sustain and transform it. Enheduana's poems point beyond themselves, inviting us to explore the connections that have sprung up around them. In the present essay I continue that "outward" movement by looking not at Enheduana herself but at some of the people who have been drawn into her circle: the high priestesses of Ur, the archaeologist who uncovered the few surviving traces of her historical life, and the modern scholars, writers, and poets who have engaged with her legacy.

THE WOMEN OF UR

On September 26, 554 BCE, a partial eclipse of the moon took place at around a quarter to five, Babylon time.[3] In cuneiform culture, as in many other cultures from around the world, lunar eclipses were traditionally seen as an evil omen, spelling death for the reigning king. But the king who was reigning over Babylon in 554 was no ordinary ruler: King Nabonidus was a man unto himself.[4] He was also the last Babylonian king to see himself as part of the cuneiform tradition. When Cyrus the Great invaded Babylon and deposed Nabonidus in 539, he ushered in a period of five centuries during which the surviving centers of cuneiform culture were ruled by either the Persians or the Greeks, who unlike previous rulers of Babylon did not assimilate themselves to its traditional customs.

Nabonidus's reign thus marked the end of an era, but the king had wanted it to be a turning point, the start of something new. He was a religious reformer who sought to make Sîn (the Akkadian equivalent of Nanna) head of the pantheon, replacing Marduk, the city god of Babylon. This dramatic upset in religious practices is clouded in mystery, as is Nabonidus's decision to leave Babylon to take up residence in the city of Tayma on the Arabian Peninsula. He stayed there for almost a decade, leaving his son Belshazzar (of "the writing on the wall" fame) to rule Babylon in his stead. Nabonidus's motives are difficult to reconstruct because he was the subject of a coordinated smear campaign by the Persian rulers, who wanted to discredit the regime they had ousted; by the priests of Marduk, who wanted to avenge Nabonidus's demotion of their god; and by the writers of the Hebrew Bible, for whom the Persian invasion marked the end of their captivity in Babylon.[5] These various writers accused Nabonidus of being an incompetent buffoon, who tried to present himself as a skilled scholar but actually was a dangerous lunatic who saw messages from the Moon God where none were to be found. Behind these scurrilous attacks lies a more complicated reality. Nabonidus was indeed a religious reformer and a devotee of the Moon God (a devotion that he may have inherited from his mother),[6] but he sought to ground his innovations in the deep past and in the rich heritage of cuneiform learning.

The eclipse is a case in point. It occurred early in his reign, during his second year on the throne, and Nabonidus had no intention of accepting it as the bad omen it appeared to be. He ignored the advice of his astrological experts and proposed a new interpretation, finding in the astrological series *Enuma Anu Enlil* an omen that—with some slight fudging—could be made to fit the eclipse. According to this omen, the eclipse meant that "Sîn desires a high priestess." This reading allowed Nabonidus to accomplish two goals at once: promoting the worship of the Moon God and restoring an ancient practice to new life. The office of Nanna's high priestess at Ur had been vacant for some ten centuries after the "great gender gap" of the mid-second millennium had curtailed the role of women in religious ceremonies. It is unclear when the office was discontinued; some evidence suggests that it persisted into the late second millennium, but the last clear evidence of a high priestess serving at Ur dates to the Old Babylonian period.[7] It was this long-gone custom that Nabonidus set out to resurrect, appointing his daughter to serve as the head of the ĝipar in Ur, just as Sargon had done with Enheduana seventeen hundred years earlier. Nabonidus gave his daughter the name Ennigaldi-Nanna, to show that he was honoring the omen he had received: the name literally means "high priestess [en], the desire [nigaldi] of Nanna."[8]

Today we are more interested in Enheduana's literary accomplishments than in her religious career, but the office of the high priestess would have shaped her life and been central to her self-perception. As described in the previous essays, Enheduana spent most of her life within the ĝipar and saw herself as part of a lineage of priestesses that extended into both past and future. Ennigaldi-Nanna brought that lineage back to life, making her part of Enheduana's legacy in a broader sense. But Ennigaldi-Nanna's engagement with the past went farther. When modern archaeologists excavated the temple complex in Ur, they discovered a series of rooms that held a curious collection of objects, including a statue of King Shulgi, a ceremonial mace head, and a Kassite stele (known as a *kudurru*).[9] These objects ranged in date from the twenty-first to the seventh century BCE but were found in the same room, which posed a puzzle for the archaeologists. As Louise Pryke puts it, "Especially unusual was that while the items were from different geographical areas and historical settings, they were neatly assembled together."[10] So how did they get there? A clue is provided by one of the objects, a copy of a royal inscription by King Amar-Suen, the son of Shulgi. A note added to this copy explains how it found its way to Ennigaldi-Nanna's home: during the renovation of a temple in Ur, it was discovered among the debris by a man named Nabu-shuma-iddin, who copied it out "for display" (*ana tāmarti*).[11] That sentence is key. If the historical artefacts were purposely assembled and displayed, then the rooms in Ennigaldi-Nanna's palace might have served as a sort of ancient museum. Of course, it would not have been a museum in the modern sense (for one thing, it would not have been accessible to the public), but it might just be the case that the city which gave us the world's first author also gave us the first museum curator—and that both were women.[12]

There is no doubt that a museum-like display of ancient objects would have fit well into the cultural mood of Ennigaldi-Nanna's time. An interest in the deep past was nothing new; as noted above, the case of Ilum-palil's ax suggests that even in Enheduana's day people may have been collecting relics of earlier centuries. But the antiquarian zeal had become particularly intense during Nabonidus's reign, to such an extent that he has been called "the archaeologist on the throne."[13] In an inscription he left behind to commemorate Ennigaldi-Nanna's appointment as high priestess, Nabonidus describes himself as worrying about the practicalities of reviving the office: "Because the rituals of the high priestess had been forgotten since ancient times, and the structure [of the ĝipar] was no longer known, I pondered the matter every day."[14] Nabonidus claims to have found a clue to the priestess's attire on a foundation stone from the twelfth century BCE, but the real breakthrough came when he turned to the building of the ĝipar itself, which in this inscription is called the E-Gipar.

> At that time, the E-Gipar—the sacred chamber, the place in which the rituals of the high priestess are perfectly performed—that place was neglected and had turned into ruins; date palms and fruit orchards grew within it. I felled the trees and cleared the rubble from its ruins, discovering the temple and revealing

its foundation. Inside it, I found inscriptions by kings of the ancient past. I also discovered ancient writings by Enanedu, high priestess of Ur, daughter of Kudur-Mabuk and sister of Rim-Sîn, king of Ur, who had renewed and restored the E-Gipar and had surrounded the burial ground of the ancient high priestesses with a wall, next to the E-Gipar's border. There, I built the E-Gipar anew as it had been in ancient times.[15]

The last statement is particularly revealing: Nabonidus says that he built the temple *kima labirim-ma eššiš*, literally "as of old, anew." This phrase is a perfect expression of his double goal of reform and return—changing religious practices, but seeking support for those changes in the remote past.[16] To build the new temple for his daughter and the Moon God, Nabonidus excavated the site back to its Old Babylonian foundations, and in doing so, he found exactly the support he needed: the testimony of an ancient high priestess.

Enanedu was indeed the daughter of Kudur-Mabuk and the sister of King Rim-Sîn. She was the successor of Enanatuma, the high priestess who rebuilt the **ĝipar** after the Elamite raid and whose statue was laid next to the Disk of Enheduana. Enanedu continued Enanatuma's project of restoring the **ĝipar**, commissioning several inscriptions to celebrate her feat—one of which was found by Nabonidus, and two of which were recovered by modern archaeologists.[17] Just as Nabonidus says, Enanedu does claim that she restored the building, adding new brickwork and plaster and thus "giving the temple a new form."[18] She also constructed a new wall to encircle the cemetery of the **ĝipar**. As we saw above, the high priestesses were originally buried beneath the building itself. When the temple ran out of space, a cemetery was set up next to it, but as Enanedu notes, this cemetery had fallen into disrepair: "It was not surrounded by a wall, its entryways and . . . had collapsed, there were no guards, and the place was no longer pure." Enanedu eagerly took up the task: "By my great wisdom, I found a place for those who in the future would go to their fate [die], establishing a great sacred precinct, larger than the graveyard of the previous high priestesses, and that ruined place I surrounded with a wall, setting up a watch and purifying it."[19]

No less than the other women discussed in this book, Enanedu cuts an impressive figure, unafraid to boast of her wisdom and skill: in the opening lines of the inscription, she claims that already in the womb she was destined for "heavenly nobility," and that Ningal herself blessed her body with the radiance that befits a high priestess.[20] In his inscription, Nabonidus refers to Enanedu as the sister of Rim-Sîn, but those are not her words: she calls herself the king's *brother*.[21] (It seems clear which of them she thought should rightfully be king.) But the reason she fits into our story is a somewhat subtler claim that emerges from her text. No less than Nabonidus and Ennigaldi-Nanna, she interweaves past and future in her account of the restoration: her building activity is aimed both at preserving the cemetery of the former high priestesses and at creating a new site for those who have yet to "go to their fate." She looks both backward and forward, and that double awareness is shared by every character I have examined in this book: each of them was conscious of the lineage she came into and the changes she wished to make to it, as when Enheduana wove her poems from existing threads of text and passed them on to the scribes who would reshape them in their turn.

In short, the high priestesses of Ur were linked in a flow of remembrance and renewal. The Disk of Enheduana was modeled on earlier depictions of high priestesses, but it added a crucial twist by inserting Enheduana's name. Enanatuma recovered that disk and used it as a metaphorical foundation for the temple she rebuilt after it had been destroyed, which was restored again in the following generation by Enanedu. In turn, Enanedu's inscriptions allowed Ennigaldi-Nanna to reinvent the office of the high priestess a millennium later. But this final reinvention proved short-lived, as the Persian invasion enabled the priests of Marduk to roll back Nabonidus's reforms. Less than a century later, in the early fifth century, droughts in southern Iraq led to Ur's being abandoned, finally bringing the chain of change and continuity to an end. The ĝipar would have to wait for more than two thousand years, buried in sand and silence, before it was once more cleared of rubble and restored to new life. But as it happened, the archaeological digs of the early twentieth century added one more chapter to the story of the women at Ur. And so, from Enheduana's successors, we now turn to her excavator.

PARALLEL LIVES

Katharine Woolley is today best remembered—if she is remembered at all—as the inspiration for Louise Leitner, the main victim of Agatha Christie's *Murder in Mesopotamia.*[22] Christie and Woolley met in 1928, when Christie was visiting the archaeological excavation at Ur, where Woolley was serving as second-in-command. During her visit to Ur, Christie struck up a romance with her future husband, Max Mallowan, with whom she would travel back to Iraq for many seasons of excavation. Woolley made a strong impression on Christie, who in her autobiography depicts her as a complicated individual:

> Katharine Woolley, who was to become one of my great friends
> in the years to come, was an extraordinary character. People
> have been divided always between disliking her with a fierce and
> vengeful hatred, and being entranced by her—possibly because
> she switched from one mood to another so easily that you never
> knew where you were with her. . . . The things she wanted to talk

about were never banal. She stimulated your mind into thinking along some pathway that had not before suggested itself to you. She was capable of rudeness—in fact she had an insolent rudeness, when she wanted to, that was unbelievable—but if she wished to charm you she would succeed every time.[23]

In *Murder in Mesopotamia*, Louise Leitner arrives at the excavation in Iraq as the wife of the expedition leader, Erich, and throughout the novel she evokes powerful, contradictory feelings in everyone around her, mixing strong love with strong hate. It is clear from Christie's autobiography that she took this trait from Woolley: the capacity to enchant and infuriate people in turn. But unlike the fictional character she inspired, Woolley was anything but a passive bystander to the excavation at Ur. While Leitner lounges around the dig house, Woolley was an indefatigable worker and administrator. It was the excavation that she helped lead which uncovered—among many other things—the temple of Nanna, the ĝipar of the high priestesses, the Disk of Enheduana, the cylinder seals of Enheduana's servants, many manuscripts of Enheduana's poems, the inscriptions of Enanedu, and the museum of Ennigaldi-Nanna. Our knowledge of Enheduana and her successors is in large part thanks to Woolley's efforts.

The credit for excavating Ur is often given entirely to Woolley's husband, Leonard, while Katharine is dismissively referred to as his difficult wife. But pigeonholing Katharine as the excavator's wife does her a double disservice. First, it underplays the extent of her involvement: she was the primary assistant at the excavation for many years and took over as its leader in 1931 while Leonard was touring the United States to promote the dig. It was Katharine who drew the illustrations that helped make the finds from "Ur of the Chaldees, Birthplace of Abraham" a sensation in the popular press. In particular, she was responsible for reconstructing the golden headdress of Queen Puabi, one of the excavation's most stunning discoveries, and she was instrumental in procuring funding for the excavation.[24] Second, Katharine only married Leonard because she was forced to do so by the museums that were financing the excavation, the British Museum and the Penn Museum. It was thought unseemly that a single woman (Katharine was a widow) should stay at a dig surrounded by men, so Leonard, desperate to keep Katharine by his side at Ur, proposed marriage. Katharine agreed but insisted that the union remain unconsummated: it was to be solely a formality.

They were married in 1927—the same year that the Disk of Enheduana was unearthed—but Leonard soon came to regret the terms he had agreed to. He had probably assumed that Katharine would eventually change her mind, but she did not, and so he wrote to his attorney requesting divorce papers. These were never filed, perhaps because Katharine was diagnosed with multiple sclerosis, of which she died in 1945. There can be no question that Katharine Woolley was a difficult person, who could be both spiteful and charming, congenial and manipulative. But it is hard not to feel that some of the vile accounts of her character, and especially the insistence that she was domineering and demanding, are at least partly due to her unusual position as a powerful woman in a male-dominated field.[25] Women in power are subjected to incompatible demands: like their male colleagues, they must be ruthless and cunning to get to the top, but unlike men, they are also expected to be guileless and nurturing. Katharine did not live according to that impossible double standard.

Katharine Woolley should rightfully feature in any account of Enheduana's legacy, since all evidence of her Old Akkadian life was uncovered under Woolley's watch, but there is also a stranger, more oblique, and more coincidental connection between the two women, or at least between their authorial personae. In 1929, Woolley published a novel, *Adventure Calls,* which combines an account of gender-subverting exploits with a staunch defense of empire in the face of revolt.[26] The novel centers on the twins Sandy and Colin Gillespie (unsubtly, their last name ends in "spy"). They are born in Baghdad, grow up in Scotland, and return to Iraq in the interwar years, when the country was under British control. Sandy, the boy, goes undercover to expose a conspiracy among the Arab population. Colin, the girl, travels to Iraq to take her twin brother's place in the (fictional) city of Kelekiyah, covering for his absence by passing as a man. In Iraq and in disguise, Colin finds relief from the oppressive sexism that otherwise limits her sense of freedom: she is constantly reminded of what women cannot do, and especially of where they cannot go. To live as a man, for Colin, is to move freely through the world. The Arab rebellion then moves its center of operations to Kelekiyah, and in what is meant to be a happy outcome, Sandy and Colin work together to put down the revolt, saving British rule in Iraq.[27] At the end, Colin's identity is found out, and in a *Mulan*-like ending, the officer under whom she had worked while disguised as a man asks for her hand in marriage.

It is a long-standing trope of Western literature set in "the Orient" that Westerners could find there a reprieve from the stuffy norms that dominated life in supposedly more "civilized" countries. That being said, Woolley's depiction of the sexist limitations that Colin endures is clearly heartfelt, and it is no doubt based on her own experience. Woolley's novel-length fantasy of the freedom that a woman might achieve by passing as a man speaks volumes to the discomfort she must have felt in her own life. But if Woolley saw Iraq as a place where she could escape Western gender norms, she felt no sympathy for the Arabs she met there or their desire for freedom. Her novel is unequivocal in its support of British rule, treating the Arabs as nothing more than a source of seething unrest. The Arab characters are described in disparaging, racist terms, full of timeworn tropes about the incorrigible ways of "the Arab mind." The revolt that is depicted in the novel is not just a literary concoction. The story is set in 1920, the year of the Great Iraqi Revolution, an uprising across the country that aimed to overthrow colonial rule. It was eventually put down by the British military forces, though it did pressure the British into adopting a more indirect form of control. Faisal I was installed as king of Iraq, but on the clear understanding that he would remain beholden to British influence. This "solution" did little to improve the life of average Iraqis, and discontent continued to simmer, occasionally bubbling into protests throughout Woolley's stay in Iraq, from 1924 to 1931. Though she witnessed the protests firsthand, the novel shows that Woolley remained disdainful of them: *Adventure Calls* can be read as an account of an alternate timeline in which Woolley's heroine managed to nip the Great Iraqi Revolution in the bud. Much like Enheduana in the *Exaltation*, her reaction to anti-imperial revolts was one of scorn.

I know that it is fanciful to draw a parallel between these women. The resemblances that one can find in their writings— both of which focus on gender-subversive servants of empire, women who were seen as not quite women by the very different standards of their time—are pure happenstance, and depend in large part on speculation. Even if we can detect scattered hints that Enheduana's authorial persona deviated from ancient gender norms, the evidence is circumstantial at best. The parallel also ignores many key differences: the two women belonged to entirely different worlds, and whatever similarities connect them cannot be more than superficial. (Also, the hymns attributed to Enheduana are a much greater literary achievement than the boilerplate novel put out by Woolley.) Still, I like to think that at least a faint echo links their lives at Ur, connecting the excavator and the excavated, the archaeologist and the priestess.

We can at least be certain that Woolley knew who Enheduana was. In Leonard's account of the excavation, he describes his excitement at discovering the disk and the cylinder seals of

Enheduana's servants. "It was an astonishing piece of luck," he wrote, because previous historians had questioned whether Sargon was a real historical figure. The disk put Sargon's existence beyond doubt, and gave the name of his daughter as an added boon. As Leonard wrote, "Now we have En-he-du-an-na, and she is a very real person; she lived at Ur and she had her court there, as beseemed a princess."[28] But even as the Woolleys had brought Enheduana's name back to light, they could not have known about her poetry. From the evidence that Katharine and Leonard had found, they were able to conclude that Enheduana was the daughter of Sargon and the high priestess of Nanna, but they knew nothing about her Old Babylonian afterlife. While the excavation at Ur did yield several manuscripts of Enheduana's poems, it would take decades for philologists to decipher them. Each tablet had to be copied by hand, the copies had to be carefully studied, the manuscripts had to be compared with one another, the differences between them had to be reconciled, the complex language of the poems had to be unknotted, and some sense had to be drawn from Enheduana's confounding metaphors.

This process is still ongoing, as new manuscripts continue to be found and our knowledge of Sumerian continues to grow. But a crucial first step was the appearance of a critical edition of the *Exaltation*, produced by the philologists William Hallo and J. J. A. van Dijk: it was this edition that marked the beginning of Enheduana's third and current life.[29] And as always with Enheduana, the circumstances of its publication were anything but peaceful.

ENHEDUANA TODAY

The long history of Enheduana and her hymns seems steeped in revolution. In the Old Akkadian Empire, Enheduana's life was haunted by uprisings, as depicted in the *Exaltation*. In the Old

Babylonian period, her poems were studied in the wake of the failed rebellion against Babylon and the social crisis that followed. Under Nabonidus, the revival of the high priestess's office was driven by religious reforms and followed by the fall of Babylon. In the 1920s, the excavations at Ur were carried out in the aftermath of the Great Iraqi Revolution. As Enheduana has made her way through history, she has repeatedly found herself surrounded by dissent. It is no surprise, then, that the critical edition of the *Exaltation*—the first book to make a poem by Enheduana available in English—was published in 1968, just as a wave of revolts swept across the world. Workers left their factories, students occupied their campuses, demonstrators filled the streets, and for a summer it seemed as if global revolution were at hand. The calls for change were as many and as varied as the contexts from which they sprang. Protesters called for an end to dictatorships, to apartheid, to the Vietnam War, to racial discrimination, to capitalism, to colonialism, to the patriarchy. In an alternate world, a newly published *Exaltation*—a paean to the goddess of change written by a nonwhite woman—would have caught the eye of some demonstrator and been hailed as a revolutionary tract for the times. But that did not happen. Instead, literary-minded students flocked to another text, which had been published the year before: "The Death of the Author" by Roland Barthes. It is one of history's odder ironies that the poem which announced the birth of authorship and the essay that called for its demise were published within twelve months of each other.[30]

As it was, the appearance of the *Exaltation* went largely unnoticed. Philologists have many fine qualities, but a keen mind for publicity is not often among them. Indeed, they have good reasons for skirting the spotlight. If studying the cultures that flourished four thousand years ago teaches you anything, it is a profound sense of historical awareness. Pandering to passing tastes can seem pointless when the past is so very large and the present so very fleeting. Philologists' aversion to publicity undoubtedly also stems from their being told over and over again that their discipline is irrelevant. This is of course not true, but the barrage of abuse does make most philologists uneager to seek public attention for their finds. Whatever the reason, Enheduana's poems remained unread by anyone but specialists for a decade. The first indication that the texts might have a wider appeal came in 1978, when the anthropologist Marta Weigle published an essay titled "Women as Verbal Artists: Reclaiming the Sisters of Enheduanna," placing Enheduana at the head of a global lineage of literary women.[31] Since then, when Enheduana's poems have managed to escape the academy, they have most often done so by circulating among feminist readers and critics, as when the *Exaltation* was included in an anthology of women poets from antiquity to the present compiled by Aliki and Willis Barnstone.[32]

Another important context for Enheduana's modern reception is the wars in Iraq. In "Triptych in a Time of War," the poet Meena Alexander places Enheduana within the war-torn Iraqi landscape of 2003: "Spring brings the golden mustard seed and clouds of war / float over the ziqqurat of Ur. / Enheduanna is poised on an alabaster disc."[33] Poems that decry the devastation of Iraq often call on images from the ancient past, such as Babylon, Gilgamesh, and (less frequently) Enheduana.[34] These ancient icons tend to appear as witnesses, immortal and unmoving, to the devastation of their country. It is as if the landscape has been emptied of human life, and only the historical characters are left to look on. Another example of this use of Enheduana comes from the Iraqi poet Amal al-Jubouri, who calls on the "Towers . . . of the Mesopotamian soil" to witness the effects of oppression: the emptiness, the silence, the dead. Like Mikhail, al-Jubouri also writes of Enheduana in relation to her own exile, and Enheduana features prominently in the collection of poems that she wrote while seeking political asylum in Germany.[35] The story of Enheduana's reception reminds us that our understanding of the poems is always shaped by the context in which we read them, and by historical developments that bring us back to the texts with new topics in mind. The feminist movement and the Gulf Wars have both changed the significance of Enheduana's hymns.

More generally, we should keep in mind that since the poems come to us in such a fragmentary state and leave so many questions unanswered, we cannot fix them in place once and for all or assign to them a definite interpretation. Any attempt to do so will quickly run into trouble. The most sustained engagements with Enheduana's poems outside of Sumerology are two books published by the Jungian psychoanalyst Betty De Shong Meador.[36] Meador sees Enheduana as crafting a conscious, coherent literary program. Accordingly, Meador slots the poems (including *Inana and Ebih,* which we have no good ground for attributing to Enheduana) into a linear narrative that reflects a progression of psycho-spiritual liberation, in which Enheduana freed herself from her father's legacy and in so doing bolstered the supposedly matriarchal worship of Inana. Attractive as they may be, Meador's readings repeatedly overstretch or misrepresent the evidence, claiming certainty where none is to be found. As I hope will be clear from this book, practically all statements about Enheduana must be festooned with ifs and maybes. Exciting possibilities abound, but they all come with caveats. I am open to all new readings of Enheduana, as long as they acknowledge that the evidence at hand is limited and full of ambiguity. That is not to say that we should not try to make sense of Enheduana's poems—indeed, we have no choice but to engage our imagination in doing so—but the questions posed by the poems can receive only partial and provisional answers. For me, this is cause for excitement, not frustration: the doubts draw me in. One moment I read Enheduana's poems and see her as a living presence whose desperate cry cuts through time to reach my ears; the next, I see her as shrouded in a thousand mysteries, her figure receding farther with each question I ask of it.

But I am also confident that many (though of course not all) of those questions will one day be answered through the painstaking work of philological research. The story of Enheduana's rediscovery is a story of steady progress, as scholar after scholar has developed key insights into her world and her poems. After the edition of the *Exaltation* by Hallo and van Dijk in 1968, the philologist Åke Sjöberg produced the first edition of the *Temple Hymns* in 1969 and of the *Hymn to Inana* in 1975.[37] The work of these scholars was impressive for the times, as they wrenched meaning from texts that bristle with cruxes. But it cannot be emphasized enough that the study of Sumerian is a still unruly scientific frontier: there is no fully agreed-upon Sumerian dictionary, and one joke among specialists is that there are as many Sumerian grammars as there are Sumerologists.[38] Still, real headway is being made, and our knowledge of the language grows with each passing year. At the same time, new manuscripts of the texts keep being found, filling holes in fragmentary compositions or forcing us to revise passages we thought we knew. As a result, new editions of the texts must be made with regular frequency, as philologists revisit the manuscripts to establish what the original text says. In 1997, Annette Zgoll published a second edition of the *Exaltation,* with a far more detailed philological analysis and literary commentary than that supplied by Hallo and van Dijk. Further work was carried out by Paul Delnero, who in 2006 published a new overview of all existent manuscripts of the *Exaltation,* and by Pascal Attinger, whose French translation proposed many new readings of the text.[39] Meanwhile, a much anticipated edition of the *Temple Hymns* is being prepared by Monica Phillips, and as always, the work is ongoing: the philological flux of the texts will never be fully stilled, and new ideas will keep emerging from this close engagement with the ancient manuscripts.

At the same time, I strongly believe that Enheduana is poised for another kind of rediscovery: a popular rediscovery, as her poems come to be much more widely read. Fifty years have passed since the *Exaltation* was first translated into English, but Enheduana's third life is only just beginning. There are two reasons why the present moment is particularly propitious for an "Enheduana revival." The first is that we are currently witnessing a surge of interest in ancient literature. Fresh translations and retellings of classic works are reaching ever-wider audiences, and people all over the world are turning to the ancient past for answers and comfort. It is my sense that when their present moment seems rocked by waves of turmoil—political disarray, social divisions, the pandemic crisis, onrushing climate change, and seismic shifts in the world order—people feel a need to step back, zoom out, and look for new perspectives in the deep past. When we feel lost and unsure about our future direction, we begin to think with renewed insistence about where we came from and how we got here. And when it comes to literary history, few pasts are as deep as Enheduana's. She does not have much to offer us in terms of reassurance, for she too lived through a time of upheaval, but for that very reason her poems appeal to us all the more strongly: her songs of chaos and flux, exile and climate change, war and violence resonate today with dark exactness. The mixture of distance and resemblance—the zoomed-out viewpoint of a long-ago past and its eerie similarity to our current situation—makes Enheduana an ideal sounding board for reflecting on future directions.

The second reason why Enheduana is now more relevant than ever is that the current return to the classics is accompanied by another, contrary motion: an expansion of the canon. There is a hunger for forgotten voices, especially those of women and those from beyond the West, which has led to a reexamination of literary history—a search for the new within the old. The past decades have brought home the realization that for far too long gender and geography have conspired to keep out of the literary canon works of great beauty and import. Enheduana should not be valued solely as a "female" or "non-Western" poet, since the significance of her hymns transcends such categories: the force of her words can appeal to anyone at any time. But if we want to show that great literature has not been written only by white men, and if we want to make our reading lists, history books, school curricula, and bookshop shelves more inclusive and diverse, we could do worse than begin with Enheduana. For me, the appeal of her poems lies not least in the alternative history they hint at. They give us a chance to step out of the well-worn track leading from the Greek classics to English modernity and explore other cultural connections and historical trajectories. A history of literature that starts with Enheduana would be a different kind of history—one whose shape we have yet to discover. The past is always changing, and who better to spearhead that change than this ancient poet of paradox and power?

CHRONOLOGY

All dates are BCE and follow a historical
reconstruction known as the Middle Chronology.

3600–3100   THE URUK PERIOD

Uruk becomes the world's first metropolis, leading to the
emergence of the earliest known states and the inven-
tion of writing. City-states begin to appear throughout
the ancient Near East.

3100–2900   THE JEMDET NASR PERIOD

This period sees major developments in the cuneiform
script, which becomes more abstract and systematic.
Writing is used mainly to record economic transactions
but also for scholarly lists of words and mathematical
calculation.

2900–2350   THE EARLY DYNASTIC PERIOD

Southern Iraq consists of a number of independent city-
states, which are locked in a complex network of con-
flicts, alliances, and trade. The region is bilingual, with
inhabitants speaking both Sumerian and Akkadian. It is
from this period—from the cities of Shuruppak and Abu
Salabikh—that we have the oldest known literary texts,
including early precursors of the *Temple Hymns*.

2334—CA. 2200   THE OLD AKKADIAN EMPIRE
A long trend toward political centralization culminates in Sargon's conquest of all the Sumerian city-states, as well as swaths of territories around them. Enheduana is installed as high priestess in Ur. The period sees great technical and artistic innovations. Sargon and his successors, especially Naram-Sîn, implement ambitious reforms, but their rule is rocked by constant rebellions. Sargon makes Akkadian the language of state administration, setting in motion the decline of Sumerian.

2112–2004   THE THIRD DYNASTY OF UR (UR III)
After a period of political disorder (one ancient chronicle asks, "Who was king? Who was not king?"), Ur-Namma founds the Third Dynasty of Ur, a heavily centralized and bureaucratic state. Its second king, Shulgi, ushers in a revival of Sumerian language and literature. But when the empire collapses, Sumerian ceases to be spoken as a native language.

2004–1763   THE ISIN-LARSA PERIOD
In the wake of the dramatic collapse of the Third Dynasty of Ur, several small states scramble to position themselves as its successors, Isin and Larsa chief among them. Sumerian is transformed from a living to a learned language: it continues to be studied in schools, used in religious rituals, and held in high regard.

1763–1595   THE OLD BABYLONIAN PERIOD
The conflicts of the Isin-Larsa period end with Hammurabi of Babylon's conquests, establishing his city's political preeminence. A revolt during the reign of Hammu-

rabi's successor, Samsu-iluna, leaves the southern cities, including Nippur and Ur, in disarray. Most Sumerian literature is known from the schools of this period: pupils were made to memorize and write out Sumerian texts, leaving behind a trove of manuscripts.

GLOSSARY

Most of the gods listed below have both a Sumerian and an
Akkadian name; the Akkadian is given in parentheses.

Abzu. *See* Deep Sea.

An (*Anu*). The god of heaven (the word "An" literally means "heaven"). He was
the ancestor of the gods, an avuncular figure whose words carried great
moral authority in the divine assembly. He was the city god of Uruk and
shared the E-ana ("House of Heaven") temple with Inana.

Anuna (*Annunaki*). A group of gods in the cuneiform pantheon and the coun-
terparts of the Igigi. In earlier sources, including Enheduana's poems, the
Anuna were the higher circle of gods and the Igigi were the lower-ranking
gods. Later, the Anuna became the underworld gods and the Igigi the heav-
enly gods.

Deep Sea or Abzu (*Apsû*). The mythical underground lake from which fresh-
water was thought to rise, nourishing the fields of southern Iraq. As the
abode of Enki, the Abzu was seen as a source of insight and wisdom.

edubba. Literally "house where tablets are given out." The schools, especially
of the Old Babylonian period, in which future priests and civil servants
learned cuneiform, Sumerian, mathematics, and literature.

Enanatuma. High priestess of Ur during the Isin-Larsa period who rebuilt the
ĝipar after it had been destroyed in a military raid. She may have been re-
sponsible for reassembling and preserving the Disk of Enheduana.

Enanedu. High priestess of Ur and successor of Enanatuma, who carried out a
further restoration of the ĝipar and left behind an inscription discovered
many centuries later by Nabonidus.

Enki (*Ea*). God of creativity and wisdom who lived in the Deep Sea. Enki was
a cunning figure, often defying the other gods with his tricks. He had a

special bond with Inana, helping her out of trouble in myths such as *Inana's Descent to the Underworld*.

Enlil. King of the gods. Together with An and Enki, he was the supreme deity of the pantheon, but literary depictions of Enlil often portray him in a somewhat negative light, as an irascible ruler.

Ennigaldi-Nanna. The last high priestess of Ur, installed by her father, Nabonidus, during the Neo-Babylonian period. Artefacts found in the palace in Ur suggest that Ennigaldi-Nanna may have presided over a museum of antiquities.

gala. Priests who performed ritual laments to prevent divine anger. In the third and early second millennium, they were sometimes depicted as departing from normative masculinity.

ĝipar. The building that housed the high priestesses, both in Ur and other cities. The **ĝipar** could also contain a temple to the wife of the city's main god, such as Ningal in Ur.

Igigi. A group of gods. See Anuna.

Inana (*Ishtar*). The central figure in Enheduana's poems and the most important goddess of the cuneiform pantheon. A challenging and complex figure, she appeared in many different and sometimes contradictory guises.

kurĝara (*kurgarrû*). See **pilipili**.

Lugal-Ane. The rebel leader who in the *Exaltation* ousts Enheduana from power and defiles Inana and An's temple in Uruk. Lugal-Ane may have been a historical figure who led a revolt against Naram-Sîn during the Great Rebellion.

me. A Sumerian concept whose range of meanings includes divine influence, existence, cultural practices, religious rituals, and destiny. The **me** are often portrayed as physical objects that the gods could hold in their hands. In my translations of Enheduana's poems, the word is consistently rendered as "power."

Nabonidus. The last king of the Neo-Babylonian empire. He carried out a series of religious reforms aimed at promoting the moon god Sîn to the head of the pantheon, and installed his daughter Ennigaldi-Nanna as high priestess in Ur.

Nanna (*Sîn*). The moon god and city god of Ur. Though he was a central god in the pantheon, there are relatively few literary texts that describe his character or relate stories about him. He was associated with cattle, due to the crescent-like shape of their horns.

Naram-Sîn. Grandson of Sargon and the fourth king of the Old Akkadian Empire. He expanded the empire, standardized the administration of the cities, suppressed revolts, and had himself declared a living god. He was later remembered as a tragic, hubristic character.

Ningal (*Nikkal*). The wife of Nanna. As with Nanna, little is known about Ningal's character.

nugig. Originally meaning "wetnurse" or "midwife," the word seems to have broadened its scope, coming to refer more generally to high-status women associated with a temple. It is used as an epithet of Inana and other goddesses.

pilipili. One of several groups of gender-subverting ritual performers associated with Inana. Similar groups included the **kurĝara** and the **saĝ-ursaĝ**. In their ritual performances, they sought to disrupt traditional gender markers, such as weapons, weaving instruments, and clothing.

saĝ-ursaĝ (*assinnu*). See **pilipili**.

Sargon. Father of Enheduana and founder of the Old Akkadian Empire. He was remembered as the ideal king, a clever and cunning leader who rose from poverty to seize universal kingship.

Shulgi. The second king in the Third Dynasty of Ur. Shulgi styled himself a literate and educated king, spearheading a renaissance in Sumerian poetry and commissioning hymns to celebrate his athletic and academic feats.

Ur-Namma (Ur-Nammu). The founder of the Third Dynasty of Ur. He carried out extensive building projects throughout his kingdom, including in Ur, where the **ĝipar** was rebuilt and a massive ziqqurat to Nanna was erected.

ziqqurat (ziggurat). A monumental stepped temple tower. It was a hallmark of Sumerian and Akkadian religious architecture, and the inspiration for the mythical Tower of Babel.

NOTES

Unless otherwise specified, all translations are my own.

INTRODUCTION

1. On Inana and her Akkadian counterpart Ishtar, see Pryke, *Ishtar;* Bahrani, *Women of Babylon,* chap. 7; Harris, "Inanna-Ishtar as Paradox"; and the references provided in Heffron, "Inana/Ištar."

2. Inana's flirtation with Dumuzi is depicted in the *Inana-Dumuzi* texts, also known as the *Love Lyrics;* Inana's crushing of skulls and eating of corpses are mentioned in the *Exaltation,* ll. 126–27.

3. The term "woman of color" is anachronistic because there was no ancient concept of race: people were not assigned separate identities based on skin color. In note 13 below, I discuss the merits of a deliberately "presentist" reading of ancient literature, which might connect Enheduana with current concerns about literature written by women of color.

4. In the case of the first fragmentary hymn, it is difficult to tell whether it is told in Enheduana's own voice or whether it describes her as a third-person character. A key problem is line 15, which seems to read "my Enheduana," en-he$_2$-du$_7$-an-na-ĝu$_{10}$, suggesting that she is a character being invoked by the narrator. But as noted by Claus Wilcke, the suffix -ĝu$_{10}$ is sometimes used in place of -**me**; see Wilcke, *Kollationen zu den sumerischen literarischen Texten,* 47. This means that the line can be read as "I am Enheduana," indicating that she herself is the narrator.

5. William Hallo, the editor of the *Exaltation,* attributed *Inana and Ebih* to Enheduana because lines 110–12 of the *Hymn* summarize the story that is told

there at greater length; see Hallo and van Dijk, *Exaltation of Inanna*, 3. But that is not in itself any kind of proof, since the *Hymn* recounts several other myths about Inana as well, such as the story of how she came to share a temple with An. Hallo further posits that *Inana and Ebih* is a mythical retelling of a real rebellion against the Old Akkadian king Naram-Sîn, which would make it more like the *Exaltation*, but there is no good reason to identify the myth as a coded representation of a historical event. As there is no proof that the ancient scribes linked *Inana and Ebih* to Enheduana, and given the doubt that clouds her authorship in general, I feel that ascribing *Inana and Ebih* to her on so slender grounds would be a bridge too far. For a similar view, see Wagensonner, "Between History and Fiction," 42.

6. Entries in the debate on Enheduana's authorship include Civil, "Limites de l'information"; Michalowski, "Sailing to Babylon," 183–85; Zgoll, *Rechtsfall der En-ḫedu-Ana;* Westenholz, "Old Akkadian Period," 76; Lambert, "Ghostwriters?"; Bahrani, *Women of Babylon*, 116; Black, "En-hedu-ana Not the Composer"; Glassner, "En-hedu-ana"; Lion, "Literacy and Gender," 97; Foster, *Age of Agade*, 207, and "Authorship in Cuneiform Literature," 13–14.

7. This is the argument I lay out at greater length in my doctoral dissertation, Helle, "First Authors." On authorship in cuneiform cultures more generally, see also Foster, "Authorship in Cuneiform Literature"; and Michalowski, "Sailing to Babylon," 183–87.

8. There are, of course, exceptions to this trend, and some studies have focused on the literary qualities of Enheduana's poems. In particular, Annette Zgoll's edition of the *Exaltation*, *Rechtsfall der En-ḫedu-Ana*, contains an extended discussion of the stylistics of the text and the framing metaphor of the court case. In the article "Nin-me-šara," Zgoll also examined Enheduana's allusions to myths about Inana, and the ways these myths are used to bolster the argument of the poem; and Zgoll has worked to make Enheduana better known in the German-speaking world, as with her translation of the *Exaltation* for the anthology *Erzählungen aus dem Land Sumer*, edited by Konrad Volk.

Another strand of interpretation, going back to the edition by Hallo and van Dijk, *Exaltation of Inanna*, has understood Enheduana's poems as a coded political thesis in the context of the Old Akkadian empire; this line of argument has especially been advanced by Claus Wilcke in "Politische Opposition nach sumerischen Quellen" and "Politik im Spiegel der Literatur." However, the attempt to interpret the poetic elements of Enheduana's poems as hidden references to specific historical circumstances and events has been criticized extensively; see Civil, "Limites de l'information," 229; Cooper, "Literature and History"; Westenholz, "Old Akkadian Period," 77.

9. Konstantopoulos, "Many Lives of Enheduana." While Robson takes a skeptical approach to Enheduana's authorship, for Konstantopoulos the point is precisely that the three lives can be studied as separate but interconnected manifestations of the same literary figure, and that the differences between the three lives should not prevent us from engaging with Enheduana's long and varied history. It is not enough to point out that the Enheduana who appears in the Old Babylonian manuscripts or in modern feminist imaginings is not "the same" as the Old Akkadian priestess, as Robson does; we must also study how the changes that led from one to the other unfolded, and what the figure of Enheduana has meant in each historical period.

10. Minamore, "Lines of Resistance," 10:45.

11. See Veldhuis, *Religion, Literature, and Scholarship*, especially page 46; Michalowski, "Literacy, Schooling and the Transmission of Knowledge," 52–53; Richardson, "Sumer and Stereotype," especially page 175; Helle, "Enheduana and the Invention of Authorship," 6–7. The *Exaltation* was part of a group of ten Sumerian texts that modern scholars have dubbed the "Decad," which also included a story about the hero Gilgamesh, hymns to various kings, gods, and temples, a pun-filled poem about agriculture, and so on. It has generally been assumed that the Decad was the final stage in Old Babylonian education, but more recently, Paul Delnero, in "Sumerian Literary Catalogues," has called this idea into question, showing that there is no solid evidence linking the grouping of the Decad to a school context. Enheduana's poems were clearly taught in schools, and clearly at an advanced stage, but the precise context of the Decad is now unclear.

12. The present book was completed while I was staying at the research center Temporal Communities in Berlin, and this account of Enheduana's literary history is shaped by the research of the center. A key argument that has

emerged from the center's activities is that literature moves through time and gains value by being circulated within a series of overlapping and often competing communities.

13. Pollock, "Philology in Three Dimensions." Pollock argues that philology is at its best when it shuttles among three ways of viewing literature: one focused on the moment in which the work was composed (historicist), one centered in its history of reception and interpretation (traditionalist), and one concerned with its significance for the current moment (presentist). I wholly concur with Pollock's theory, but I have a reservation about his analysis. He too offers feminist readings as an example of a presentist reading, noting how his students react with dismay at the enfeebling depiction of the heroine Shakuntala in the Sanskrit play of the same name. Pollock is oddly dismissive of this reaction, speaking of his students' "failure" to engage in historical thinking (408). Surely if we are to appreciate *Shakuntala* in three dimensions, the feminist perspective of the present is indispensable, and the same holds true for Enheduana and her poetry.

14. See my analysis of the multiple voices that make up the "I" of the *Exaltation* in "Voices Intertwined" in "The Honeyed Mouth," below.

15. This is merely a conventional pronunciation among specialists, since we do not know how Sumerian was actually spoken. Jagersma, "Descriptive Grammar," chap. 3, has proposed a tentative reconstruction of Sumerian phonology, but his views are not universally accepted.

16. See Farber-Flügge, *Mythos "Inanna und Enki"*; Farber, "me." In a recent assessment, Selz, "Mesopotamian Path to Abstraction," 425, concludes that "a sensible translation of the word is not yet in sight and perhaps altogether impossible."

17. *Exaltation*, lines 7–8; see also *Enki and Inana*, where Inana steals the **me** from Enki and loads them onto her boat.

18. In my translation, the *Exaltation* and the *Hymn* seem to start with the same word, "queen." This is not quite the case in Sumerian: **nin** and **innin** can both mean "lady, mistress," but **innin** is a rarer, more literary term.

19. As noted in "Power and Chaos" in "The Honeyed Mouth," the crucial point here is that Inana is not considered to be a supreme deity *according to the*

internal narrative of the poem. That is, in the Old Akkadian period, many people may well have seen her as the most powerful deity of the cosmos, since she was the patron goddess of the empire, a view that made the poem's attempt to elevate her status unnecessary. One may compare this situation to the epic *Enuma Elish*, which describes how the city god of Babylon, Marduk, was exalted among the other gods, but the epic was probably written around the eleventh century BCE, well after Babylon had achieved political supremacy and so cemented Marduk's position as the head of the pantheon. What matters here is thus not whether the *Exaltation* changed how Inana was perceived by people in the Old Akkadian or Old Babylonian periods, but that the plot of the poem, as I understand it, relies on Enheduana exalting Inana to a more powerful position than she previously held. See also note 17 to "The Honeyed Mouth," below.

20. For the sake of convenience, I here offer a phonemic transcription that attempts to capture roughly how the lines might have sounded. However, it should be made clear that phonemic transcriptions of Sumerian are educated guesses at best. In the case of Akkadian, we can at least draw inferences from other languages in the same family, but Sumerian is an isolate, and it died out as a native language four thousand years ago, making it extraordinarily difficult to reconstruct how the language would have been pronounced. See note 15 above.

21. Readers who want to learn more about the original text can consult the website enheduana.org, where they will find each line of the *Exaltation* and the *Hymn* in cuneiform, transliteration, phonemic transcription, and word-by-word translation, followed by analysis and commentary. This resource is meant to guide readers with no knowledge of Sumerian to a basic understanding of the original texts, giving them a chance to appreciate how the poems are structured. The website also contains study tools, informational videos, and suggestions for further reading. Other useful websites for the study of Sumerian poetry include the Electronic Text Corpus of Sumerian Literature, at etcsl.orinst.ox.ac .uk, which offers literal translations of most Sumerian poetry; the Cuneiform Digital Library Initiative, which includes a vast catalogue of cuneiform texts as well as a useful wiki on Assyriological matters, at cdli.ox.ac.uk/wiki/; and the Open Richly Annotated Cuneiform Corpus (ORACC) Project List, which

brings together many digital projects that help students and researchers access cuneiform texts, at oracc.museum.upenn.edu/projectlist.html.

22. See Jagersma, "Descriptive Grammar," 63–67. Note that some scholars also use the character ẖ in transcribing Sumerian, as in **En-ẖedu-ana**. The ẖ represents a sound like the *ch* in Scottish *loch* or the *x* in *Mexico*. It is commonly used in transcribing Akkadian, but most philologists now prefer a plain *h* for Sumerian.

23. Enheduana's name is written with the cuneiform signs en-he$_2$-du$_7$-an-na: hence the spelling with the double *n*, which is now traditional, but cuneiform writing is not that straightforward. As described in "Daughter of Sargon" in the essay "Enheduana's World," below, Enheduana's name means "High priestess who is the ornament of heaven." The word for heaven is **an**, which is also the name of the god of heaven. The genitive ending, "*of* heaven," is -a (actually -ak, but the **k** is elided when not followed by a vowel). The signs **an-na** are therefore to be read **ana**: the first sign is an ideographic sign representing the word "heaven," the second is a phonetic sign representing how that word was to be pronounced—that is, with the case ending -a. The same logic underlies the difference between Inana and Inanna.

THE EXALTATION OF INANA

1. The text was first edited by Hallo and van Dijk: *Exaltation of Inanna*; a revised edition was published by Zgoll: *Rechtsfall der En-ẖedu-Ana*; and a synoptic edition by Delnero, "Variation in Sumerian Literary Compositions," 2030–2108. In my translation I often follow the interpretation given in Attinger, "Innana B." I have divided the translation into six sections. The transition between sections is marked by different invocations of Inana. The first and last sections are both short and invoke Inana with "Queen!" (**nin**) as their first word. The second section consists of five blocks of seven lines each, four of which begin with the words "My queen!" (**nin-ĝu$_{10}$**). The third section has a chiastic structure, as it begins and ends with similar invocations ("great daughter of Nanna . . . who can rob you of your rule?"). The fourth section zigzags between appeals to the

gods and autobiographical vignettes, while the fifth section is structured by the repetition of the invocation "Queen, beloved of heaven!" (**nin ki-aĝ₂ an-na-ĝu₁₀**). I discuss these further in Helle, "Enheduana's Invocations."

2. See Zgoll, *Rechtsfall der En-ḫedu-Ana.*

3. For some of the other interpretations of the *Exaltation,* see the sources listed in note 8 to the Introduction.

4. This is the logic of what is called *performative sentences.* The classic example of a performative sentence is the verdict of the judge, who does not merely describe the state of the defendant but enacts a new social reality with his or her speech. But crucially, the judge must be empowered to pronounce a performative sentence: if I were to proclaim somebody guilty right now, it would have no effect whatsoever. The power of performative words thus relies on social recognition. I argue that a similar logic underlies the *Exaltation:* Inana must have her status recognized if she is to judge Enheduana's case. That is why the poem ends with the climactic list that repeats the refrain "Let them know" (ll. 123–33). Enheduana tells Inana that she should let her powers be known to the audience, but in the same breath, she does what she is asking the goddess to do. By reading the text, the audience comes to know of Inana's might, thus establishing the goddess's performative authority.

5. Pryke, "Hidden Women of History."

6. This line can be understood in several different ways. Part of its complexity lies in the ambiguity of the word **nam-ena**, "en-ship." En can mean both "ruler" and "high priestess," so the phrase "suitable for **en**-ship" can imply that Inana is fit to rule the land (hence my translation "to rule is your right") or that she is fit to preside as high priestess, which would establish a strong connection between Inana and Enheduana herself. The sentence can also be read differently, as a description of the crown in the first part of the line, leading to a translation such as, "you love the good crown that befits the high priestess." This would form a parallel to line 107, in which Lugal-Ane takes away Enheduana's **aga zi nam-en-na**, literally her "righteous crown of high priestesshood." As always in the *Exaltation,* this ambiguity is probably deliberate, as the line establishes Inana's right to rule, her connection with Enheduana, and her love for the office of high priestess all at the same time.

7. The number 7 is not to be taken literally here; it refers more generally to a collection of many **me**. More subtly, the number hints at the structure of the following section: the passage that begins in the next line (ll. 6–40) can be divided into stanzas of seven lines, each beginning with the phrase "My queen" (**nin-ĝu₁₀**). See Helle, "Enheduana's Invocations."

8. The mythical creature **ušumgal**, often translated "dragon" or "basilisk," was a giant horned serpent with four fanged feet and a venomous spit.

9. This is a cryptic line, not least because Inana's name is otherwise carefully avoided: she is named only four times in a poem that is entirely dedicated to her greatness. Some translators understand the word "Inana" here as a general designation of goddesses, rendering it as "you are their goddess," or the like. Pascal Attinger ("Innana B," 3) proposes taking the line as an attempt to explain Inana's name, which was in antiquity thought to mean "Queen of Heaven" ([n]in-an-a). According to this explanation, the line can be rendered as "You are the leader in heaven and earth: this Queen-of-Heaven is you."

10. The line is unclear, but it may turn on a pun on **zu**, "tooth," and **zu**, "flint."

11. Following a suggestion by Benjamin Foster, *Age of Agade*, 332, I take the feet as the subject of this line, but it may also be the people, the Storm God, or even the winds. For the "harps," see "Grief and Gender" in the essay "The Honeyed Mouth," below.

12. Inana's destruction of the mountain calls to mind the story of *Inana and Ebih*, in which Inana obliterates the mountain Ebih for refusing to bow down to her. Note the contrast between the invaded mountain and the rebellious city, an external and an internal enemy, respectively, both of which are brought to heel by Inana.

13. This is a particularly difficult line, whose reading is far from certain. I follow the interpretation proposed by Attinger, "Innana B," 6.

14. The aurochs (ur-ox) is a breed of now-extinct wild cattle, larger and fiercer than domesticated cows.

15. Literally: "For you, I entered my holy **ĝipar**." On the **ĝipar** as the home of the high priestess, see "Priestess of the Moon" in "Enheduana's World."

16. On the funeral meals that were brought to high priestesses in the ĝipar, see "Priestess of the Moon."

17. As I understand this passage, Enheduana here asks Nanna to petition An on her behalf, so that he may condemn Lugal-Ane to death (a punishment to be meted out by Inana). It was common in cuneiform culture to ask a god with whom one had a personal connection to intercede on one's behalf with a higher-ranking god: Enheduana has a connection with Nanna as his high priestess, and An is one of the supreme gods in the pantheon, alongside Enlil. For other understandings of this line, see note 4 to "The Honeyed Mouth," below.

18. The temple described in these lines is the E-ana, "House of Heaven," which stood in Uruk, implying that Lugal-Ane's rebellion included this city as well. The E-ana was shared by An and Inana, and various interpretations were offered by the ancient scholars as to why this was the case—including the one relayed by Enheduana in the *Hymn*, ll. 106-8. But in the *Exaltation*, the E-ana is mentioned in part to show that Lugal-Ane's insurrection has reached Inana's temple as well.

19. I take this line to mean that Lugal-Ane wanted to usurp Enheduana's position out of jealousy, and as suggesting that even now, when he has presumably become her equal, he cannot shake this feeling of envy at her superior skill: the envy (**ninim**) literally follows him, it "draws near" (**te**) to him. However, some translators have seen in this line a suggestion of sexual violence. Foster, *Age of Agade*, 334, translates it as, "Forcing his way in as if he were an equal, he dared approach me in his lust!" Other attestations of the word **ninim** do not allow for the meaning "lust"; in her study of Sumerian words for emotions, Margaret Jaques concludes that **ninim** probably denoted a feeling between anger and jealousy; see Jaques, *Vocabulaire des sentiments*, 249-50. Still, it remains possible that a sexual assault is, if not directly described, then implied in this line.

20. Lugal-Ane's offer of the knife and dagger may be read as an invitation for Enheduana to commit suicide, but it could also be a gendered insult (or both at once). In cuneiform cultures, weapons were closely associated with masculinity, and the gender-subverting ritual performers who appear in the *Hymn* are often described as carrying knives and daggers (see ll. 86-91 and "Grief

and Gender"). Lugal-Ane might be rebuking Enheduana for having assumed a traditionally masculine position of power, or he might be comparing her to the gender-subverting performers, who were associated with ritual grief and lamentations, but these suggestions remain speculative.

21. Inana's youthful love affair with the shepherd god Dumuzi (who in the Sumerian is referred to by his mythical epithet, "the ušumgal of heaven") was one of the central myths about the goddess, and a collection of poems known as the *Love Lyrics* details their dalliance. The story of *Inana's Descent to the Underworld* tells of how Inana, who had become trapped in the underworld, had to give up another person to take her place, so that she might return to the land of the living. Finding that Dumuzi had not mourned her in her absence, Inana became enraged and sacrificed Dumuzi to the underworld demons.

22. The exact meaning of this line is unclear. As high priestess of Nanna, Enheduana would sometimes ritually embody his wife Ningal, and some scholars maintain that she would have performed a ritual known as the Sacred Marriage (see "Priestess of the Moon"). It is possible, though highly uncertain, that the "shining bed" and the divulged words of Ningal refer to this practice.

23. The Holy Inn was one of Inana's temples. Inana was often portrayed as a patron goddess of inns, which were seen as places of transformation, magic, and sexuality.

24. These obscure lines were stock phrases of the lamentation genre, indicating that the lamenter has taken over as the narrator. See "Grief and Gender"; and Zgoll, *Rechtsfall der En-ḫedu-Ana*, 431–35. But who is this spouse and child? Inana has a spouse of sorts, her lover Dumuzi (l. 111), and the god Shara is said to be her son (see *Temple Hymn* no. 25); but neither of them seems relevant to this passage. Zgoll argues that the spouse refers to the king (in this case Naram-Sîn), who is sometimes described as the husband of Inana, and the child refers to Dumuzi, taking the term "child" in the metaphorical sense of "darling" or "dear one" (431–35). I am not sure that her interpretation is of much help in this narrative context, in which neither Naram-Sîn nor Dumuzi seems to be prominent. The obscurity and ambiguity of the couplet might well be intentional, and either way many meanings must be in play at once. Might the spouse refer to

Enheduana, who has become Inana's symbolic wife during their marriage-like communion in the Holy Inn, and could the child then be the song itself?

25. This line echoes the opening of the text, repeating the words e_3-a, which I translate as "downpour" but which literally means "emerging, coming forth," and gur_3, which here means "wrapped in, laden with." The poem thus returns to the beginning, rounding off the narrative and marking a transition from daylight to moonlight.

26. This line has been understood in opposite ways by previous translators, as described in "Voices Intertwined" in "The Honeyed Mouth": it can refer to Inana's order that Enheduana be restored as high priestess, or Enheduana's celebration of Inana, or both, showing how the two women have magnified each other's power with their words.

THE HYMN TO INANA

1. The text is sorely in need of a new edition, as we are still reliant on Sjöberg's treatment from 1975, and many manuscripts of the poem have been discovered since; see Sjöberg, "in-nin šà-gur$_4$-ra." An updated, but still incomplete transliteration can be found on the ETCSL website: see Krecher, "A Hymn to Inana."

2. In the *Exaltation*, Inana's dependence on Enlil and especially An is suggested by lines 14 ("It was An who gave you power") and 18–19 ("Enlil loves you for teaching the land how to fear, An has ordered you to stand by for battle"). Discussing the *Hymn*, Jeremy Black and the other editors of *Literature of Ancient Sumer* write that "the tone of the hymn is so emphatic as to Inana's superiority to all other gods that the composition can only have issued from a religious milieu fanatically devoted to her cult" (92). Though I take issue with its disparaging tone, the gist of their description is certainly accurate.

3. Eco, *Vertigine della lista*.

4. Lines 175 through 187, after which the text breaks, mostly begin with the same grammatical structure: one to three words followed by the possessive

pronoun "your"; the last word before the pronoun is then typically a nominalized verb.

5. The translation offered here is very tentative, as the line is difficult to make sense of.

6. The text here alludes to a group of gender-subverting individuals who were associated with the worship of Inana and performed ritual lamentations. Similar groups are the **kurĝara** and the **saĝ-ursaĝ**, who are mentioned in l. 88. See "Grief and Gender" in "The Honeyed Mouth," below.

7. As also alluded to in the *Exaltation* (see note 18 to that text), An and Inana shared a temple in Uruk, the E-ana, or "House of Heaven." Though other Sumerian deities also shared temples with one another, they would usually each have a main center of worship as well. But An and Inana had the same main temple, and this was clearly seen as unusual in the ancient world, since several attempts were made to explain it. The *Hymn* contains one such explanation—namely, that An became so terrified of Inana's might that he offered her his own house, adding in the rituals that established divine and royal power for good measure.

8. The *Hymn* here tells an abbreviated version of the myth that is presented at greater length in the poem *Inana and Ebih*, which some modern scholars have also attributed to Enheduana, though the grounds for doing so seem to me too tenuous. In that text, Ebih is described as a magnificent mountain, but it fails to do obeisance to Inana, who therefore sets out to destroy it. Inana ignores An's attempts to dissuade her from this plan, promptly shreds Ebih to pieces and announces that she has killed the mountain. At the end of the text, Inana recounts how she created the same ritual performers also mentioned in the *Hymn* and the *Exaltation*: the **pilipili**, the **kurĝara**, and the lamentation priests (**gala**).

9. Here begins a long section (ll. 175–99) in which each line opens with a similar phrase, typically consisting of a body part, a verb, and the pronoun "your": for example, the first line reads **ka ba-zu**, "at your opening of the mouth." This template does not stay exactly the same in all the lines, but the repetition of the pronoun "your" early in each line is remarkably consistent.

10. This is once more a reference to the E-ana.

11. The word I here translate as "high priestess" is **nunuz-zi**, for which see note 26 to "Enheduana's World," below.

THE TEMPLE HYMNS

1. A frequently repeated metaphor is that of the temple as a mountain, while a repeated construction is the contrast between two parts of the temple, typically the inside and outside (ša₄ and **bar**) or the front and rear (**igi** and **aga**). For lines repeated wholesale, see the discussion of lines 253–54 and 385–86 in "Power and Chaos" in the essay "The Honeyed Mouth," below.

2. Monica Phillips's edition of the *Temple Hymns* is forthcoming. Note that the central importance of names in the *Temple Hymns* stands in stark contrast to the *Exaltation*, which almost completely avoids mentioning Inana's name—see note 9 to that text, above.

3. My reconstruction is based on the entries for the respective temples in George, *House Most High*: see p. 151, no. 1113, for the E-Tummal as a byname for the E-kiur; p. 125, no. 1113, on the E-meurana as part of the E-shumesha; and p. 78, no. 191, and p. 86, no. 296, for Shuziana's temples.

4. The individual hymn introductions are based primarily on Black and Green, *Gods, Demons, and Symbols*; and the online resource "Ancient Mesopotamian Gods and Goddesses," http://oracc.museum.upenn.edu/amgg/index .html.

5. Southern Iraq was divided into two regions, Sumer to the south and Akkad to the north, though the regions were never clearly defined and most often appear as a conceptual pair. By claiming that Nippur lies between the two, the hymn places the city at the midpoint of the cultured world. Today we take the main cardinal direction to be north, but in the ancient world, it was the east (hence the verb "to orient," meaning "to face east"). If one stood in Nippur and faced east, Sumer would be to the right and Akkad to the left.

6. This is an unusual metaphor. Mountains are often said to have roots in cuneiform literature, so this is not in itself odd, but the notion that these roots toil—doing what?—is striking. The line also contains an allusion to the traditional epithet of Nippur, "the bond of heaven and earth," **dur-an-ki**, referring to the city's placement in the middle of southern Iraq: it was the *axis mundi* that tied together the cosmos. This is alluded to in the phrase, "your roots (**ur₂**) with heaven (**an**) and earth (**ki**) . . . "

7. For House of Tummal as a byname of the E-kiur, see George, *House Most High*, 151, no. 1113. The story of Ninlil's age-old sanctuary is related in *Tummal Chronicle*; for which see Glassner, *Mesopotamian Chronicles*, 156–59.

8. The meaning of the temple's name, e$_2$-šu-me-ša$_4$, is unclear. Literally, it means "house hand power heart," but this probably reflects an unclear idiomatic expression.

9. The ending of these two lines is unclear. Literally, the phrases mean "your brickwork is your birth-giving" (šeg$_{12}$-zu tu-tu-zu) and "your form (or exterior) is your creation" (bar-zu du$_3$-a-zu). Bricks were often associated with birth because women would deliver while standing on two large bricks, and this association is, of course, particularly salient in a hymn to the goddess of birth. One way to interpret the line is that it reads this association back onto the brickwork of the temple, imbuing its architecture with the force of childbirth: the whole temple becomes a site of creation.

10. The meaning of the name "Ekishnugal" in Sumerian, e$_2$-kiš-nu-ĝal$_2$, is unclear. The name could also be written e$_2$-ĝiš-nu$_{11}$-gal, as noted in George, *House Most High*, p. 114, no. 653: this would give us the straightforward meaning "House of Alabaster." But that is unlikely to be the original meaning of the temple's name; perhaps it was a folk etymology used to explain a name that was already obscure in antiquity. One possibility is to interpret e$_2$-kiš-nu-ĝal$_2$ as "House Sending Light to the Earth (?)"; see Krecher, "Temple Hymns." That would make line 110—translated here as "your shimmering moonlight shines over the country"—an explication of the temple's name. For the sake of clarity, I use the derivative sense "House of Alabaster" in the translation.

11. This line is unclear. A literal translation would be something like: "Your oxen lie down by (on? as?) the giš-bur$_2$ of your nest." The word giš-bur$_2$ can mean "snare," but that does not yield much sense. It can also refer to a door decoration of an unidentified kind. I would cautiously suggest that it might refer to guardian statues and other decorative objects placed next to ceremonial entrances, such as the statues of winged bulls that flanked the doors of Assyrian palaces. The oxen in this hymn would thus be a living version of the guardian statues.

12. The word I translate as "home of high priestesses" is ĝipar, for which see "Priestess of the Moon" in the essay "Enheduana's World," below.

13. It is worth noting that Shulgi's name is not written with the divine determinative, a cuneiform sign that would normally precede the name of a god. This suggests that his deification was not complete when this hymn was written, even if a temple had been dedicated to him. On divine kingship in the ancient Near East, see Brisch, "Introduction"; and Michalowski, "Mortal Kings."

14. The Seven Sages were a group of semi-divine figures, known as the **abgal**, who were said to have founded civilization and brought wisdom and science to the human population.

15. The heavy-handed rhyme in my translation is meant to reflect an equally intense patterning in the Sumerian, which in a phonemic transcription would read: **nunzu am gal amsi aniše hula / sumun si mu simušaniše hula** (ll. 151–52; on the difficulties of phonemic transcription, see note 20 to the Introduction, above). A literal translation would be, "Your lord is a great wild bull, an elephant that rejoices in its strength, / an aurochs sprouting horns, rejoicing in his brilliance." We find here a chain of sounds, leading from **am**, "wild bull," through **am-si**, "elephant," to **si mu$_2$**, "sprouting horns," and finally to **si-muš$_3$**, "brilliance."

16. The word I translate as "underworld" here is in fact the city of Kutha, which, as is made clear by hymn 36, was associated with the worship of Nergal, god of death. This hymn uses Kutha as a reference to the underworld, and then immediately puns on its name, by turning **gu$_2$-du$_8$-a**, "Kutha," into **gu$_2$ si-a**, "gather."

17. The hymn is framed by two lines that begin with similar words: **ki ul**, "ancient land," and **siki ul**, "joyful hair." The shift in the meaning of the word **ul**, from "ancient" to "joyful," brings out a more general shift in the hymn, from the dread and terror of the opening lines to the sunshine and abundance of its end.

18. It is unclear what this passage refers to and what the seven "desires" (**kurku$_2$**) are.

19. This line is unclear, and the proposed translation is a tentative suggestion. (Note that the phrase "countless ewes," **u$_{18}$ lu-a**, is a pun: the word I translate as "countless" can also mean "sheep.")

20. Here and in the rest of the *Temple Hymns*, I use the phrase "holy woman" to render the Sumerian **nugig**, for which see "Voices Intertwined" in "The Honeyed Mouth," below.

21. A translation of the story of Ninurta's battle against Anzu can be found in Foster, *Before the Muses*, 555–78.

22. The manuscript has "seven" but there are eight lines.

23. The text's mention of both "dawn" and "dusk" is a reference to an astronomical curiosity of the planet Venus, with which Inana was identified. Venus has a narrower orbit than earth, and this proximity to the sun means that the planet is for the most part invisible to the naked eye, since it is blotted out by sunlight. From earth, Venus can be observed in two situations: when it rises before the sun does, so that it appears shortly before dawn on the eastern horizon, and when it lingers in the sky after the sun has set, so that it appears shortly after sundown on the western horizon. In these two appearances it is known as the "morning star" and the "evening star," respectively. Inana's association with Venus may have shaped how the goddess was perceived, a theory that would explain why Inana was assigned incompatible aspects (such as her "masculine" role as a warrior and her "feminine" role as the goddess of sex and love). That explanation seems to me unlikely. It is more probable that things happened the other way round: Inana was from the beginning viewed as a goddess of paradox and transformation and was therefore linked to a suitably binary planet.

24. Pronouns in Sumerian are not marked for gender as male and female, but as person and nonperson, so since the name of the deity has been lost, we do not know whether it was a god or a goddess. The choice of *her* is thus merely a guess.

25. The line, "she holds the great gems of the **nugig**," recalls line 2 of the *Exaltation*, where Inana is described as, in a literal translation, "the **nugig** of An, who holds the mighty gems." The second type of priestess mentioned in this hymn, in line 390, is the **nubar**, but this word is even more obscure, and it is likewise unclear what it means for Ninisina to set aright their breasts.

26. This is the first of two echoes of the *Exaltation*. Compare the phrase "pour poison on the enemy" in line 432 of the *Temple Hymns* to line 9 of the

Exaltation, and the image of the "south wind" as "shrouding" or "enveloping" (u$_{18}$-lu dul) in line 435 of the *Temple Hymns* and line 71 of the *Exaltation*, in addition to more general similarities such as the comparison to a basilisk and a lion.

27. The phrase "house built amid abundance," **e$_2$ nam-he$_2$-a du$_3$-a**, is primarily a reference to the temple's name, House of the Granary—a place full of abundance. But given that the hymn was attributed to Enheduana, it is hard not to hear an echo of her name in these words.

28. The phrase "fierce god," **diĝir er$_9$-ra**, is an allusion to one of Nergal's other names, Erra.

29. This line is in fact a juxtaposition of two of Nergal's names; literally, it reads, "Nergal, Meslamtea." In my translation, I avoid using multiple names for each god, so I have translated the literal meaning of the name Meslamtea: "he who comes forth from the Meslam."

30. The word **urun**, which I translate as "towering" or "soaring," is one of the most frequently recurring words in the *Temple Hymns*, but it is here put to particularly good use, in the phrase **Urum urun**.

31. The significance of this reversal—from the beard below Utu's head to the crown atop it—is unclear to me, but it may refer to the Sun God's movement around the earth.

32. The line consists of two of Nisaba's names, and literally reads, "Great Nanibgal, Nisaba" (compare note 29 above).

33. As befits the goddess of writing, this line has a pun on the spelling of her name: "Nisaba" was written with the signs **še-naga**, and **naga** on its own meant "soap." It is only natural that Nisaba should be associated with the reed stylus, the main instrument for writing cuneiform, but the idea that she is the *child* of a stylus—and the specification that this stylus is "upright" or "erect," **du$_3$**—suggests that the English pun on "pen" and "penis" here finds a Sumerian forerunner.

34. The ending of this hymn differs from the rest of the collection, because it was customary to end a hymnic poem with the name of the deity followed by **za$_3$-mi$_2$**, "be praised." This is also the case in the *Exaltation*, which ends with the words ⁿInana za$_3$-mi$_2$, which I translate as "All praise Inana."

FRAGMENTARY HYMNS

1. The two hymns were edited by Joan Westenholz in "Enheduanna," 552–56; see also Wilcke, *Kollationen zu den sumerischen literarischen Texten*, 47; and Hall, "Study of the Sumerian Moon-God," 764–75, on the first hymn.

2. See the discussion of ritual feeding in "'The Disk of Enheduana" in the essay "Enheduana's World," below.

3. The first line of the text is tricky, and my reading of it is uncertain: I take it to be a metaphor comparing the temple rising from the ground with the rising of the dawn, an image reinforced by Ur's position in the eastern part of Sumer. But however one reads the line, it is the first of several references to the *Exaltation*, as the opening lines of both hymns juxtapose the words u_4, "daylight," and e_3-a, which here means "emerging" but in the *Exaltation* is combined with **dalla** to mean "shining."

4. On the name of the Ekishnugal, see note 10 to the *Temple Hymns*, above.

5. This line contains a further reference to the *Exaltation*: in both texts, Enheduana describes herself "setting aright the **šuluh**," which were rituals of purification. In the *Exaltation*, line 136, I give the simpler translation, "I have purified myself," but in both cases the implication is that Enheduana does not just perform the ritual, she performs it perfectly.

6. For the reading of this line, see Wilcke, *Kollationen zu den sumerischen literarischen Texten*, 47.

7. The word I here translate as "high priestess" is **nunuz-zi**, for which see note 26 to "Enheduana's World," below.

8. Sumerian does not differentiate grammatically between the male and female gender, so it is unclear if the miller is a man or woman.

9. The juxtaposition of the two words **masab** (basket of offerings) and **asila** (hymns of joy) is another reference to the *Exaltation*, line 68, where the same two words are given together.

10. This verse looks in translation as if it breaks the pattern of verses beginning with **en**, "high priestess." But Nanna is here called by his Akkadian name Suen, which is written **en-zu**, so this verse also begins with **en**.

ENHEDUANA'S WORLD

1. For introductions to the Old Akkadian Period, see Foster, *Age of Agade;* Schrakamp, "Kingdom of Akkad"; Michalowski, "Kingdom of Akkad"; and Westenholz, "Old Akkadian Period."

2. A key obstacle in establishing the degree of power held by the Old Akkadian high priestess is that we have no administrative texts that would prove their direct involvement in the running of the temple. But then again, priestesses could easily have given oral orders for their scribes to implement, and these would not have left behind a written record. A new and much-needed study of Sumerian and Babylonian priestesses in the third to second millennium is currently being prepared by Nicole Brisch.

3. The name of Sargon's wife, Tashlultum, is recorded on an alabaster bowl belonging to her steward; see Frayne, *Sargonic and Gutian Periods,* 36–37. But it is possible that Sargon had several wives, and we do not know whether Enheduana, Rimush, and Manishtushu were siblings or half-siblings.

4. Note that some ancient chronicles list these two kings in reverse order, so Manishtushu may have ruled before Rimush. See Steinkeller, "Ur III Manuscript," 278–79.

5. On divine kingship in the ancient Near East, see Brisch, "Introduction"; and Michalowski, "Mortal Kings."

6. On the Victory Stele of Naram-Sîn, as it is called, see especially Winter, "Sex, Rhetoric"; Bänder, *Siegesstele des Naramsîn;* and Foster, *Age of Agade,* 200, including the references collected on 241–42nn44–50.

7. See the discussion in Haul, *Stele und Legende,* 38–57. As Haul notes, this text, MAD 1 172, purports to be a copy of a real inscription by Naram-Sîn, but it is clearly a literary reimagining of such an inscription from the Old Babylonian period. Its mention of Lugal-Ane could therefore easily have been taken from Enheduana's *Exaltation,* which was widely read at that time. Haul parses the evidence for and against the possibility that this text reflects a kernel of historical information about Lugal-Ane, but ultimately the question remains open.

8. Aage Westenholz, "Assyriologists, Ancient and Modern," 555, offers a chronological reconstruction that would place the events of the *Exaltation* in the thirtieth year of Naram-Sîn's reign, concluding that Enheduana would have been around seventy-four years old at the time and died a few years later.

9. The technical advances and material culture of the Old Akkadian period are summarized with flair in Foster, *Age of Agade*, chaps. 4 and 5.

10. See Foster, *Age of Agade*, 21–22.

11. The exact date and cause of the death of Sumerian is a matter of debate among scholars—see especially Woods, "Bilingualism, Scribal Learning, and the Death of Sumerian"; Michalowski, "Lives of the Sumerian Language"; and Rubio, "Šulgi and the Death of Sumerian."

12. See C. Leonard Woolley, *Royal Cemetery*, 490–91. Some of the objects can be viewed online in the Penn Museum's digital collection: go to upmaa -pennmuseum.netdna-ssl.com/collections/ and search for "PG 503" (quotation marks included).

13. For an introduction to cylinder seals, see Collon, *First Impressions*. For lost seals, see Hallo, "Seals Lost and Found."

14. Frayne, *Sargonic and Gutian Periods*, 38. The seal can be found in the British Museum's online collection, britishmuseum.org/collection, by searching for the museum number 120572.

15. On the elaborate hairstyles of the Old Akkadian period, see Foster, *Age of Agade*, 122 and 194; on the tools found in PG 503, see 238. The contents of PG 503 are listed in C. Leonard Woolley, *Royal Cemetery*, 491.

16. Sagadu's seal is a recent discovery, published in Seligson, *She Who Wrote*; I am grateful to Sidney Babcock for alerting me to it. The other two seals are published in Frayne, *Sargonic and Gutian Periods*, 38–39. The seal of the scribe whose name ends in "-kitushdu" is also available in the British Museum's online collection, where it has the museum number 123668.

17. C. Leonard Woolley, *Royal Cemetery*, 27.

18. See Weadock, "The *giparu* at Ur."

19. As noted in Weadock, "The *giparu* at Ur," 124, the orientation of the older archaeological layers suggests that the home of the high priestess, the cemetery, and the temple of Ningal were separate buildings in Enheduana's lifetime, and

that they were brought together into one architectural unit by Ur-Namma's reconstruction of the temple area.

20. Joan Westenholz, "Enheduanna," 544.

21. Weadock, "The *giparu* at Ur," 116–18. The ritual of the "Sacred Marriage" is a controversial topic. Some Sumerian literary texts, such as *Iddin-Dagan A*, seem to depict ceremonies where the king symbolically marries the goddess Inana. Older scholarship posited that these accounts reflect a real historical practice, including a sexual union between the king and the high priestess of Inana. But no extant reliable references outside literary texts attest to such a ritual ever being performed, and if it was, there is little reason to think that it entailed an actual consummation. See Cooper, "Sacred Marriage"; Nissinen and Uro, *Sacred Marriages*; and Jones, "Embracing Inana."

22. As noted below, some high priestesses clearly evaded this ban, but that does not mean that the ban did not exist—only that it could be evaded. The mythological justification for the ban is given in the Akkadian epic *Atra-hasis*: according to Babylonian tradition, the gods decided to unleash the mythical Flood not because humans had become sinful, as in the Bible, but because they had become too numerous, and so kept the gods awake with their noise. After the Flood, the gods re-created the human race with a limited lifespan, and further installed a number of measures to prevent overpopulation—including offices such as the high priestess, whose childlessness would protect humanity from future disasters. A much later text, *The Birth Legend of Sargon*, dating from the first millennium BCE, gives Sargon a Moses-like background, claiming that he was the son of a high priestess who gave birth to him in secret, setting him adrift on the river in a casket of reeds. Translations of both texts can be found in Foster, *Before the Muses*, 227–80 and 912–13.

23. The reference in question is from a divinatory text in which an omen in the liver of a sacrificed sheep is given the following interpretation: "The high priestess will allow anal sex so as to avoid pregnancy" (CT 31 44, obv. ll. 10–11, from the omen series *Isru*, to be edited by Nils Heeßel and Ulla Koch, forthcoming).

24. Weadock, "The *giparu* at Ur," 109.

25. On the Disk of Enheduana, see especially Winter, "Women in Public"; Joan Westenholz, "Enheduanna"; and Hansen, "Art of the Akkadian Dynasty,"

128–29. For the inscription on the disk, see Frayne, *Sargonic and Gutian Periods*, 35–36.

26. On the identification of Inana-Zaza with the deity Ashtar, see Lambert, "Pantheon of Mari," 537. The word translated here as "priestess" is **nunuz-zi**, possibly to be read **zirru**: the same word appears in the *Hymn*, where Enheduana introduces herself with the words "I am Enheduana, the **nunuz-zi**," and in the first of the fragmentary hymns. Beginning in the Old Akkadian period, this title seems to have become synonymous with **en**, "high priestess," and Joan Westenholz, "Enheduanna," argues that it refers specifically to the high priestesses' role as human embodiments of Ningal.

27. See line 1 of the *Chronicle of Ancient Kings* in Glassner, *Mesopotamian Chronicles*, no. 39, pp. 268–69.

28. C. Leonard Woolley, *Excavations at Ur*, 115.

29. As noted in Wagensonner, "Between History and Fiction," 40, it is possible to restore this section of the disk differently: it may show not a temple tower but the statue of a god.

30. Drawing on a parallel to a plaque from the Early Dynastic period, Claudia Suter, in "On Images, Visibility, and Agency," 346, argues that the two fragmentary figures may have been the governor of Ur and his wife.

31. For the importance of food offerings in ancient Near Eastern religion, see Brisch, "To Eat Like a God."

32. Winter, "Women in Public."

33. See McHale-Moore, "Mystery of Enheduanna's Disk."

34. The inscription that identifies the statuette as Enanatuma is given in Frayne, *Old Babylonian Period*, 43–44. The statue is on display in the Middle East Galleries of the Penn Museum, and can be viewed in its online collection, upmaa-pennmuseum.netdna-ssl.com/collections/, by searching for its excavation number U.6352.

35. See Weadock, "The *giparu* at Ur," 104 and 108. It appears that Enanatuma's fame was so great that she was deified after her death: together with her successor Enmegalana, she appears in a list of offerings to various minor gods of Ningal's temple, meaning that she was effectively treated as a local deity herself.

36. See Frayne, *Old Babylonian Period,* 114-17.

37. See Frayne, *Old Babylonian Period,* 44-45.

38. See McHale-Moore, "Mystery of Enheduanna's Disk," 71.

39. McHale-Moore, "Mystery of Enheduanna's Disk," 72-74.

40. Bahrani, *Women of Babylon,* chap. 5.

41. See Bahrani, *Graven Image,* chaps. 4 and 5; see also Radner, *Macht des Namens.*

42. See Guinan and Leichty, "Tasteless Tablets."

43. The phrase "eat dust and live on clay" is a standard refrain in Babylonian accounts of the underworld, found, e.g., in *Gilgamesh* VII 188.

44. The gender-neutral language of this and the following paragraphs is meant to emphasize that not all the students and scribes were men: on female scribes in the Old Babylonian period, see Lion, "Literacy and Gender"; and Lion and Robson, "Quelques textes scolaires."

45. The name of the schools is also sometimes rendered **edubba'a**. Because of the number of school texts that have been preserved, much has been written on the Old Babylonian education. See especially Robson, "Tablet House"; Tinney, "On the Curricular Setting"; George, "In Search of the é.dub.ba.a"; Michalowski, "Literacy, Schooling and the Transmission of Knowledge"; and Delnero, "Literature and Identity."

46. The tablet is published as no. 79 in Wilson, *Education in the Earliest Schools.*

47. The tablet in question is Plimpton 322. For an introduction to Babylonian mathematics, see Robson, *Mathematics in Ancient Iraq,* which discusses Plimpton 322 on 110-15.

48. On the death of Sumerian, see the references collected in note 11, above.

49. On this building, see Robson, "Tablet House." This serendipitous find was made under the worst imaginable circumstances. For a brief and tragicomic sketch of the catastrophic excavation at Nippur, see Aage Westenholz, "Sins of Nippur."

50. As with the ĝipar, we do not know whether Old Babylonian private houses had one or more stories, since only their ground plans have survived. But terracotta models of houses from this period generally have more than

one story, and the walls of houses like the one in Nippur were certainly thick enough to support an upper story. See Leick, *Dictionary of Ancient Near Eastern Architecture,* 229.

51. See Robson, "Tablet House," 42. The board game is known as the Royal Game of Ur.

52. See Robson, "Tablet House," 53 and 56. On the implicit pedagogical significance of the *Exaltation,* see Helle, "Enheduana and the Invention of Authorship," 13–14.

53. See Veldhuis, *Religion, Literature, and Scholarship,* especially 46; Michalowski, "Literacy, Schooling and the Transmission of Knowledge," 52–53; Richardson, "Sumer and Stereotype," especially 175; Helle, "Enheduana and the Invention of Authorship," 6–7.

54. In Helle, "Enheduana and the Invention of Authorship," I argue that Enheduana's position in the Old Babylonian schools also reflected a desire to imagine the Sumerian past as a coherent cultural whole, specifically one that Akkadian speakers could learn and appropriate for their own uses. In reality, there never was such a thing as "Sumerian culture": each city was its own cultural and political unit, and the people who lived in these cities saw themselves as Urukean, Nippurian, or the like, never as Sumerian. The idea of Sumer as a bounded cultural entity was created in the Old Babylonian schools, where the Sumerian literary heritage was refashioned to yield an ideal image of cultural stability, coherence, and unity—see especially Veldhuis, *Religion, Literature, and Scholarship,* chap. 3; Rubio, "Inventions of Sumerian"; Cooper, "Sumerian Literature." I would add that Enheduana's poems became popular in the Old Babylonian schools precisely because they fit so neatly into this cultural program. The *Temple Hymns* gathered all Sumerian-speaking cities into one anthology, creating a single text out of a wealth of traditions. The *Exaltation* displays Enheduana using her mastery of the Sumerian language to save herself—depicting Sumerian eloquence as something that Akkadian-speaking scribes could learn, appropriate, and employ.

55. Zgoll, *Rechtsfall der En-ḫedu-Ana,* 40: "der erste Bestseller der Weltliteratur."

56. The myth of Sargon's father being a gardener is first found in the *Sumerian King List*, l. v 32; later tradition, as evinced by *The Birth Legend of Sargon*, claimed instead that Sargon himself had been a gardener before Ishtar fell in love with him and promoted him to kingship. The legends concerning Sargon and Naram-Sîn are gathered in Joan Westenholz, *Legends*; see also Foster, *Age of Agade,* chap. 11, for the place of the Old Akkadian period in Babylonian cultural memory.

57. See Foster, *Age of Agade,* 270.

58. See Brisch, "Rebellions and Peripheries."

59. Brisch, "Rebellions and Peripheries," 39. See also Michalowski, "Literacy, Schooling and the Transmission of Knowledge," 49–50.

60. This argument is presented in further detail in Helle, "Enheduana and the Invention of Authorship." See also note 54, above.

61. On Sumerian-Akkadian translation, see Crisostomo, *Translation as Scholarship.*

62. This line presents several problems, and the Sumerian text given here is pieced together from two equally baffling manuscripts.

63. Readers who wish to go beyond this series of puns to better understand the Sumerian—both its sound games and its frequently contested meaning—can consult the website enheduana.org, where they will find word-for-word translations, transliterations, and discussions of the original.

64. The text was first edited by Groneberg, *Lob der Ištar,* who notes the connection to Enheduana's *Hymn* (123); an updated edition was published by Streck and Wasserman, "Man Is Like a Woman."

65. Streck and Wasserman, "Man Is Like a Woman," 15–20.

66. For *Izi,* see Crisostomo, "Writing Sumerian"; for *Erimhush,* see Michalowski, "Literature as a Source," and Boddy, *Composition and Tradition,* especially 99–108 and 171–74.

67. I am unconvinced by the argument given in Black, "En-hedu-ana Not the Composer," that the line refers only to the last of the forty-two hymns. Even granting that Black is right and these lines are not to be taken as a postscript to the collection but as the last lines of the last hymn—about which I have my

doubts, as noted in Helle, "First Authors," 327–29—it would not make much of a difference. Surely the entire collection would still end with a claim that Enheduana composed it all, even if that claim is internal to the last hymn and not an appended postscript. In the Babylonian epic *Erra and Ishum*, for example, the poet Kabti-ili-Marduk announces his authorship in the last of the epic's five Tablets, but that claim undoubtedly refers to the whole text, not just to its final section.

68. See Helle, "What Is an Author?"

69. See the references collected in note 6 to the Introduction, above.

70. See Rubio, *Sumerian Literary Texts*, chap. 4.3. The second of the fragmentary hymns does offer an intriguing and overlooked piece of evidence regarding Enheduana's authorship, but its meaning is not clear to me. The text mentions that Enheduana should bring Nanna's prayers to the Deep Sea, the Abzu, but this comment is baffling in light of the other texts attributed to her. Since the second fragmentary text has been dated to the Third Dynasty of Ur, it might reflect an earlier tradition about Enheduana from before her authorial figure solidified into the form that we know from the Old Babylonian texts. This could be taken as evidence against her authorship of the better-known poems—since it shows that the literary tradition about her was in flux in the intervening centuries—but with so fragmentary a hymn, it is impossible to draw definitive conclusions.

71. See Biggs, "Archaic Sumerian Version," especially 196.

72. See Huber, "Correspondance Royale d'Ur"; Michalowski, *Correspondence of the Kings of Ur*, chap. 8.

73. See Lambert, "Ghost-writers?"

74. Lion, "Literacy and Gender," 97.

75. This line of thinking goes back to the text edition by Åke Sjöberg; see especially Sjöberg and Bergmann, *Collection of the Sumerian Temple Hymns*, 7–8. In several cases, the argument relies on royal inscriptions by later kings who claim to have built temples included in the collection. For example, hymn 12 to the Karzida, Nanna's temple in Gaesh, mentions a ĝipar in l. 161. But as noted by Sjöberg (8), King Amar-Suen of the Third Dynasty of Ur (centuries after Enheduana's death) claims to have built the Karzida's ĝipar, explicitly stating

that "from ancient times no ĝipar had been built (and) no **en** had dwelt (there)";
see Frayne, *Ur III Period*, 264, text no. 16, ll. 16–18. This is a compelling argu-
ment against Enheduana's authorship of that hymn, but it should be noted that
royal inscriptions are by no means exempt from misrepresentation, either: the
kings frequently overstate their achievements, for example, by claiming to be
the first to have accomplished a given task. In this case, it is Amar-Suen's word
against Enheduana's, and the former is not inherently more reliable. A fuller
appraisal of which buildings mentioned in the *Temple Hymns* existed during
the Old Akkadian period will have to await the forthcoming new edition by
Monica Phillips.

76. For the text's allusion to the *Exaltation*, see notes 3, 5, and 9 to the Frag-
mentary Hymns, above.

77. See, e.g., Delnero, "'Inana and Ebiḫ,'" 670–71. Note that some texts,
such as royal inscriptions from the third millennium, were copied in the Old
Babylonian period with great reverence and attention to detail, reproducing
the original orthography (this is also the case with the copy of the Disk of
Enheduana). However, it seems that literary texts were generally seen as more
amenable to revision.

78. See Delnero, "Memorization and Transmission."

79. See Biggs, *Inscriptions from Tell Abū Ṣalābīkh*, 45–56; on the relation be-
tween the two collections, see Sjöberg and Bergmann, *Collection of the Sumerian
Temple Hymns*, 6.

80. A famous cuneiform example of a textile metaphor being used to de-
scribe the creation of new text out of old material is "Esagil-kin-apli's Mani-
festo," in which the scholar Esagil-kin-apli describes how he created the Baby-
lonian medical compendia *Sagig* and *Alamdimmû* by weaving anew material
"that had not been bound in a new edition since days of old, but was tangled like
threads"; see Wee, "Phenomena in Writing," 251–55. On the significance of the
textile metaphor in a cuneiform context, see Helle, "First Authors," 109–12 and
116–22; on its significance in the literary history of authorship more generally,
see Helle, "What Is an Author?"

81. See Helle, "Birth of the Author," 69. It is a now well-established truth in
authorship studies that the notion of the author as a "lonely genius" is untenable:

literary works are created through collaboration with other authors, editors, publicists, and readers. Multiple authorship is the rule, not the exception, as established in Stillinger, *Multiple Authorship*. But the case I am making is subtly different. It is not just that many people must work together to create a given text, but that many people must work together to create the authorial figure: the "I" of the *Exaltation* emerges from a series of conversations and re-creations. More generally, in the ancient world the image of a given author was circulated and cocreated by a host of people, often in an effort to frame, explain, or popularize the texts attributed to that author. This is also the case today, where publicists endeavor to construct a specific narrative around the author whose books they are trying to promote; see Puksar, "Institutions: Writing and Reading."

82. Hoskote, "Introduction," xxxiii.

83. Hoskote, "Introduction," xxxvi.

THE HONEYED MOUTH

1. The understanding of literary readings presented here is shaped by the field of reader-response theory; a good introduction to this field is the anthology edited by Andrew Bennett, *Readers and Reading*.

2. I first presented the analysis given in this section in Helle, "Birth of the Author."

3. My understanding of the constitutive role of dialogue in the *Exaltation* is based on the philosophy of Judith Butler, who in *Giving an Account of Oneself* argues that we are socially constituted by our attempts at self-description. When we tell our life stories, we create the self we set out to describe, by giving our "I" a fixed existence in the social world of discourse. But this self-creation is shaped by the fact that when we "give an account of ourselves," we are directing our words at somebody else, and our self-narration will accordingly be shaped by the listener's implicit presence, as we modify our telling to suit each hearing. This is but one of the many ways in which Butler argues that we are first and foremost social relations, and that our individuality is established by those relations, rather than the other way around. My description of

Enheduana's monologue as shaped by an awareness of the words of others is based on Mikhail Bakhtin's notion of "doubled-voiced discourse"; see Bakhtin, *Problems of Dostoevsky's Poetics*, 186.

4. Note that this line can also be understood differently. I follow Foster, *Age of Agade*, 333, and Black et al., *Literature of Ancient Sumer*, 318, in taking the line as an address to Nanna about Lugal-Ane. However, Zgoll, "Nin-me-šara," 62, and Attinger, "Innana B," 7, take the line to be addressed to Inana, with both Nanna and Lugal-Ane being described as Enheduana's "fate."

5. My understanding of the **nugig** is based on conversations with Nicole Brisch, who is preparing a new study of priestesses in the third and early second millennia.

6. The word appears first as **nu-gig**, then as **nu-u$_8$-gig**, but it is unclear whether this difference in spelling is significant.

7. Compare the translation by Foster, *Age of Agade*, 336, "What she commanded for her consecrated woman prevailed," in which the subject is Inana, with that by Hallo and van Dijk, *Exaltation of Inanna*, 35, "Her (Enheduanna's) speaking to the Hierodule was exalted."

8. See Hallo and van Dijk, *Exaltation of Inanna*, 62, who note that "the exaltation of Inanna implies at the same time the restoration of Enheduanna, their two fates being so closely linked that in lines 146 f. it is hard to decide whether the narrator, who takes over in this stanza, is speaking of one or the other." Note also the symmetry of the two uses of the word **nugig**, which appears in the third and the third-to-last line of the *Exaltation.*

9. See Helle, "Birth of the Author," 66–67. My analysis here builds on Michel Foucault's notion of a "pluralité d'ego," that is, the fact that texts inevitably contain a number of different voices, which cannot be reconciled by the figure of the author; see Foucault, "Qu'est-ce qu'un auteur?," 88. Also relevant is Jonathan Culler's concept of a "complexity of the enunciative apparatus": the idea that lyric poems are characterized by a highly patterned arrangement of voices spoken and overheard; see Culler, *Theory of the Lyric*, 16.

10. Delnero, "Texts and Performance."

11. All cuneiform signs carry more than one meaning, and it is the context in which they are used that determines how they are to be read. These two

lines take full advantage of that fact: in line 13, the thrice-repeated sign NE disambiguates into the words **izi bar$_7$-bar$_7$-ra**, which literally means "fire (**izi**) that flares up (**bar$_7$-bar$_7$-ra**)"; in line 15, the repeated sign is KA, which forms the phrase **inim dug$_4$-dug$_4$**, meaning "you speak (**dug$_4$-dug$_4$**) orders (**inim**)."

12. Some literary texts were stored in archives, either personal tablet collections or state libraries, such as the famous royal library that was housed in the Assyrian capital of Nineveh. A more touching example of cuneiform tablets that were cared for beyond their immediate usefulness comes from the archive of the Old Babylonian **gala** priest Ur-Utu. As shown by Michel Tanret, "Learned, Rich, Famous," 280–82, Ur-Utu's archive of business documents included a box of no longer relevant contracts, which Ur-Utu kept as mementos of key developments in his career.

13. See Farber-Flügge, *Der Mythos Inanna und Enki*; Farber, "me."

14. Farber, "me," 610: "Alle Bereiche von Zivilisation und Kultur, seien es staatliche oder religiöse Institutionen, geistige oder Gefühlswerte, seien es soziale Zustände, Berufe, Ämter oder auch irgendwelche Gegenstände oder Geräte, sind durchdrungen von den von Göttern geplanten und verwirklichten 'göttlichen Kräften.'"

15. The text was edited by Farber-Flügge, *Inanna und Enki*. An English translation can be found on the Electronic Text Corpus of Sumerian Literature: https://etcsl.orinst.ox.ac.uk/cgi-bin/etcsl.cgi?text=t.1.3.1.

16. In Akkadian epics such as *Anzû* and *Enuma Elish*, the Tablet of Destinies (which does not appear in Sumerian stories) seems to play a role similar to the **me**: it is an otherwise inert object that divine beings can hold in their hands and use to control the cosmos. Reasoning backward, one might suspect that the **me** were also imagined as akin to cuneiform tablets.

17. Since Inana was the patron deity of the Old Akkadian Empire, she was presumably given a paramount position in the pantheon of the time. As noted by Aage Westenholz, "Old Akkadian Period," 38, some scholars have viewed the *Exaltation*'s praise of Inana as nothing more than a promulgation of the empire's ideology. However, such a reading of the poem is unduly reductive, as it takes into account neither its literary complexity nor the difficulty of dating it to the Old Akkadian period. The correlation between historical reality and

the internal dynamics of this piece of fiction is almost impossible to establish. As noted by Schrakamp, "Kingdom of Akkad," 624, it is unclear whether Inana's status in Ur changed during the Old Akkadian period. But again, these questions seem to me secondary: I am not arguing that Enheduana's poems really did change religious beliefs of the Old Akkadian period, or even that they reflect the political milieu in which they were written (as we cannot be sure when they were written). Rather, I am arguing that in order to understand the narrative of the poem on its own terms, we must see the text as elevating Inana from a previously inferior position to divine supremacy.

18. A literal translation would be: "for queens (**in-nin$_9$**) and ladies (**nin-e-ne**), the destinies (**nam**) you decide (**nam-ma-tar-re**); for ladyship (**nam-nin-a**) you are fit (**tum$_2$-ma**)." On the problems of phonemic transcriptions, see note 20 to the Introduction, above.

19. See the summary in Foster, *Age of Agade*, 17–21.

20. See Helle, "Enheduana and the Invention of Authorship," 9–11; Aage Westenholz, "Old Akkadian Period," 38–39.

21. See Helle, "Enheduana and the Invention of Authorship," 5–8. On the reinvention of the Sumerian world in the Old Babylonian period, transforming what was once a disunited medley of cities into an ordered, homogenous cultural entity, see Veldhuis, *Religion, Literature, and Scholarship*, 66–79; Rubio, "Invention of Sumerian"; Cooper, "Sumerian Literature"; Brisch, "Rebellions and Peripheries."

22. Note that the text presents a view of the Sumerian world that is specifically focused on the city of Nippur, from which most of the manuscripts of Enheduana's poems come; see Helle, "Enheduana and the Invention of Authorship." Our knowledge of Old Babylonian education in general is heavily skewed toward Nippur, which is where most of our sources were found, but as shown in Delnero, "Literature and Identity," local differences can also be detected: the school curriculum at Ur, for example, had a different structure and set of priorities. This Nippur-centric bias is clear from the preserved version of the *Temple Hymns*. Having begun with Eridu, traditionally held to be the oldest city in Sumerian cosmology, the text moves on to Nippur, giving it pride of place in the collection, and more hymns are dedicated to temples in Nippur than to any other city.

23. See Cullen et al., "Climate Change"; and the studies collected in Weiss, *Seven Generations*; and in Kuzucuoğlu and Marro, *Sociétés humaines et changement climatique*.

24. This notion of war as instigated by the machinery of warfare itself (the ancient equivalent of the military-industrial complex) is echoed in a much later cuneiform text, the Babylonian epic *Erra and Ishum*, for which see George, "Poem of Erra and Ishum," esp. 53.

25. Dunya Mikhail speaks of her relation to Enheduana on the second episode of the podcast series *Ishtar Diaries*, a project that brought together poets, musicians, and artists from the Middle East to reflect on and respond to the appeal of ancient literature in the modern world. The podcast can be accessed at globalcenters.columbia.edu/events/ishtar-diaries-podcast-series.

26. Delnero, *How to Do Things with Tears*, 6. For the genre of lamentations, see also Gabbay, *Pacifying the Hearts*.

27. See Zgoll, *Rechtsfall der En-ḥedu-Ana*, 431–35.

28. Gabbay, "Balaĝ Instrument."

29. The classic work on Emesal is Schretter, *Emesal-Studien*. My understanding of Emesal follows Whittaker, "Linguistic Anthropology."

30. See, for example, the treatment of the **gala** in the Sumerian Proverb Collection 2, nos. 97–106, which allude to them as figures of ridicule, in Alster, *Proverbs of Ancient Sumer*, 1:65–67. Entry no. 100 in the collection has been used as evidence that the **gala** were perceived as homosexual, but it is hard to know what to make of it: "A **gala** priest wiped his anus and said: 'I must not stir up that which belongs to the Queen of Heaven, my lady.'"

31. On the gender liminality of the **gala**, see Gabbay, "Akkadian Word for Third Gender"; Cooper, "Genre, Gender, and Sumerian Lamentation." On the history of the **gala** more generally, see Gabbay, *Pacifying the Hearts*, chap. 5; Shehata, *Musiker*, chap. 6; and Michalowski, "Love or Death."

32. See, for example, the texts *Iddin-Dagan A* and *Lob der Ishtar*, both of which described gender-subverting rituals that glorify Inana; respectively, Reisman, "Iddin-Dagan's Sacred Marriage Hymn," and Streck and Wasserman, "Man Is Like a Woman." I have discussed nonbinary gender identities in cuneiform sources in Helle, "Only in Dress?" and "Weapons and Weaving

Instruments"; see also Nissinen and Svärd, "(Re)constructing the Image"; and Assante, "Bad Girls."

33. Some scholars have argued that it is possible to disambiguate the gender of the **kurĝara** and the **saĝ-ursaĝ**, who are known in Akkadian as *kurgarrû* and *assinnu:* see, e.g., Zsolnay, "Misconstrued Role"; and Peled, "*assinnu* and *kurgarrû*." Zsolnay argues that the *assinnu* have only a masculine warrior role, Peled that they have only a feminine role (he assigns the warrior role to the *kurgarrû*). I find these arguments unconvincing, as they rely on either a selective use of evidence or highly specious readings of that evidence; see Helle, "Only in Dress?," 50–51n39. It is not enough to point to the fact that the *assinnu* or *kurgarrû* sometimes present in ways that are typical of one or the other gender, such as the masculine warrior role. The point is that their gendering is not consistent across attestations: they appear in multiple, contradictory roles in different contexts, clearly indicating that their gender presentation involved a degree of playful subversion.

34. Streck and Wasserman, "Man Is Like a Woman," 20.

35. I have chosen the neutral term "burden" to translate the Sumerian šer₇-da, because I believe that it is here being used in a metaphorical sense. The word (which is a loanword from Akkadian *šērtu*) can mean "vice, transgression, crime" but also "punishment." Crime and punishment may seem like opposite concepts to modern English speakers, but several Akkadian terms, such as *arnu*, connote both. (Guy Deutscher, *Through the Language Glass*, 2, jokes that "the Babylonians would have been hard-pressed to understand *Crime and Punishment*, because their language used one and the same word to describe both of these concepts.") One can think of a term like *šērtu* as akin to the English expression "burden of guilt": when one commits an offense, it can be experienced as an emotional weight on one's body. It is this kind of burden that the **pilipili**—and, later, Enheduana herself—are said to carry. Perhaps the explanation is to be found in the fragmentary section in lines 74–79: did the future **pilipili** commit some form of transgression that made Inana transform their bodies and enlist them in her ritual service? Or were the rituals that they performed for Inana seen as transgressions, a deliberate breaking of taboos and so a "crime" that the goddess imposed on them?

36. A similar connection between Enheduana and nonbinary gender identities can be found in line 108 of the *Exaltation*, where Lugal-Ane hands her a ĝiri₂ and **ba-da-ra**, translated as "knife and dagger." These specific weapons were often brandished by the **kurĝara** and **saĝ-ursaĝ** as part of their subversion of traditional gender symbols; see Helle, "Weapons and Weaving Instruments." On the meaning of Lugal-Ane's action, see note 20 to the *Exaltation*.

37. For the ideal of femininity promoted in Old Babylonian schools, see Matuszak, "'She Is Not Fit for Womanhood.'"

38. See Standard Babylonian *Gilgamesh*, I 185 and 192 (women); and Old Babylonian *Gilgamesh*, Schøyen₂ l. 18 (men).

39. Bahrani, *Women of Babylon*, chap. 7.

40. Some key studies of women in the ancient Near East include Bahrani, *Women of Babylon*; Harris, *Gender and Aging*; and Svärd, *Women and Power*. See also the essays collected in Fink and Droß-Krüpe, *Powerful Women in the Ancient World*; Svärd and Garcia-Ventura, *Studying Gender*; Budin et al., *Gender and Methodology*; and Lion and Michel, *Role of Women*. The comparison with the status of women in ancient Athens is taken from Scurlock, "Status of Women." For female literacy, see Lion, "Literacy and Gender"; and Lion and Robson, "Quelques textes scolaires."

41. The importance of the *nadītu* was first made clear by Rivkah Harris; see Harris, "*nadītu* Woman." They have been the subject of numerous studies since then; a useful introduction is given in Jeyes, "Nadītu Women." A recent reassessment of their economic significance is given in De Graef, "*Cherchez la femme!*," which confirms the long-standing notion that they were leading figures in ancient trade.

42. The classic study of this mid-millennium transformation is Frymer-Kensky, *In the Wake of the Goddesses*. But a new and more detailed study of the Babylonian "great gender gap" is sorely needed; in the meantime, see Brisch, "Marginalization of Priestesses"; and Sonik, "Minor and Marginal(ized)?," 784–86, especially the references collected in note 39. For misogyny in Sumerian sources—which speaks against the notion of a "Sumerian matriarchy"—see Matuszak, "'She Is Not Fit for Womanhood.'"

43. On the gendered dynamics of creation in *Enuma Elish*, see Helle, "Marduk's Penis"; Sonik, "Gender Matters"; and Metzler, "Tod, Weiblichkeit und Ästhetik."

44. On authorship in the first millennium, see Lambert, "Catalogue of Texts and Authors"; Michalowski, "Sailing to Babylon," 83–87; and Helle, "First Authors," chaps. 10–11. On female authorship in the ancient Near East, see Svärd, "Female Agency and Authorship," but note that Svärd discusses authorship of various kinds of texts, not literary authorship specifically, which in the first millennium BCE does seem to be restricted to men. Zsombor Földi, "Bullussa-rabi," has recently argued that Bullussa-rabi, the author of the "Gula Hymn," was probably a woman because the name is exclusively used for women in the Kassite period; but in all first-millennium sources, Bullussa-rabi is depicted as a man.

THE PRIESTESS RETURNS

1. Bennett, *The Author*, 30.

2. Bennett, *The Author*, 30.

3. I take the time and date (and the phrase "Babylon time") from Michalowski, "Doors of the Past," 138.

4. The authority on Nabonidus is Beaulieu, *Reign of Nabonidus.*

5. The main negative accounts of Nabonidus are the "Cyrus Cylinder" and the "Verse Account of Nabonidus," both edited in Schaudig, *Die Inschriften Nabonids*, 550–56 and 563–78. In the Hebrew Bible, Nabonidus is conflated with Nebuchadnezzar II.

6. Nabonidus's mother was named Adad-guppi, and two stelae preserve an extended account of her life in the first person. Confusingly, however, the account ends by switching to a third-person narrator who relates that Adad-guppi has died, describing Nabonidus's ample funerary offerings to her. Adad-guppi may have dictated the text at the end of her life, with a scribe adding the final section, or the whole thing may have been composed after her death. Either

way, the stela, edited in Weiershäuser and Novotny, *Royal Inscriptions*, 223–28, tells us that Adad-guppi had a lifelong devotion to the Moon God, repeatedly praying to him and receiving visions from him about her son's career. She says that she lived to be 104—and would thus have been alive to witness her grand-daughter Ennigaldi-Nanna's installment as high priestess—and that old age had treated her well: "My eyesight was still bright, my intellect exceptional, my hands and feet healthy, my words well-chosen, food and drink agreeable to me, my body was good, my heart full of joy. I saw my children's children's children's children alive, up to the fourth generation: I attained a very old age"; Weiershäuser and Novotny, 226–27, ll. ii 29–34. On Adad-guppi's inscription, see Yun, "Mother of Her Son."

7. Part of the problem in identifying when the office of the high priestess ceased is that the terminology used to denote these priestesses changed over time. Though the **ereš-diĝir** priestesses seem to be identical with the **en** priest-esses in some periods, they may have been distinct in the Middle Babylonian period, when the latter office may have ceased to exist: as Michalowski, "Doors of the Past," 149n24, points out, the Middle Babylonian **ereš-diĝir** priestesses seem to be a larger group, not singular heads of a temple.

8. Nabonidus's installment of Ennigaldi-Nanna is described in two sources: a royal inscription on a cylinder, edited in Weiershäuser and Novotny, *Royal Inscriptions*, 165–69, and a historical chronicle, edited in Glassner, *Mesopotamian Chronicles*, 312–16. Convincing analyses of these sources can be found in Micha-lowski, "Doors of the Past"; and Reiner, *Your Thwarts in Pieces*, 1–16. The omen was "fudged" because the relevant entry in *Enuma Anu Enlil* reads: "If Sîn [i.e., the moon] is eclipsed in the month of Ululu during the last watch of the night [i.e., at dawn], then Sîn desires a high priestess." The month was right, but the time of day was not—the eclipse took place in the afternoon.

9. See C. Leonard Woolley, *Neo-Babylonian and Persian Periods*, 17; see also Pryke, "Hidden Women of History: Ennigaldi-Nanna."

10. Pryke, "Hidden Women of History: Ennigaldi-Nanna."

11. The copyist's note is edited in Frame, *Rulers of Babylonia*, 246–47; the Sumerian inscription is in Frayne, *Ur III Period*, 256–57.

12. See Pryke, "Hidden Women of History: Ennigaldi-Nanna."

13. Schaudig, "Nabonid, der 'Archäologe auf dem Königsthron.'" For antiquarianism in cuneiform culture generally, see Beaulieu, "Mesopotamian Antiquarianism"; for the later periods of Babylonian culture specifically, see Beaulieu, "Antiquarianism and the Concern for the Past."

14. L. i 26–27, Weiershäuser and Novotny, *Royal Inscriptions,* 167.

15. L. i 39—ii 5, Weiershäuser and Novotny, 167–68. For the stele of Nebuchadnezzar I that Nabonidus saw as providing a depiction of the priestesses' attire, see Michalowski, "Doors of the Past," 139–43, which plausibly identifies it as a *kudurru* that may not originally have had anything to do with high priestesses, but which fit well with Nabonidus's political program.

16. See Michalowski, "Doors of the Past," 142; see also Beaulieu, *Reign of Nabonidus,* 138–41, on Nabonidus's political use of his antiquarian findings.

17. Enanedu's inscriptions are edited in Frayne, *Old Babylonian Period,* 224–31 and 299–301.

18. L. 33, Frayne, *Old Babylonian Period,* 300.

19. L. 36–43, Frayne, *Old Babylonian Period,* 300.

20. See l. 1–4, Frayne, *Old Babylonian Period,* 300.

21. See Frayne, *Old Babylonian Period,* 257, text no. 32, l. 5, and 226, text no. 15, frag. 9, l. 6'.

22. On the life and legacy of Katharine Woolley, see Luby, "Backward Glance"; Melman, *Empires of Antiquities,* 211–12; and Kaercher, "Adventure Calls."

23. Christie, *Autobiography,* 364. For a similar description, see the account by Christie's husband, the archaeologist Max Mallowan, in Mallowan, *Memoirs,* 36–38.

24. On the popular reception of the excavations at Ur in the interwar period, see Melman, *Empires of Antiquities,* chaps. 5 and 6. On Woolley's role in securing funding, see Mallowan, *Memoirs,* 37.

25. Examples of these vile reports are collected in Luby, "Backward Glance," including references to Woolley as "demanding," "ruthless," "calculating," "poisonous," and "dangerous."

26. Katharine Woolley, *Adventure Calls.*

27. The only contemporary review of the novel I was able to find is a short notice by Kermit Roosevelt, the ill-fated son of Theodore Roosevelt. He

NOTES TO PAGES 174-178

was enthusiastic about the novel's realistic depiction of a revolt successfully squashed by a family "who have 'taken up the white man's burden,'" but spared no words to mention the themes of sexism and cross-dressing. See Roosevelt, "In Mesopotamia."

28. C. Leonard Woolley, *Excavations at Ur*, 115.

29. Hallo and van Dijk, *Exaltation of Inanna*.

30. Barthes's essay is often mistakenly dated to 1968, when the French version of the text appeared. But the English translation of the essay appeared first, in the 1967 issue of the experimental magazine *Aspen*. See Barthes, "Death of the Author"; Logie, "1967."

31. Weigle, "Women as Verbal Artists." For an overview of Enheduana's modern reception, see Konstantopoulos, "Many Lives of Enheduana."

32. Barnstone and Barnstone, *Book of Women Poets*, 1-8.

33. Alexander, "Triptych in a Time of War," 1593.

34. For the elegiac recollection of the ancient past in modern Iraqi literature, see Musawi, *Reading Iraq*, 27-29.

35. al-Jubouri, "Enheduanna"; al-Jubouri, *Laka hādhā*.

36. Meador, *Inanna, Lady of Largest Heart*, and *Princess, Priestess, Poet*.

37. Sjöberg and Bergmann, *Temple Hymns*; Sjöberg, "in-nin šà-gur$_4$-ra."

38. A brief overview of the Sumerian language is given in Michalowski, "Sumerian"; two useful guides for beginners (both freely available online) are Foxvog, *Introduction to Sumerian Grammar*; and Zólyomi, *Introduction to the Grammar of Sumerian*. The most ambitious attempt to build up a complete Sumerian grammar is Jagersma, "Descriptive Grammar," but many of the finer points remain debated. The only complete, but again debated, Sumerian lexicon is Attinger, *Glossaire sumérien-français*; to be consulted alongside the electronic glossaries by Sallaberger, "Münchner Sumerischer Zettelkasten"; and Tinney, Jones, and Veldhuis, "Electronic Pennsylvania Sumerian Dictionary."

39. Zgoll, *Rechtsfall der En-ḫedu-Ana*; Delnero, "Variation in Sumerian Literary Compositions," 2030-2108; Attinger, "Innana B." Further philological studies of Enheduana's poems include Michalowski, "Literature as a Source"; Krecher, "A Hymn to Inana (Inana C)"; Wilcke, *Kollationen zu den sumerischen literarischen Texten*, 48; and Wilcke, "nin-me-šár-ra."

BIBLIOGRAPHY

Alexander, Meena. "Triptych in a Time of War." *PMLA* 121, no. 5 (2006): 1593–95.

al-Jubouri, Amal. "Enheduanna." Translated by Salih J. Altoma. *World Literature Today* 77, nos. 3/4 (2003): 40.

———. *Laka hādhā al-jasad lā khawf ʿalayy.* London: Dār al-Sāqī, 1999.

Alster, Bendt. *Proverbs of Ancient Sumer: The World's Earliest Proverb Collections.* 2 vols. Bethesda, Md.: CDL Press, 1997.

Assante, Julia. "Bad Girls and Kinky Boys? The Modern Prostituting of Ishtar, Her Clergy and Her Cults." In *Tempelprostitution im Altertum: Fakten und Fiktionen,* edited by Tanja Susanne Scheer and Martin Lindner, 23–54. Berlin: Verlag Antike, 2009.

Attinger, Pascal. *Glossaire sumérien-français, principalement des textes littéraires paléobabyloniens.* Wiesbaden: Harrassowitz Verlag, 2021.

———. "Innana B (Ninmešara) (4.7.2)," 2019. Zenodo. https://zenodo.org/record/2667768#.XhScnRdKgWo.

Bahrani, Zainab. *The Graven Image: Representation in Babylonia and Assyria.* Philadelphia: University of Pennsylvania Press, 2003.

———. *Women of Babylon: Gender and Representation in Mesopotamia.* London: Routledge, 2001.

Bakhtin, Mikhail M. *Problems of Dostoevsky's Poetics.* Translated by Caryl Emerson. Theory and History of Literature 8. Minneapolis: University of Minnesota Press, 1984.

Bänder, Dana. *Die Siegesstele des Naramsîn und ihre Stellung in Kunst- und Kulturgeschichte.* Idstein: Schulz-Kirchner, 1995.

Barnstone, Aliki, and Willis Barnstone, eds. *A Book of Women Poets from Antiquity to Now.* Revised edition. New York: Schocken, 1992.

Barthes, Roland. "The Death of the Author." Translated by Richard Howard. *Aspen* 5–6 (1967). http://www.ubu.com/aspen/aspen5and6/threeEssays.html #barthes.

Beaulieu, Paul-Alain. "Antiquarianism and the Concern for the Past in the Neo-Babylonian Period." *Bulletin of the Canadian Society for Mesopotamian Studies* 28 (1994): 37–42.

———. "Mesopotamian Antiquarianism from Sumer to Babylon." In *World Antiquarianism: Comparative Perspectives*, edited by Alain Schnapp, 121–39. Los Angeles: Getty Research Institute, 2013.

———. *The Reign of Nabonidus, King of Babylon, 556–549 B.C.* Yale Near Eastern Researches 10. New Haven: Yale University Press, 1995.

Bennett, Andrew. *The Author*. The New Critical Idiom. London: Routledge, 2005.

Bennett, Andrew, ed. *Readers and Reading*. London: Routledge, 1995.

Biggs, Robert D. "An Archaic Sumerian Version of the Kesh Temple Hymn from Tell Abū Ṣalābīkh." *Zeitschrift für Assyriologie* 61, no. 2 (1971): 193–207.

———. *Inscriptions from Tell Abū Ṣalābīkh*. Oriental Institute Publications 99. Chicago: University of Chicago Press, 1974.

Black, Jeremy A. "En-hedu-ana Not the Composer of *The Temple Hymns*." *Nouvelles assyriologiques brèves et utilitaires* 2002, no. 1 (2002): 2–4, n. 4.

Black, Jeremy A., Graham Cunningham, Eleanor Robson, and Gábor Zólyomi, eds. *The Literature of Ancient Sumer*. Oxford: Oxford University Press, 2004.

Black, Jeremy A., and Anthony Green. *Gods, Demons, and Symbols of Ancient Mesopotamia: An Illustrated Dictionary*. London: British Museum Press, 1992.

Boddy, Kaira. *The Composition and Tradition of Erimḫuš*. Cuneiform Monographs 22. Leiden: Brill, 2020.

Brisch, Nicole M. "Introduction." In *Religion and Power: Divine Kingship in the Ancient World and Beyond*, edited by Nicole M. Brisch, 1–11. University of Chicago Oriental Institute Seminars 4. Chicago: Oriental Institute of the University of Chicago, 2008.

———. "The Marginalization of Priestesses in Ancient Mesopotamia." In *Pearls, Politics and Pistachios: Essays in Anthropology and Memories on the Occasion of Susan Pollock's 65th Birthday*, edited by Aydin Abar, et al., 585–94. Berlin: Ex Oriente, 2021.

———. "Rebellions and Peripheries in Sumerian Royal Literature." In *Rebellions and Peripheries in the Cuneiform World*, edited by Seth Richardson, 29–45. American Oriental Series 91. New Haven: American Oriental Society, 2010.

———. "To Eat Like a God: Religion and Economy in Old Babylonian Nippur." In *At the Dawn of History: Ancient Near Eastern Studies in Honour of J. N. Postgate*, edited by Yağmur Heffron, Adam Stone, and Martin Worthington, 43–53. Winona Lake, Ind.: Eisenbrauns, 2017.

Budin, Stephanie, Megan Cifarelli, Agnès Garcia-Ventura, and Adelina Millet Albà, eds. *Gender and Methodology in the Ancient Near East: Approaches from Assyriology and Beyond*. Barcino 10. Barcelona: Edicions de la Universitat de Barcelona, 2018.

Butler, Judith. *Giving an Account of Oneself*. New York: Fordham University Press, 2005.

Christie, Agatha. *An Autobiography*. London: Collins, 1977.

Civil, Miguel. "Les limites de l'information textuelle." In *L'Archéologie de l'Iraq: Du début de l'époque néolithique à 333 avant notre ère*, edited by Marie-Thérèse Barrelet, 225–32. Colloques internationaux du CNRS 580. Paris: Éditions du CNRS, 1980.

Collon, Dominique. *First Impressions: Cylinder Seals in the Ancient Near East*. London: British Museum Press, 2005.

Cooper, Jerrold S. "Genre, Gender, and the Sumerian Lamentation." *Journal of Cuneiform Studies* 58 (2006): 39–47.

———. "Literature and History: The Historical and Political Referents of Sumerian Literary Texts." In *Historiography in the Cuneiform World*, edited by Tzvi Abusch, Paul-Alain Beaulieu, John Huehnergard, Peter Machinist, and Piotr Steinkeller, 131–48. Compte Rendu de la Rencontre Assyriologique Internationale 45. Bethesda, Md.: CDL Press, 2001.

———. "Sacred Marriage and Popular Cult in Early Mesopotamia." In *Official Cult and Popular Religion in the Ancient Near East*, edited by Eiko Matsushima, 81–96. Heidelberg: Universitätsverlag Winter, 1993.

———. "Sumerian Literature and Sumerian Identity." In *Problems of Canonicity and Identity Formation in Ancient Egypt and Mesopotamia,* edited by Kim Ryholt and Gojko Barjamovic, 1–18. Carsten Niebuhr Institute Publications 43. Copenhagen: Museum Tusculanum Press, 2016.

Crisostomo, C. Jay. *Translation as Scholarship: Language, Writing, and Bilingual Education in Ancient Babylonia.* Studies in Ancient Near Eastern Records 22. Berlin: De Gruyter, 2019.

———. "Writing Sumerian, Creating Texts: Reflections on Text-Building Practices in Old Babylonian Schools." *Journal of Ancient Near Eastern Religions* 15, no. 2 (2016): 121–42.

Cullen, H. M., P. B. deMenocal, S. Hemming, G. Hemming, F. H. Brown, T. Guilderson, and F. Sirocko. "Climate Change and the Collapse of the Akkadian Empire: Evidence from the Deep Sea." *Geology* 28, no. 4 (2000): 379–82.

Culler, Jonathan. *Theory of the Lyric.* Cambridge: Harvard University Press, 2015.

De Graef, Katrien. "*Cherchez la femme!* The Economic Role of Women in Old Babylonian Sippar." In *The Role of Women in Work and Society in the Ancient Near East,* edited by Brigitte Lion and Cécile Michel, 270–95. Studies in Ancient Near Eastern Records 13. Berlin: De Gruyter, 2016.

Delnero, Paul. *How to Do Things with Tears: Ritual Lamenting in Ancient Mesopotamia.* Studies in Ancient Near Eastern Records 26. Berlin: De Gruyter, 2020.

———. "'Inana and Ebiḫ' and the Scribal Tradition." In *A Common Cultural Heritage: Studies on Mesopotamia and the Biblical World in Honor of Barry L. Eichler,* edited by Grant Frame, Erle Leichty, Karen Sonik, Jeffrey H. Tigay, and Steve Tinney, 123–49. Bethesda, Md.: CDL Press, 2011.

———. "Literature and Identity in Mesopotamia During the Old Babylonian Period." In *Problems of Canonicity and Identity Formation in Ancient Egypt and Mesopotamia,* edited by Kim Ryholt and Gojko Barjamovic, 19–50. Carsten Niebuhr Institute Publications 43. Copenhagen: Museum Tusculanum Press, 2016.

———. "Memorization and the Transmission of Sumerian Literary Compositions." *Journal of Near Eastern Studies* 71, no. 2 (2012): 189–208.

———. "Sumerian Literary Catalogues and the Scribal Curriculum." *Zeitschrift für Assyriologie* 100 (2010): 32–55.

———. "Texts and Performance: The Materiality and Function of the Sumerian Liturgical Corpus." In *Texts and Contexts: The Circulation and Transmission of Cuneiform Texts in Social Space*, edited by Paul Delnero and Jacob Lauinger, 87–118. Studies in Ancient Near Eastern Records 9. Berlin: De Gruyter, 2015.

———. "Variation in Sumerian Literary Compositions: A Case Study Based on the Decad." Ph.D. Diss. University of Pennsylvania, 2006. https://repository.upenn.edu/dissertations/AAI3246150/.

Deutscher, Guy. *Through the Language Glass: How Words Colour Your World*. London: Heinemann, 2010.

Eco, Umberto. *Vertigine della lista*. Milan: Bompiani, 2009.

Farber, Gertrud. "me (ĝarza, parṣu)." *Reallexikon der Assyriologie* 7 (1990): 610–13.

Farber-Flügge, Gertrud. *Der Mythos "Inanna und Enki" unter besonderer Berücksichtigung der Liste der me*. Studia Pohl 10. Rome: Biblical Institute Press, 1973.

Fink, Sebastian, and Kerstin Droß-Krüpe, eds. *Powerful Women in the Ancient World: Perception and (Self)Presentation; Proceedings of the 8th Melammu Workshop, Kassel, 30 January—1 February 2019*. Melammu Workshops and Monographs 4. Münster: Zaphon, 2021.

Földi, Zsombor J. "Bullussa-rabi, Author of the Gula Hymn." *Kaskal* 16 (2019): 81–83.

Foster, Benjamin R. *The Age of Agade: Inventing Empire in Ancient Mesopotamia*. London: Routledge, 2016.

———. "Authorship in Cuneiform Literature." In *The Cambridge Handbook of Literary Authorship*, edited by Ingo Berensmeyer, Gert Buelens, and Marysa Demoor, 13–26. Cambridge: Cambridge University Press, 2019.

———. *Before the Muses: An Anthology of Akkadian Literature*. 3rd edition. Bethesda, Md.: CDL Press, 2005.

Foucault, Michel. "Qu'est-ce qu'un auteur?" *Bulletin de la Société française de philosophie* 63, no. 3 (1969): 73–104.

Foxvog, Daniel A. *Introduction to Sumerian Grammar*. Revised edition. Scotts Valley: CreateSpace, 2014.

Frame, Grant. *Rulers of Babylonia: From the Second Dynasty of Isin to the End of Assyrian Domination (1157–612 BC)*. Royal Inscriptions of Mesopotamia, Babylonian Periods 2. Toronto: University of Toronto Press, 1995.

Frayne, Douglas. *Old Babylonian Period, 2003–1595 BC.* Royal Inscriptions of Mesopotamia, Early Periods 4. Toronto: University of Toronto Press, 1990.

———. *Sargonic and Gutian Periods, 2334–2113 BC.* Royal Inscriptions of Mesopotamia, Early Periods 2. Toronto: University of Toronto Press, 1993.

———. *Ur III Period, 2112–2004 BC.* Royal Inscriptions of Mesopotamia, Early Periods 3/2. Toronto: University of Toronto Press, 1997.

Frymer-Kensky, Tikva. *In the Wake of the Goddesses: Women, Culture, and the Biblical Transformation of Pagan Myth.* New York: Free Press, 1992.

Gabbay, Uri. "The Akkadian Word for Third Gender: The *kalû* (gala) Once Again." In *Proceedings of the 51st Rencontre Assyriologique Internationale*, edited by R. D. Biggs, J. Myers, and M. T. Roth, 49–56. Studies in Ancient Oriental Civilization 62. Chicago: Oriental Institute of the University of Chicago, 2008.

———. "The Balaĝ Instrument and Its Role in the Cult of Ancient Mesopotamia." In *Music in Antiquity: The Near East and the Mediterranean*, edited by Joan Goodnick Westenholz, Yossi Maurey, and Edwin Seoussi, 129–47. Yuval 7. Berlin: De Gruyter Oldenbourg, 2014.

———. *Pacifying the Hearts of the Gods: Sumerian Emesal Prayers of the First Millennium BC.* Heidelberger Emesal-Studien 1. Wiesbaden: Harrassowitz Verlag, 2014.

George, Andrew R. *House Most High: The Temples of Ancient Mesopotamia.* Mesopotamian Civilizations 5. Winona Lake, Ind.: Eisenbrauns, 1993.

———. "In Search of the é.dub.ba.a: The Ancient Mesopotamian School in Literature and Reality." In *"An Experienced Scribe Who Neglects Nothing": Ancient Near Eastern Studies in Honor of Jacob Klein*, edited by Yitschak Sefati, Pinhas Artzi, Chaim Cohen, Barry L. Eichler, and Victor A. Hurowitz, 127–37. Bethesda, Md.: CDL Press, 2005.

———. "The Poem of Erra and Ishum: A Babylonian Poet's View of War." In *Warfare and Poetry in the Middle East*, edited by Hugh Kennedy, 39–71. London: I. B. Tauris, 2013.

Glassner, Jean-Jacques. "En-hedu-ana, une femme auteure en pays de Sumer, au IIIᵉ millenaire?" *Topoi Suppléments* 10 (2009): 219–31.

———. *Mesopotamian Chronicles*. Edited by Benjamin R. Foster. Writings from the Ancient World 19. Atlanta: Society of Biblical Literature, 2004.

Groneberg, Brigitte R. M. *Lob der Ištar: Gebet und Ritual an die altbabylonische Venusgöttin: "Tanatti Ištar."* Cuneiform Monographs 8. Groningen: Styx, 1997.

Guinan, Ann, and Erle Leichty. "Tasteless Tablets." In *Gazing on the Deep: Ancient Near Eastern and Other Studies in Honor of Tzvi Abusch*, edited by Jeffrey Stackert, Barbara N. Porter, and David P. Wright, 49–50. Bethesda, Md.: CDL Press, 2010.

Hall, Mark Glenn. "A Study of the Sumerian Moon-God, Nanna/Suen." Ph.D. Diss. University of Pennsylvania, 1985.

Hallo, William W. "Seals Lost and Found." In *Seals and Sealing in the Ancient Near East*, edited by McGuire Gibson and Robert D. Biggs, 55–60. Bibliotheca Mesopotamica 6. Malibu, Calif.: Undena, 1977.

Hallo, William W., and J. J. A. van Dijk. *The Exaltation of Inanna*. Yale Near Eastern Researches 3. New Haven: Yale University Press, 1968.

Hansen, Donald P. "Art of the Akkadian Dynasty." In *Art of the First Cities: The Third Millennium B.C. from the Mediterranean to the Indus*, edited by Joan Aruz and Ronald Wallenfels, 189–209. New York: Metropolitan Museum of Art, 2003.

Harris, Rivkah. *Gender and Aging in Mesopotamia: The Gilgamesh Epic and Other Ancient Literature*. Norman: University of Oklahoma Press, 2000.

———. "Inanna-Ishtar as Paradox and a Coincidence of Opposites." *History of Religions* 30, no. 3 (1991): 261–78.

———. "The *nadītu* Woman." In *Studies Presented to A. Leo Oppenheim*, edited by Robert D. Biggs and John A. Brinkman, 106–35. Chicago: Oriental Institute of the University of Chicago, 1964.

Haul, Michael. *Stele und Legende: Untersuchungen zu den keilschriftlichen Erzählwerken über die Könige von Akkade*. Göttinger Beiträge zum alten Orient 4. Göttingen: Universitätsverlag Göttingen, 2009.

Heffron, Yağmur. "Inana/Ištar." Ancient Mesopotamian Gods and Goddesses, 2016. http://oracc.museum.upenn.edu/amgg/listofdeities/inanaitar/.

Helle, Sophus. "The Birth of the Author: Co-Creating Authorship in En-heduana's *Exaltation.*" *Orbis Litterarum* 75, no. 2 (2020): 55–72.

———. "Enheduana and the Invention of Authorship." *Authorship* 8, no. 1 (2019): 1–20.

———. "Enheduana's Invocations: Form and Force." In *Women in Religion in the Ancient Near East and Asia: Goddesses, Empresses, Priestesses, and Business-women,* edited by Nicole M. Brisch and Fumi Karahashi. Studies in Ancient Near Eastern Records. Berlin: De Gruyter, forthcoming.

———. "The First Authors: Narratives of Authorship in Akkadian Literature." Ph.D. Diss. Aarhus University, 2020.

———. "Marduk's Penis: Queering *Enūma Eliš.*" *Distant Worlds Journal* 4 (2020): 63–77.

———. "'Only in Dress?' Methodological Concerns Regarding Non-Binary Gender." In *Gender and Methodology in the Ancient Near East: Approaches from Assyriology and Beyond,* edited by Stephanie Budin, Megan Cifarelli, Agnès Garcia-Ventura, and Adelina Millet Albà, 41–53. Barcino 10. Barce-lona: Edicions de la Universitat de Barcelona, 2018.

———. "Weapons and Weaving Instruments as Symbols of Gender in the An-cient Near East." In *Fashioned Selves: Dress and Identity in Antiquity,* edited by Megan Cifarelli, 105–15. Oxford: Oxbow Books, 2019.

———. "What Is an Author? Old Answers to a New Question." *Modern Lan-guage Quarterly* 80, no. 2 (2019): 113–39.

Hoskote, Ranjit. "Introduction." In *I, Lalla: The Poems of Lal Děd,* ix–lxxvii. Pen-guin Classics. London: Penguin Books, 2013.

Huber, Fabienne. "La Correspondance Royale d'Ur, un corpus apocryphe." *Zeitschrift für Assyriologie* 91 (2001): 169–206.

Jagersma, Bram. "A Descriptive Grammar of Sumerian." Ph.D. Diss. Universi-teit Leiden, 2010. https://scholarlypublications.universiteitleiden.nl/handle/1887/16107.

Jaques, Margaret. *Le vocabulaire des sentiments dans les textes sumériens: Recherche sur le lexique sumérien et akkadien.* Alter Orient und Altes Testament 332. Münster: Ugarit-Verlag, 2006.

Jeyes, Ulla. "The Nadītu Women of Sippar." In *Images of Women in Antiquity*, edited by Averil Cameron and Amélie Kuhrt, 260–72. Detroit: Wayne State University Press, 1983.

Jones, Philip. "Embracing Inana: Legitimation and Mediation in the Ancient Mesopotamian Sacred Marriage Hymn Iddin-Dagan A." *Journal of the American Oriental Society* 123, no. 2 (April 2003): 291.

Kaercher, Kyra. "Adventure Calls: The Life of a Woman Adventurer." Penn Museum Blog, February 29, 2016. https://www.penn.museum/blog/museum/adventure-calls-the-life-of-a-woman-adventurer/.

Konstantopoulos, Gina. "The Many Lives of Enheduana: Identity, Authorship, and the 'World's First Poet.'" In *Powerful Women in the Ancient World: Perception and (Self)Presentation; Proceedings of the 8th Melammu Workshop, Kassel, 30 January—1 February 2019*, edited by Sebastian Fink and Kerstin Droß-Krüpe, 55–74. Melammu Workshops and Monographs 4. Münster: Zaphon, 2021.

Krecher, Joachim. "A Hymn to Inana (Inana C)." Electronic Text Corpus of Sumerian Literature, 1996. https://etcsl.orinst.ox.ac.uk/cgi-bin/etcsl.cgi?text=t.4.07.3.

———. "The Temple Hymns." Electronic Text Corpus of Sumerian Literature, 1996. https://etcsl.orinst.ox.ac.uk/cgi-bin/etcsl.cgi?text=t.4.80.1.

Kuzucuoğlu, Catherine, and Catherine Marro, eds. *Sociétés humaines et changement climatique à la fin du troisième millénaire: Une crise a-t-elle eu lieu en Haute Mésopotamie? Actes du Colloque de Lyon (5–8 décembre 2005)*. Varia Anatolica 19. Istanbul: Institut Français d'Études Anatoliennes-Georges Dumézil, 2007.

Lambert, Wilfred G. "A Catalogue of Texts and Authors." *Journal of Cuneiform Studies* 16, no. 3 (1962): 59–77.

———. "Ghost-writers?" *Nouvelles assyriologiques brèves et utilitaires* 2001, no. 3 (2001): 77, n. 83.

———. "The Pantheon of Mari." *Mari* 4 (1985): 525–39.

Leick, Gwendolyn. *A Dictionary of Ancient Near Eastern Architecture*. London: Routledge, 1988.

Lion, Brigitte. "Literacy and Gender." In *The Oxford Handbook of Cuneiform Culture*, edited by Karen Radner and Eleanor Robson, 90–112. Oxford: Oxford University Press, 2011.

Lion, Brigitte, and Cécile Michel, eds. *The Role of Women in Work and Society in the Ancient Near East*. Studies in Ancient Near Eastern Records 13. Berlin: De Gruyter, 2016.

Lion, Brigitte, and Eleanor Robson. "Quelques textes scolaires paléo-babyloniens rédigés par des femmes." *Journal of Cuneiform Studies* 57 (2005): 37–54.

Logie, John. "1967: The Birth of 'The Death of the Author.'" *College English* 75, no. 5 (2013): 493–512.

Luby, Edward M. "Backward Glance: The Ur-Archaeologist." *Biblical Archaeology Review* 23, no. 2 (1997): 60–61.

Mallowan, Max. *Mallowan's Memoirs*. New York: Dodd, Mead, 1977.

Matuszak, Jana. "'She Is Not Fit for Womanhood': The Ideal Housewife According to Sumerian Literary Texts." In *The Role of Women in Work and Society in the Ancient Near East*, edited by Brigitte Lion and Cécile Michel. Studies in Ancient Near Eastern Records 13. Berlin: De Gruyter, 2016.

McHale-Moore, Rhonda. "The Mystery of Enheduanna's Disk." *Journal of the Ancient Near Eastern Society* 27 (2000): 69–74.

Meador, Betty De Shong. *Inanna, Lady of Largest Heart: Poems of the Sumerian High Priestess Enheduanna*. Austin: University of Texas Press, 2000.

———. *Princess, Priestess, Poet: The Sumerian Temple Hymns of Enheduanna*. Austin: University of Texas Press, 2009.

Melman, Billie. *Empires of Antiquities: Modernity and the Rediscovery of the Ancient Near East, 1914–1950*. Oxford: Oxford University Press, 2020.

Metzler, Kai A. "Tod, Weiblichkeit und Ästhetik im mesopotamischen Weltscöpfungsepos *Enūma eliš*." In *Sex and Gender in the Ancient Near East*, edited by Simo Parpola and Robert M. Whiting, 393–411. Compte Rendu de la Rencontre Assyriologique Internationale 47. Helsinki: Neo-Assyrian Text Corpus Project, 2002.

Michalowski, Piotr. *The Correspondence of the Kings of Ur: An Epistolary History of an Ancient Mesopotamian Kingdom*. Mesopotamian Civilizations 15. Winona Lake, Ind.: Eisenbrauns, 2011.

———. "The Doors of the Past." *Eretz-Israel* 2003 (2003): 136–52.

———. "The Kingdom of Akkad in Contact with the World." In *The Oxford History of the Ancient Near East*, edited by Karen Radner, Nadine Moeller, and Daniel T. Potts, 686–764. Oxford: Oxford University Press, 2020.

———. "Literacy, Schooling and the Transmission of Knowledge." In *Theory and Practice of Knowledge Transfer: Studies in School Education in the Ancient Near East and Beyond*, edited by Wolfert S. van Egmond and Wilfred H. van Soldt, 39–57. PIHANS 121. Leiden: Nederlands Instituut voor het Nabije Oosten, 2012.

———. "Literature as a Source of Lexical Inspiration: Some Notes on a Hymn to the Goddess Inana." In *Written on Clay and Stone: Ancient Near Eastern Studies Presented to Krystyna Szarzynska*, edited by Jan Braun, Krystyna Łyczkowska, Maciej Popko, and Piotr Steinkeller, 65–74. Warsaw: Agade, 1998.

———. "The Lives of the Sumerian Language." In *Margins of Writing, Origins of Cultures*, edited by Seth L. Sanders, 163–88. University of Chicago Oriental Institute Seminars 2. Chicago: Oriental Institute of the University of Chicago, 2006.

———. "Love or Death? Observations on the Role of the Gala in Ur III Ceremonial Life." *Journal of Cuneiform Studies* 58 (2006): 49–61.

———. "The Mortal Kings of Ur: A Short Century of Divine Rule in Ancient Mesopotamia." In *Religion and Power: Divine Kingship in the Ancient World and Beyond*, edited by Nicole M. Brisch, 33–45. University of Chicago Oriental Institute Seminars 4. Chicago: Oriental Institute of the University of Chicago, 2008.

———. "Sailing to Babylon, Reading the Dark Side of the Moon." In *The Study of the Ancient Near East in the Twenty-First Century: The William Foxwell Albright Centennial Conference*, edited by Jerrold S. Cooper and Glenn M. Schwartz, 177–93. Winona Lake, Ind.: Eisenbrauns, 1996.

———. "Sumerian." In *A Companion to Ancient Near Eastern Languages*, edited by Rebecca Hasselbach-Andee, 83–105. Hoboken, N.J.: Wiley, 2020.

Minamore, Bridget. "Lines of Resistance." *BBC Sounds*. London: BBC, 2017. https://www.bbc.co.uk/sounds/play/b098h0f3.

Musawi, Muhsin Jasim. *Reading Iraq: Culture and Power in Conflict.* Library of Modern Middle East Studies 51. London: I. B. Tauris, 2006.

Nissinen, Martti, and Saana Svärd. "(Re)constructing the Image of the Assinnu." In *Studying Gender in the Ancient Near East,* edited by Saana Svärd and Agnès Garcia-Ventura, 373–411. Winona Lake, Ind.: Eisenbrauns, 2018.

Nissinen, Martti, and Risto Uro, eds. *Sacred Marriages: The Divine-Human Sexual Metaphor from Sumer to Early Christianity.* Winona Lake, Ind.: Eisenbrauns, 2008.

Peled, Ilan. "*assinnu* and *kurgarrû* Revisited." *Journal of Near Eastern Studies* 73, no. 2 (2014): 283–97.

Pollock, Sheldon. "Philology in Three Dimensions." *postmedieval* 5, no. 4 (2014): 398–413.

Pryke, Louise M. "Hidden Women of History: Enheduanna, Princess, Priestess and the World's First Known Author." *The Conversation,* February 12, 2019. https://theconversation.com/hidden-women-of-history-enheduanna -princess-priestess-and-the-worlds-first-known-author-109185.

———. "Hidden Women of History: Ennigaldi-Nanna, Curator of the World's First Museum." *The Conversation,* May 21, 2019. https://theconversation .com/hidden-women-of-history-ennigaldi-nanna-curator-of-the-worlds -first-museum-116431.

———. *Ishtar.* Gods and Heroes of the Ancient World. London: Taylor and Francis, 2017.

Puksar, Jason. "Institutions: Writing and Reading." In *The Cambridge Handbook of Literary Authorship,* edited by Ingo Berensmeyer, Gert Buelens, and Marysa Demoor, 429–43. Cambridge: Cambridge University Press, 2019.

Radner, Karen. *Die Macht des Namens: Altorientalische Strategien zur Selbsterhaltung.* Santag 8. Wiesbaden: Harrassowitz Verlag, 2005.

Reiner, Erica. *Your Thwarts in Pieces, Your Mooring Ropes Cut: Poetry from Babylonia and Assyria.* Ann Arbor: Horace H. Rackham School of Graduate Studies at the University of Michigan, 1985.

Reisman, Daniel. "Iddin-Dagan's Sacred Marriage Hymn." *Journal of Cuneiform Studies* 25, no. 4 (1973): 185–202.

Richardson, Seth. "Sumer and Stereotype: Re-Forging a 'Sumerian' Kingship in the Late Old Babylonian Period." In *Conceptualizing Past, Present and Future*, edited by Sebastian Fink and Robert Rolliger, 145–86. Melammu Symposia 9. Münster: Ugarit-Verlag, 2018.

Robson, Eleanor. *Mathematics in Ancient Iraq: A Social History*. Princeton: Princeton University Press, 2008.

———. "The Tablet House: A Scribal School in Old Babylonian Nippur." *Revue d'Assyriologie* 93, no. 1 (2001): 39–66.

Roosevelt, Kermit. "In Mesopotamia." *Saturday Review of Literature*, June 29, 1929.

Rubio, Gonzalo. "The Inventions of Sumerian: Literature and the Artifacts of Identity." In *Problems of Canonicity and Identity Formation in Ancient Egypt and Mesopotamia*, edited by Kim Ryholt and Gojko Barjamovic, 231–57. Carsten Niebuhr Institute Publications 43. Copenhagen: Museum Tusculanum Press, 2016.

———. "Šulgi and the Death of Sumerian." In *Approaches to Sumerian Literature Studies in Honour of Stip (H. L. J. Vanstiphout)*, edited by Piotr Michalowski and Niek Veldhuis, 167–79. Cuneiform Monographs 35. Leiden: Brill, 2006.

———. *Sumerian Literary Texts from the Ur III Period*. Mesopotamian Civilizations. Winona Lake, Ind.: Eisenbrauns, forthcoming.

Sallaberger, Walther. "Münchner Sumerischer Zettelkasten," 2020. https://www .assyriologie.uni-muenchen.de/forschung/zettelkasten/index.html.

Schaudig, Hanspeter. *Die Inschriften Nabonids von Babylon und Kyros' des Grossen samt den in ihrem Umfeld entstandenen Tendenzschriften: Textausgabe und Grammatik*. Alter Orient und Altes Testament 256. Münster: Ugarit-Verlag, 2001.

———. "Nabonid, der 'Archäologe auf dem Königsthron': Erwägungen zum Geschichtsbild des ausgehenden neubabylonischen Reiches." In *Festschrift für Burkhart Kienast zu seinem 70. Geburtstage, dargebracht von Freunden, Schülern und Kollegen*, edited by Gerbhard J. Selz, 447–97. Alter Orient und Altes Testament 256. Münster: Ugarit-Verlag, 2003.

Schrakamp, Ingo. "The Kingdom of Akkad: A View from Within." In *The Oxford History of the Ancient Near East*, edited by Karen Radner, Nadine Moeller, and Daniel T. Potts, 612–85. Oxford: Oxford University Press, 2020.

Schretter, Manfred K. *Emesal-Studien: Sprach- und literaturgeschichtliche Untersu-chungen zur sogenannten Frauensprache des Sumerischen.* Innsbrucker Beiträge zur Kulturwissenschaft 69. Innsbruck: Verlag des Instituts für Sprachwis-senschaft der Universität Innsbruck, 1990.

Scurlock, JoAnn. "The Status of Women in Ancient Mesopotamia." In *The West-ern Perspective: A History of Civilization in the West,* edited by Philip V. Can-nistraro and John H. Reich, 62–64. Fort Worth, Tex.: Harcourt, Brace, 1999.

Seligson, Joelle, ed. *She Who Wrote: Enheduanna and Women of Mesopotamia, ca. 3400–2000 BC.* New York: Morgan Library and Museum, 2022.

Selz, Gebhard J. "A Mesopotamian Path to Abstraction? On Sumerian 'Ontolo-gies.'" In *Conceptualizing Past, Present and Future: Proceedings of the Ninth Symposium of the Melammu Project, Held in Helsinki / Tartu, May 18–24, 2015,* edited by Robert Rolliger, 409–33. Melammu Symposia 9. Münster: Ugarit-Verlag, 2018.

Shehata, Dahlia. *Musiker und ihr vokales Repertoire: Untersuchungen zu Inhalt und Organisation von Musikerberufen und Liedgattungen in altbabylonischer Zeit.* Göttinger Beiträge zum Alten Orient 3. Göttingen: Göttingen University Press, 2009.

Sjöberg, Åke W. "in-nin šà-gur$_4$-ra: A Hymn to the Goddess Inanna by the en-Priestess Enheduanna." *Zeitschrift für Assyriologie* 65, no. 2 (1975): 161–253.

Sjöberg, Åke W., and Eugen S. J. Bergmann. *The Collection of the Sumerian Temple Hymns.* Texts from Cuneiform Sources 3. Locust Valley, N.Y.: J. J. Augustin, 1969.

Sonik, Karen. "Gender Matters in *Enūma Eliš.*" In *In the Wake of Tikva Frymer-Kensky,* edited by Richard H. Beal, Steven W. Holloway, and JoAnn Scurlock, 85–101. Piscataway, N.J.: Gorgias Press, 2009.

———. "Minor and Marginal(ized)? Rethinking Women as Minor Characters in the *Epic of Gilgamesh.*" *Journal of the American Oriental Society* 141, no. 4 (2021): 779–802.

Steinkeller, Piotr. "An Ur III Manuscript of the Sumerian King List." In *Li-teratur, Politik und Recht in Mesopotamien,* edited by Walther Sallaberger, Konrad Volk, and Annette Zgoll, 267–92. Orientalia Biblica et Christiana 14. Wiesbaden: Harrassowitz Verlag, 2003.

Stillinger, Jack. *Multiple Authorship and the Myth of Solitary Genius.* Oxford: Oxford University Press, 1991.

Streck, Michael P., and Nathan Wasserman. "The Man Is Like a Woman, the Maiden Is a Young Man: A New Edition of Ištar-Louvre." *Orientalia Nova Series* 87, no. 1 (2018): 1–38.

Suter, Claudia E. "On Images, Visibility, and Agency of Early Mesopotamian Royal Women." In *The First Ninety Years: A Sumerian Celebration in Honor of Miguel Civil,* edited by Lluís Feliu, Fumi Karahashi, and Gonzalo Rubio, 337–62. Studies in Ancient Near Eastern Records 12. Berlin: De Gruyter, 2017.

Svärd, Saana. "Female Agency and Authorship in Mesopotamian Texts." *Kaskal* 10 (2013): 269–80.

———. *Women and Power in Neo-Assyrian Palaces.* State Archives of Assyria Studies 23. Helsinki: Neo-Assyrian Text Corpus Project, 2015.

Svärd, Saana, and Agnès Garcia-Ventura, eds. *Studying Gender in the Ancient Near East.* Winona Lake, Ind.: Eisenbrauns, 2018.

Tanret, Michel. "Learned, Rich, Famous, and Unhappy: Ur-Utu of Sippar." In *The Oxford Handbook of Cuneiform Culture,* edited by Karen Radner and Eleanor Robson, 270–87. Oxford: Oxford University Press, 2011.

Tinney, Steve. "On the Curricular Setting of Sumerian Literature." *Iraq* 61 (1999): 159–72.

Tinney, Steve, Phillip Jones, and Niek Veldhuis. "Electronic Pennsylvania Sumerian Dictionary," 2017. http://oracc.museum.upenn.edu/epsd2/index.html.

Veldhuis, Niek. *Religion, Literature, and Scholarship: The Sumerian Composition Nanše and the Birds, with a Catalogue of Sumerian Bird Names.* Cuneiform Monographs 22. Leiden: Brill, 2004.

Volk, Konrad, ed. *Erzählungen aus dem Land Sumer.* Wiesbaden: Harrassowitz Verlag, 2015.

Wagensonner, Klaus. "Between History and Fiction—Enheduana, the First Poet in World Literature." In *Women at the Dawn of History,* edited by Klaus Wagensonner and Agnete W. Lassen, 38–45. New Haven: Yale Babylonian Collection, 2020.

Weadock, Penelope N. "The *giparu* at Ur." *Iraq* 37, no. 2 (1975): 101–28.

Wee, John Z. "Phenomena in Writing: Creating and Interpreting Variants of the Diagnostic Series Sa-Gig." In *In the Wake of the Compendia: Infrastructural Contexts and the Licensing of Empiricism in Ancient and Medieval Mesopotamia*, edited by J. Cale Johnson, 247–87. Science, Technology, and Medicine in Ancient Cultures 3. Berlin: De Gruyter, 2015.

Weiershäuser, Frauke, and Jamie Novotny. *The Royal Inscriptions of Amēl-Marduk (561–560 BC), Neriglissar (559–556 BC), and Nabonidus (555–539 BC), Kings of Babylon*. Royal Inscriptions of the Neo-Babylonian Empire 2. University Park, Pa.: Eisenbrauns, 2020.

Weigle, Marta. "Women as Verbal Artists: Reclaiming the Sisters of Enheduanna." *Frontiers: A Journal of Women Studies* 3, no. 3 (1978): 1–9.

Weiss, Harvey, ed. *Seven Generations Since the Fall of Akkad*. Studia Chaburensia 3. Wiesbaden: Harrassowitz Verlag, 2012.

Westenholz, Aage. "Assyriologists, Ancient and Modern, on Naramsin and Sharkalisharri." In *Assyriologica et Semitica: Festschrift für Joachim Oelsner anläßlich seines 65. Geburtstages am 18. Februar 1997*, edited by Joachim Marzahn and Hans Neumann, 545–56. Alter Orient und Altes Testament 252. Münster: Ugarit-Verlag, 2000.

———. "The Old Akkadian Period: History and Culture." In *Akkade-Zeit und Ur III-Zeit*, edited by Walther Sallaberger and Aage Westenholz, 11–110. Orbis Biblicus et Orientalis 160/3. Freiburg: Vandenhoeck & Ruprecht, 1999.

———. "The Sins of Nippur." In *In Context: The Reade Festschrift*, edited by Irving L. Finkel and St John Simpson, 82–100. Oxford: Archaeopress Archaeology, 2020.

Westenholz, Joan Goodnick. "Enheduanna, En-Priestess, Hen of Nanna, Spouse of Nanna." In *Dumu-e₂-dub-ba-a: Studies in Honor of Åke W. Sjöberg*, edited by Hermann Behrens, Darlene Loding, and Martha Tobi Roth, 539–56. Occasional Publications of the Samuel Noah Kramer Fund 11. Philadelphia: Samuel Noah Kramer Fund, 1989.

———. *Legends of the Kings of Akkade: The Texts*. Mesopotamian Civilizations 7. Winona Lake, Ind.: Eisenbrauns, 1997.

Whittaker, Gordon. "Linguistic Anthropology and the Study of Emesal as (a) Women's Language." In *Sex and Gender in the Ancient Near East,* edited by Simo Parpola and Robert M. Whiting, 2:1–12. Compte Rendu de la Rencontre Assyriologique Internationale 47. Helsinki: Neo-Assyrian Text Corpus Project, 2002.

Wilcke, Claus. *Kollationen zu den sumerischen literarischen Texten aus Nippur in der Hilprecht-Sammlung Jena.* Abhandlungen der Sachsischen Akademie der Wissenschaften zu Leipzig, Philologisch-historische Klasse 65, no. 4. Berlin: Akademie-Verlag, 1976.

———. "nin-me-šár-ra—Probleme der Interpretation." *Wiener Zeitschrift für die Kunde des Morgenlandes* 68 (1976): 79–92.

———. "Politik im Spiegel der Literatur, Literatur als Mittel der Politik im älteren Babylonien." In *Anfänge politischen Denkens in der Antike: Die nahöstlichen Kulturen und die Griechen,* edited by Kurt A. Raaflaub, 29–75. Schriften des Historischen Kollegs, Kolloquien 24. Munich: R. Oldenbourg Verlag, 1993.

———. "Politische Opposition nach sumerischen Quellen: Der Konflikt zwischen Königtum und Ratsversammlung: Literaturwerke als politische Tendenzschriften." In *La voix de l'opposition en Mesopotamie: Colloque organisé par l'Institut des Hautes Études de Belgique, 19 et 20 mars 1973,* edited by André Finet, 37–65. Brussels: Institut des Hautes Études, 1975.

Wilson, Mark. *Education in the Earliest Schools: Cuneiform Manuscripts in the Cotsen Collection.* Los Angeles: Cotsen Occasional Press, 2008.

Winter, Irene. "Sex, Rhetoric, and the Public Monument: The Alluring Body of Naram-Sîn of Agade." In *Sexuality in Ancient Art: Near East, Egypt, Greece, and Italy,* edited by Natalie Kampen, 11–26. Cambridge: Cambridge University Press, 1996.

Winter, Irene J. "Women in Public: The Disk of Enheduanna, the Beginning of the Office of En-Priestess, and the Weight of Visual Evidence." In *La femme dans le Proche-Orient Antique,* edited by Jean-Marie Durand, 189–201. Compte Rendu de la Rencontre Assyriologique Internationale 33. Paris: Éditions Recherches sur les Civilisations, 1987.

Woods, Christopher. "Bilingualism, Scribal Learning, and the Death of Sumerian." In *Margins of Writing, Origins of Cultures,* edited by Seth L. Sanders, 95–124. University of Chicago Oriental Institute Seminars 2. Chicago: Oriental Institute of the University of Chicago, 2006.

Woolley, C. Leonard. *Excavations at Ur.* Apollo Edition. New York: Crowell, 1965.

———. *The Neo-Babylonian and Persian Periods.* Ur Excavations 9. London: British Museum, 1962.

———. *The Royal Cemetery: A Report on the Predynastic and Sargonid Graves Excavated Between 1926 and 1931.* Ur Excavations 2. London: British Museum, 1934.

Woolley, Katharine. *Adventure Calls.* London: John Murray, 1929.

Yun, Sungduk. "Mother of Her Son: The Literary Scheme of the Adad-guppi Stele." *Acta Orientialia Academiae Scientiarum Hungaricae* 70, no. 3 (2017): 277–94.

Zgoll, Annette. "Nin-me-šara—Mythen als argumentative Waffen in einem rituellen Lied der Hohepriesterin En-ḫedu-Ana." In *Weisheitstexte, Mythen und Epen,* edited by Bernd Janowski and Daniel Schwemer, 55–67. Texte aus der Umwelt des Alten Testaments, Neue Folge 8. Gütersloh: Gütersloher Verlagsaus, 2015.

———. *Der Rechtsfall der En-ḫedu-Ana im Lied nin-me-šara.* Alter Orient und Altes Testament 246. Münster: Ugarit-Verlag, 1997.

Zólyomi, Gábor. *An Introduction to the Grammar of Sumerian.* Budapest: Eötvös University Press, 2017.

Zsolnay, Ilona. "The Misconstrued Role of the *Assinnu* in Ancient Near Eastern Prophecy." In *Prophets Male and Female: Gender and Prophecy in the Hebrew Bible, the Eastern Mediterranean and the Ancient Near East,* edited by Jonathan Stökl and Corrine Carvalho, 81–99. Atlanta: Society of Biblical Literature Press, 2013.

ACKNOWLEDGMENTS

MY FIRST AND GREATEST THANKS GO TO MY PARTNER, Aya Labanieh. Without her support, I would not have had the courage to pursue this project. Gina Konstantopoulos was an invaluable help as I made my way through the brambles of Sumerian grammar, and the always kind Louise Pryke generously guided me to the still unexplored life of Ennigaldi-Nanna.

This book is the culmination of a long engagement with Enheduana and her poems that began when Seraina Nett first introduced me to the world of Sumerian literature with infectious enthusiasm. Nicole Brisch—a teacher unmatched in kindness—first taught me Sumerian and was later the adviser for my Ph.D. dissertation on the cuneiform origins of literary authorship. My other adviser was Mads Rosendahl Thomsen, who offered indispensable help as I made my way into literary studies and the field of world literature. Countless colleagues have helped me develop my ideas about Enheduana over the years—in conversations over conference coffees, workshop dinners, and symposium drinks—but I would like to single out Paul Delnero, whose insights are always particularly illuminating. This book builds on my Danish translation of the *Exaltation*, which I completed at the instigation of Shëkufe Tadayoni Heiberg, my editor at the indie publishing house Forlaget Uro. Her dedication in promoting the poetry of Enheduana and other neglected women writers is an inspiration to us all. My friends and family, who read and responded to the translations and lent a generous ear to my rantings about Enheduana over the years, have given me both fresh perspectives and valuable encouragement: in particular, I would like to thank Rakel Haslund-Gjerrild; Alexandra O'Sullivan Freltoft; my parents, Merete Pryds Helle and Morten Søndergaard; and my sister, Agathe Søndergaard Helle.

This is my second book with Yale University Press, and it has once more been a delight to work with my editor Jennifer Banks, who shepherded this book from proposal to publication with wonderful keenness. My copyeditor, Susan Laity, made countless improvements to the text; her wit and her ear make her a marvelous collaborator. The Penn Museum generously allowed me to reprint images of the Disk of Enheduana and of a manuscript of the *Exaltation*. The anonymous reviewers supplied many helpful additions and corrections to strengthen my argument. The project was further supported by the J. and H. Kruuse Memorial Fund, the Danish Institute in Damascus, and the European Young Researcher Association. I completed the book while staying at the excellent research cluster Temporal Communities at Freie Universität Berlin; my stay there was made possible by a grant from the Carlsberg Foundation.

Thank you all.

INDEX

abgal (Seven Sages), 66, 203n14

Abu Salabikh, 131, 181

Abzu (Deep Sea), 57, 59, 64, 66, 73, 77, 96, 99, 214n70

Adab, temple of Ninhursanga in, 82

Adad-guppi (Nabonidus's mother), 223–24n6

Adventure Calls (K. Woolley), 171–73

afterlife, 112. *See also* underworld

Akkad, 55, 107, 149; temple of Ilaba in, 92; temple of Inana in, 79, 91

Akkadian Empire. *See* Old Akkadian Empire

Akkadian language, 106, 107–8, 120–21, 124–25, 144, 181–82, 201n5, 212n54, 221n35

Akkil, temple of Ninshubur in, 72–73

Alamdimmû (medical series), 215n80

Alexander, Meena, 176

Altar (the Table of Heaven), 113, 115

Amar-Suen (king), 165, 214–15n75

An (*Anu*; grandfather of the gods), 21, 70–71, 136–37, 142, 189–90n5, 197n17; in *Inana and Ebih*, 200n8; **nugig** of, 137; temple of, 197n18, 199n2, 200n7

"Ancient Mesopotamian Gods and Goddesses" (Heffron), 201n4

Anuna gods (*Annunaki*), 150

Anzû, 218n16

Anzu (Thunder Bird), 74, 204n21

Asarluhi (god of magic and incantations), temple of, 66

Ashgi (son of Ninhursanga), 82

Ashimbabbar, 55. *See also* Nanna

Ashtar, 113, 210n26

Atra-hasis, 160, 209n22

Attinger, Pascal, 178, 196n9, 217n4, 226n38

aurochs, 11, 14, 25, 43, 67, 75, 78, 80, 84, 88, 150, 196n14, 203n15

authorship: in ancient times, 131–32, 160, 223n44; concept of, xi, xii–xiii, 131–32, 135, 141, 162, 215–16n81; death of author, 175; of Enheduana's hymns, vii, xi, xiii, xiv, 126, 127, 129–32, 135, 140, 189–190n5, 191n9, 214–15n75, 214n70; in *Exaltation*, 135, 138, 140, 142, 162, 175; self-reflective, xi, 135, 138, 140; as weaving, 127, 132

Enheduana (*continued*)
162–63, 165–69, 174, 194n23,
195n6, 197n17, 198n22, 199n26;
historical context, vii, xiv–
xvi; modern scholarship on,
174–80; predecessors of, 110,
116, 132–33, 165; rebuilding the
ĝipar, 110–12, 117, 129; spelling
of name, 194nn22–23; succes-
sors of, 107, 113, 133, 162–63;
"three lives" of, xiv–xvi, 191n9,
192n13. *See also* Disk of Enhe-
duana; Enheduana's poetry

Enheduana's poetry, vii, xvi–xxii;
authorship of, xii–xiv, 126–33,
129, 138–40, 189n4, 191n9, 213–
14n67, 214n70, 214–15n75, 215–
16n81; and the author's voice,
135–36; in Babylonian schools,
xv, 119–26, 142–43, 149, 161,
163, 191n11, 212n54; as coded
political thesis, 190–91n8; cre-
ation of, 127, 132–33; dating of,
129–30, 131; grief and gender
in, 154–61; imagery in, xvi–xvii;
language of, 130–31; modern
editions of, 174–80; nature, war,
and exile in, 149–54; popularity
of, 123, 126; power and chaos
in, 143–49; translation of, xvi,
xviii–xxi, 22, 103, 104, 124–25,
137, 142, 144, 156, 163, 178–79,
193n21, 194–95n1, 195n6, 196n9,

197n19, 199nn25,26, 200n11,
202nn10,11, 203n12, 203nn15,16,
203n19, 204n25, 205nn29,30,
205n34, 206n5, 206n7, 210n26,
217n7, 219n18, 221n35, 222n36;
use of metaphor in, x, xi, xvi,
53–54, 127, 140, 141, 149–50,
152, 153, 158, 168, 174, 190n8,
198n24, 201n1, 201n6, 206n3,
215n80, 221n35. *See also Exalta-
tion of Inana;* hymns: fragmen-
tary; *Hymn to Inana;* Temple
Hymns

E-ninnu, 74–75

Enki (*Ea*), 144–45; daughter of, 76;
sons of, 66. *See also* Ea

Enki, House of, 58

Enki and Inana, 192n17

Enlil (king of the gods; Great
Mountain), 21, 53, 55, 58,
199n2; servant of, 60; son of,
61–62; sons of, 74, 86; temple
of, 54; wife of, 59, 62. *See also*
Nunamnir

Enmegalana, 210n35; as local deity,
210n35

Enmenana, 107

Ennigaldi-Nanna, 165–66, 168–69,
223–24n6, 224n8

Enuma Anu Enlil, 164, 224n8

Enuma Elish, 192–93n19, 218n16,
223n43

Eresh, temple of Nisaba in, 92–93

Ereshkigal (queen of the dead), 69, 143; sons of, 86

Eridu, 57–58; temple of, 53, 58, 149, 219n22

Erra, 205n28. *See also* Nergal

Erra and Ishum, 213–14n67, 220n24

Esagil-kin-apli, 215n80

E-sherziguru, 79–80

Eshnunna, temple of Ninazu in, 86–87

E-shumesha, 55, 61–62, 201n3

E-sikil, 86–87

E-Sirara, 76

E-tarsirsir, 75–76

E-temen-ni-guru, 95, 130

E-Tummal, 55, 58, 59, 201n3, 202n7

E-ugalgala, 80–81

E-Ulmash, 91

E-unir, 53, 54, 57

Exaltation of Inana, viii–xii, xiii, xviii, xix, 3–5, 95, 105–6, 113, 122, 129, 132, 147, 174; authorship of, 162–63; depictions of war in, 152; ending of, 205n34; first publication of, 175; importance of, 135–36; lamentation in, 155–56; literary readings of, 134–36; modern editions of, 178; possible performance of, 142; power of words in, 136–37; role of dialogue in, 135–36, 216–17n3; school copies of, 140, 141; structure of, 194–95n1,

196n7; study tools, 193–94n21; text, 7–19; translation(s) of, 103, 190–91n8, 195n6, 196n9, 196n10, 197n19, 197–98n20, 199n25, 199n26, 217n4

exile, 153–54

E-zagin, 92–93

4.2 kiloyear event, 151

Fara period, 128, 131

Farber (Farber-Flügge), Gertrud, 144, 218nn14,15

feminism, xiv–xv, 147, 176–77, 191n9, 192n13

Flood, 209n22

Földi, Zsombor, 223n44

Foster, Benjamin, 196n11, 213n56, 217n4, 217n7

Foucault, Michel, 217n9

Foxvog, Daniel A., 226n38

Frayne, Douglas, 214–15n75

funeral meals, 112

Gabura, 67

Gaduda, 55

Gaesh, 214–15n75; temple of Nanna in, 67–68

Gagimah, 62

gala (lamentation priest), 141, 156–57, 200n8, 218n12, 220nn30,31

gender issues, 156–61, 220nn30,31, 220–21n32, 221n33, 222n36; in Sumerian language, 206n8

Ur, 53, 64, 104, 123, 153, 163,
183; archaeology in, 108–10,
170–71, 225n24; as port city,
106; priestesses of, 165, 168–
69; temple in, 95, 105, 165;
temple of Inana-Zaza at, 113;
temple of Nanna in, 64–65;
temple of Shulgi in, 65–66;
Third Dynasty of (Ur III),
116–17, 119, 127, 128–29, 130,
182, 214n70, 214–15n75;
women of, 163–69
Urash (goddess of the earth), 85
Ur-Namma (Ur-Nammu; king), 116,
117, 130, 182, 208–9n19
Uruk, 68, 104, 181, 197n18, 200n7;
temple of Inana in, 70–71, 79
Uruk period, 181
Urum, 56; temple of Nanna in,
88–89
Ur-Utu, 218n12
ušumgal, 196n8, 198n21
Utu (sun god), 55, 205n31; temple
of, 68–69, 89–90

Veldhuis, Niek, 149, 226n38
Venus, 204n23
Victory Stele, 207n6

Wagensonner, Klaus, 210n29
warfare, 151–53, 220n24
Weadock, Penelope, 111, 208–9n19
weapons, 197–98n20, 222n36

Weiershäuser, Frauke, 223–24n6,
224n8
Weigle, Marta, 175
Westenholz, Aage, 208n8,
218–19n17
Westenholz, Joan, 206n1, 210n26,
213n56
Wilcke, Claus, 189n4, 190–91n8
Winter, Irene, 116
women: in ancient Iraq, 160; as
archaeologists, 169–71; as
authors, 179–80, 223n44; of
color, xi, 189n3; and the "great
gender gap," 164–65, 222n42;
as museum curators, 166; as
scribes, 160, 211n44; of Ur,
163–69. See also priestesses
Woolley, C. Leonard, 110, 114,
170–71, 173–74
Woolley, Katharine, 169–74,
225n25

Zababa (patron of war), temple
of, 87
Zabalam, temple of Inana in,
79–80
Zgoll, Annette, 123, 178, 190–91n8,
217n4
ziqqurat (ziggurat), 53–54, 57–58,
78, 114, 176; on Disk of Enhe-
duana, 115
Zólyomi, Gábor, 226n38
Zsolnay, Ilona, 221n33